ELLIS ROWAN

The Flower Hunter

ELLIS ROWAN

The Flower Hunter

*The adventures,
in Northern Australia and
New Zealand, of flower painter
Ellis Rowan*

ANGUS & ROBERTSON

An imprint of HarperCollins*Publishers*

AN ANGUS & ROBERTSON BOOK
An imprint of HarperCollinsPublishers

First published in Australia by Angus & Robertson Publishers in 1898
This edition published by
CollinsAngus&Robertson Publishers Pty Limited (ACN 009 913 517)
A division of HarperCollinsPublishers (Australia) Pty Limited
4 Eden Park, 31 Waterloo Road, North Ryde, NSW 2113, Australia

William Collins Publishers Ltd
31 View Road, Glenfield, Auckland 10, New Zealand

Angus & Robertson (UK)
77-85 Fulham Palace Road, London W6 8JB, United Kingdom

Copyright this edition © CollinsAngus&Robertson Publishers

This book is copyright.

Apart from any fair dealing for the purposes of private study, research, criticism or review, as permitted under the Copyright Act, no part may be reproduced by any process without written permission. Inquiries should be addressed to the publishers.

National Library of Australia
Cataloguing-in-Publication data:

Rowan, Ellis, 1848 – 1922.
  [A flower hunter in Queensland and New Zealand]. The
  flower hunter: letters and adventures of Marian Ellis Rowan.
  ISBN 0 207 17050 9.

  1. Rowan, Ellis, 1848 – 1922 — Correspondence. 2.
  Queensland — Description and travel. 3. New Zealand —
  Description and travel. I. Title. II. Title: The flower hunter.
919.43

Internal black and white illustrations by Karen Carter
Cover border illustration: Karen Carter
Cover panel illustration:
  Ruth Sutherland 1884 – 1948 Australian
  Girl in a Hammock
  Oil on canvas on panel
Reproduced by permission of the National Gallery of Victoria, Melbourne
Typeset in Australia by Midland Typesetters Pty Limited
 Printed in the People's Republic of China
5 4 3 2 1
95 94 93 92 91

Preface

My love for the *flora* of Australia, at once so unique and so fascinating, together with my desire to complete my collection of floral paintings, has carried me into other colonies, Queensland, and some of the remotest parts of the great Continent of Australia. The excitement of seeking and the delight of finding rare or even unknown specimens[1] abundantly compensated me for all difficulties, fatigue, and hardships. The pursuit has made me acquainted with many strange phases of colonial life; it has carried me into the depths of jungles, to distant islands, to wild mountain districts, and has brought me in contact with the aboriginal races, often in peculiar circumstances.

The experiences gained in this pursuit form the subject of my letters, written to my friends from the places they describe, and transcribing impressions while they were still in all their freshness. The letters contained in the first part of this volume were written to my husband in 1890–1892, at a time when the state of my health compelled me to pass the winter months in the tropical climate of North Queensland. To him, who encouraged me in my work of collecting and painting the flora of Australia, they owe whatever interest they possess. The task, which I undertook at first to please him, soon became my greatest interest and an unfailing source of pleasure. The latter part of the book consists of a selection of my letters from New Zealand, written years later in sadder days and altered circumstances. Portions of some of these letters appeared in the Sydney *Town and Country Journal*, and for permission to reprint these passages I am indebted to the kind courtesy of the proprietor.

It only remains for me to express my gratitude to the many friends in Queensland and New Zealand for their kindness to me, and for the generous and ungrudging help given me in my work.

E.R.

November 1897.

---

[1] Those specimens hitherto unknown were named by the late Sir Frederick Meuller.

Contents

PREFACE   V

Letters from Northern Australia

A TROPICAL PLANTATION   3
DISAGREEABLE INSECTS   15
A DANGEROUS VOYAGE   24
A MIDNIGHT CORROBOREE   33
A TEDIOUS JOURNEY   41
CHILLAGOE CAVES   52
OFF THE TRACK OF CIVILISATION   69
ENCOUNTER WITH AN ALLIGATOR   80
AN ABUNDANCE OF FLOWERS   97
BRILLIANT SEA FLOWERS   107
THE SKELETON IN THE TREE   120
TORRES STRAIT ISLANDS   127

Letters from New Zealand

THE CRADLE OF NEW ZEALAND   145
HOT SPRINGS AND MUD GEYSERS   150
MAORI MYTHOLOGY   155
A LUSH BEAUTY   165
REMINISCENCES   169
SHEEP-SHEARING, PHYSICKING AND DIPPING   180
RUTHLESS DEFORESTING   184
CLIFFS OF ICE   197
A LAND OF OLIVES AND HONEY   208

Letters from Northern Australia

A Tropical Plantation

Rockhampton, Queensland

We are at last really on our way to Thursday Island. I find that a steamer leaves here for the South early to-morrow, so if my letter is rather disjointed and shaky, you must put it down to my sea journey; for you know as of old that "a life on the ocean wave" is about the last that I would choose. I cannot, however, grumble, for, so far, we have sailed on a sea of glass for days—not even a ripple upon the water—and I have been dreaming the sunny days away, while we skimmed past the numerous islands, too lazy even to read or to do anything but watch the sea-birds passing and the porpoises chasing each other; now and then a turtle basked on the top of the water, or a black and yellow sea-snake lay coiled asleep, but at the sound of the engine, like a flash, it disappeared. Then there was the endless amusement of silently studying one's fellow-passengers—the lucky digger with his universal "shouts" to all on board, the woman with the ubiquitous infant, the fussy old party whom nothing satisfies, the new chum with his innumerable questions and insatiable desire for information, and, best of all, two bright unaffected Australian girls, whose hospitable father has already asked me to break my journey at their station.

But, "Not so quick," I hear you say; "I left you last in Brisbane, planning a trip to Thursday Island." Very well, I will begin at the beginning. My month's visit to Mr. Casey's station at Normanby had made "such a man of me" that I was ready for anything and everything, and when at last you managed reluctantly to say "yes", and pretended you meant it, I was more than content. We left Brisbane on the 3rd, after having spent a very pleasant ten days there, as usual turning two days into one. Our trip in the mountains to Towoomba, the sanatorium of the town, gave us enough cool air to double our energies. Eric and I made another trip to One Tree Hill, where he hunted butterflies and I flowers. There is a magnificent panoramic view from the top, of the whole town and its surroundings. To the south lies the great dividing range between Queensland and New South Wales, and far away in blue misty distance one can see the outline of Moreton Bay, and the long reaches of the river winding its way to the sea. Another excursion which we made was to the Enoggera Reservoir, ten miles from the town, a beautiful drive the whole way. The lake itself is a very picturesque one, with surroundings of semi-tropical vegetation; Eric, boy-like, managed to tumble in; he rather enjoyed the fun of a ducking, and my discomfiture in fearing he might be drowned.

Last, but not least, I must not forget to give you a description of the exciting kangaroo-hunt that was arranged for me one day before I left Brisbane. We went by train the night before to Mr. ———'s station, and we were a goodly muster as we drew up at the stockyard gates at 11 that bright morning, with just touch enough of frost in the air to redden our cheeks and our noses. There was plenty of muscle and go in the horses; each man was on his finest jumper, each lady on hers. Eric, who joined in the fun, rode on the pony "Paddy" beside my grey mare. After handshakes and greetings as much as our fretting horses would allow, we were off and away, ambling, trotting, cantering, spreading, and driving, as we bore to the left, then on to the fern and over the brow of the hill, where soon, with a shrill chorus, the dogs spoke to a find; we halted for a second as five or six kangaroos scattered in front of us, turning in a dazed way from right to left, as they dodged in such close quarters among us that with the butt-end of his whip a horseman knocked one over, then the hounds bend and falter, doubling back and landing another with a scrimmage on his back on the ground; now up the hill and away like the wind the rest go, clearing yards at a bound; through the thick fern we steeplechase over logs, squeezing, dodging, crashing in and out of the gums, then "for'ard" on the wide sweep of the valley to a bit of galloping ground, where, with desperate speed, "long, limber, and grey", the hounds in full cry flash past; the kangaroos, leaping ten yards at a stretch, disappear; with the sun and wind in our faces, with wild halloas from every side, and a chorus of "hold ups", we swish through a swamp; a fallen branch and a stumble, and Paddy is on his nose, but before we have time to dismount, both pony and rider are up again, and away now, with snap and crash, cheating falls we dodge through a network of saplings and flying logs. Neck to neck the horses rattle their hoofs through the fern, a yelping sound, a cracking of whips, then a mass of draggled fur and the last two six-footers clear the fence and make for the edge of the swamp—a crashing and splitting of timber, a critical moment, some meet their fate on the ground; with bold hearts, strong muscles and luck others are over, and Paddy is "in at the death"; but I can't look where, clasping, gripping, and tearing at the dogs with his strong hind legs, one kangaroo stands at bay in the water, fighting tooth and nail for life.

My last afternoon I spent at the Acclimatisation Society Gardens, where they have a splendid collection of native plants. Mr. Soutter, the curator, a most enthusiastic botanist, gave me an armful of tropical flowers, some of which I sat up painting until well into daylight next morning—how shocked you would have been at my burning the candle at both ends! After wishing Eric good-bye, and handing him over into safe custody for the overland journey by train back to Sydney, I drove down to catch my steamer, the *Maranoa*. My cabin was already filled with flowers, and there and then, between my qualms of sea-sickness, I painted some of them in.

It was a glorious moonlight night, and the phosphorescent waves lapping against the ship's side and sending out live flashes of fire, kept me so fascinated by their beauty, that it was eleven o'clock before I stirred to go below. Just outside my cabin door two men were discussing, in rather loud tones, the merits and demerits of Mr. Tyson, the richest man in Australia. Then followed an animated conversation between two circus men travelling with a "show"; they were relating their experiences, and I was unwillingly let into some of the secrets of the trade. I learned how the boa-constrictor, when he was dead, was carried backwards and forwards to the different colonies stuffed with tobacco and cigars, how the mermaid was "built up" out of the monkey and the fish's tail, and how the Chinaman whom they wanted to prepare as a New Guinea mummy wouldn't die, and eventually "spited" them all by getting well. With their voices still jingling in my ears I fell asleep, and did not awake until I heard the engines stop, the shrill whistle ring out, and the rattling of anchor going down at three next morning. Then we were unceremoniously bundled out of our berths, and had to sit waiting for two hours more in the stuffy, dimly-lighted saloon for the tender which was to take us up to the town. We were a draggled and limp-looking set of beings when she finally started. I rolled myself into a berth and tried to get some more sleep, but some one in the berth below me snored so lustily that this was impossible, and something running over my face brought visions of cockroaches, which grow to an alarming size along this coast, so, wrapping round me my sealskin cloak, which I was most thankful you insisted on my bringing, I went on deck, where they gave us coffee while we sat and watched the cold grey dawn of the morning break as we steamed up the bends of the flat, uninteresting river.

We passed the central works of the Queensland Preserving and Refrigerating Company, and saw droves of cattle on their way, and I was not sorry when we came to the end of our thirty-five mile journey. We reached Rockhampton at nine—a two minutes' drive to the Criterion Hotel, breakfast, with plenty of good, unwatered milk, a bath, and all our morning's discomforts were forgotten. Here, to my astonishment, I met Mr. A. in the

breakfast-room, and, later on, several other friends, so we hired a trap and did the lions of the town together.

We drove first to the Crescent lagoon, two miles away, on the top of the Athelstone Range, where the water is pumped into an artificial reservoir to supply the town, then round about the streets, which are broad and well planted with trees. The town is flat and lies very low, and I am glad that my visit is in spring instead of in the summer, for the crisp air now is just warm enough to be pleasant and the sky absolutely cloudless. We bought books, sugar-plums, and papers, and I dined in the evening with Mrs. P., whose husband is lucky enough to own many thousands of shares in the Mount Morgan Mine. Of course I went to see it; who does not? and thoroughly enjoyed the twenty-five-mile drive, notwithstanding the roughness of the road; for the last nine miles it was very break-neck work, and our leader (we had three horses) had a pleasant way of turning round and facing us just at the most critical moments, to see how we were taking things. We were taking them very badly; for Mrs. P., who kindly drove me there, was even more nervous than I was. At the Razorback Hill we came upon the body of a smashed coach, then a pair of wheels, and finally the top part of the "Royal Mail Coach" itself. The drive from the railway station—eight miles—is generally taken in this coach, and we heartily congratulated ourselves that we had not joined it that time.

We passed more and larger teams of horses and bullocks than I had ever seen before. Driving the former seems warranted to produce more strong language than any other occupation going, judging from the snatches that we quickly got in passing. Twenty-eight bullocks or seventeen or eighteen horses were not unusual numbers in one team. The sight of a mob of wild cattle farther on crossing a swollen stream, the roaring and bellowing, the tossing forest of horns above the heaving mass of beasts and the cracking of stock-whips, as the riders pressed them forward, shouting and urging them on, took me back to the old station life. How angrily they looked at us, tossing their shaggy heads; how they plunged and snorted, and then, with dripping sides and reddened nostrils, eyed us defiantly from the other side of the stream, as if we had been the cause of all their woes. But let them toss their heads, for we are now over the shallow crossing, which in winter time has been the camping-ground of many a broken-down, mud-stuck waggon, and where not a few bones of wretched animals have been left behind, bleaching in the sun and rain.

The first glimpse of Mount Morgan gives one the idea of a huge red landslip, for the top has all been quarried away. Suddenly, numerous chimneys and the scattered bandbox-looking town come into sight. A quick sweep round the Chinamen's gardens and we are in front of the pretty cottage occupied by the manager of the famous mine, where, after our long drive, we do full justice to a sumptuous lunch. An hour's rest afterwards and we start for the mine, partly walking, but doing the steepest bits in trollies. Everything wears the busiest of airs, everything is in motion, and we see all that is to be seen, even to the bars of precious metal ready for the escort to take into town. Candles in hand, we go through the tunnels of white pipeclay, one after another. Enough of this clay is in sight, they say, to last for seven years, giving all round 2 oz. to the ton. Then we go on to the top, where the men just now are busy blasting, and we have to hide ourselves for a minute or two until the explosion is over and the blackened, bubbly, burnt-up looking stuff is exposed, which gives, we are told, sometimes 20 and 30 oz. to the ton. The bright yellow-looking clay just beside it is richer still, while other stuff close alongside yields nothing at all, and so they go on in a delightful state of uncertainty as to what is coming next.

Twelve hundred men are employed in the mine, and it costs from £8000 to £10,000 a month to work the whole concern, but even with this large amount for expenses the mine has, in seven years or less, paid two and a half million pounds in dividends.

We left early next morning again and reached Rockhampton in time for lunch. I drove to the Botanical Gardens on the Murray Lagoon in the afternoon, to see the native lilies there in full blossom, blue, white, yellow, and pink, the latter a lotus: some of them being as large as a cheese-plate. Numbers of big dragonflies were skimming over the surface of the water, and several small birds near us were turning over the lily-leaves hunting for insects. Two large grey cranes peered at us through the rushes, and there were dozens of wild ducks looking quite at home and secure in the knowledge that here they are not

A Tropical Plantation

Sir John Longstaff, Memorial portrait of Mrs Ellis Rowan, flower painter and authoress, 1926, oil on canvas, 148 x 101 cm Reproduced by permission of the National Library of Australia

allowed to be shot. We finished up our day in a garden on the other side of the river, almost entirely filled with native plants, and had our afternoon tea under the shade of a jujuba tree with the golden yellow fruit hanging in bunches everywhere, and we came home laden with enough new flowers to keep me contented for a week.

The Criterion is a capital hotel, prettily situated on the bank of the Fitzroy River, and I was most comfortable there. Mrs. Eaton, the hostess, was kindness itself and couldn't do enough for us, and the ever-smiling Bridget was ready to wait upon me day and night. She even went so far as to cut the stems of my flowers each day to keep them fresher, a piece of thoughtful devotion I did not forget. "You're never idle, mum," and "You'll wear yourself out entoirely," she was always saying, but I felt fresh again, and ready for anything, notwithstanding the remark which a passenger made on board, that I looked as if I had been through one famine and was half-way through another. But who could fail to get well in such a winter climate?

From Rockhampton I caught the *Wodonga* to Mackay, and what a different from the *Maranoa*; she is a large, comfortable steamer, and I found myself in a cabin with a handsome, fresh-looking English girl, going to join her husband at Townsville. He is taking up land in the far north, and I cannot help thinking how soon her roses will fade, and how little she knows of the life she is going to.

The next morning we reached Mackay, but were too late to catch the tide, and could not steam up the Pioneer River, there are so many sandbanks at its mouth. The pilot, who is also the harbour-master, offered me a seat in his boat, up to the town. There were a good many of us in her, and she began to leak so badly that we had to get on to a tender anchored near and wait until she was baled out: then into her again, and for five weary miles these poor men had to row us against wind and tide, under a hot tropical sun—every now and then having to stop and bale out again to keep us from sinking altogether.

We were exceedingly glad to find ourselves on dry land at last. The town of Mackay is small, flat and uninteresting, but there are a great many sugar plantations round it, and now that this industry has taken a new lease of life it will probably become an important town. The first person who greeted us was a Kanaka, paddling a small boat (these are the people who are mostly employed on the plantations). The next scene we came upon was a man trying to drive a buck-jumping horse in a cart, a novel sort of amusement of which we never saw the end, for we had to hurry on. The vegetation along the roads was thoroughly tropical, quantities of bananas and several South Sea Island plants were growing wild, and a Mexican fruit called papaw, the milky juice of which is said to be a great specific for diphtheria.

At Mackay, Mr. R. met me and drove me to "The Rocks". On both sides of the road were sugar-cane plantations, and I saw numbers of creeping plants in blossom which were quite new to me. We stopped half-way for tea with Mr. and Mrs. K.—such a pretty bungalow house theirs was—and the climbing plants over it, in full blossom, were a sight not easily forgotten; an old grey stump of a tree was one glorious mass of crimson bougainvilleas, against a background of forest jungle, almost as beautiful as that at Colombo. The house inside was so like an Indian bungalow that it was hard to realise that it was not one. It was half-past five before we reached our destination, and until we were actually in through the garden gate, I did not know what a view awaited me. At the foot of a hill on which the house stands runs the winding river, the Pioneer. It eddies round great rocks (from which the house takes its name) and small islands, just now splendid with the crimson flowers of the bottle brush—then it tosses and tumbles away into the distance over the stones, with a fall here, another there, and again plunges or glides into deep pools, the homes of alligators, which occasionally come out to bask upon its sandy banks. On the opposite shore there is a wonderfully varied bit of jungle, and far away in the distance are ranges of blue mountains.

The wide verandah is furnished with easy-chairs, comfortable lounges, cushions, books, tables, and nick-nacks; everything is left there at night, and the doors and windows are never shut. There is a great chattering of birds from the aviary, and a magpie struts along the verandah and calls for Rover, the dog. Outside, on a stand, there is a young eagle who likes fresh food every day, and requires a hunter to himself to keep his appetite satisfied. Several other tame birds run loose about the garden. Six months ago a pet curlew disappeared. At the commencement of the spring he suddenly appeared again, accompanied by a wife, and came as usual into the verandah to be fed; his little mate at first kept at a safe distance, but by degrees she too gained confidence and became even tamer than the other; as the summer advanced, they both disappeared again, probably to return in the spring.

At the foot of the garden a beautiful umbrella tree, with its large leaves and crimson-brown flowers, hangs over the rocky cliff, and beyond it is a group of palm leaves with long tassels of red berries, and the Pandanus, with its crimson fruit, all in sections and as large as a cocoa-nut; and last, but not least, in the bend of the river spreads a bed of blue water-lilies, each open flower as large as a cheese-plate, and of the most delicate shades of pale blue and purple, with a bright centre of yellow stamens and large floating leaves lined with pink, double the size of those of our English lilies.

My first walk in the wild tropical jungle next morning I cannot forget. I entered, sketch-book in hand, by a narrow little pathway, probably made by an alligator. I kicked, as I thought, a grey stick aside—it was a snake, and quick as lightning it darted off, while I grew hot and cold by turns. There was such a death-like silence about me that I felt an intruder there, and the thick and tangled mass of rank vegetation completely hid the sun from sight. A few steps farther on I came to an opening, and below me lay a miniature lake, its water covered with large blue lilies floating amid their leaves on which the sun shone through a network of graceful palms. Scarlet, yellow-eyed dragonflies skimmed over its surface, while presently a great butterfly tremulously fluttered past, and the sunlight, catching the metallic lustre of its wings, changed them to every rainbow hue. The trees were clasped and linked together by delicate tendrils, and climbing ferns and huge caladiums covered the ground. It was a scene of wild, mysterious beauty, but in the distance there was the hum of a thousand gossamer-winged and hungry insects, and I hurried on with my sketch, for the mosquitoes had already found me out. Too much wrapped up in my work to turn round, I push twice aside from my cheek what I took to be a hanging tendril; but surely it moved too quickly—one wild jump and I was yards away! It was a long tree snake that had fastened is tail to a branch, and, curious to find out what manner of being this might be that had disturbed its solitude, was gracefully swaying backwards and forwards. This was the climax, and with a good deal of slipping and scrambling,

A Tropical Plantation

I left the scene without a regret. That same night I heard a great fluttering in the aviary, and going out, found a large copper-coloured snake hanging from a beam. It had already swallowed one bird, and was in the act of crushing another. I called Mr. R. who caught it with a pair of shears, but not before I had made a rough sketch of it. Next day I filled in the sketch in colour, getting also correctly the scales from the corner of its mouth to the tip of its nose, which, according to their number, are said to indicate its degree of venom. The larger and fewer the scales, the more deadly they say it is. Birds seem almost mesmerised by these reptiles, and I have many times watched them fluttering round as if powerless to fly away.

I had the pleasurable excitement here of being introduced to the nettle tree, some branches of which I picked, not knowing what it was. My hand and arm ached for many a day afterwards.

It is a charming house to stay in. I am allowed to do just as I like. If I am very busy I don't come in to lunch, no one wonders, and I go quietly on painting until five-o'clock tea, when I generally finish the whole of the chocolate or cocoa-nut cakes that we always have. I take plenty of milk, and am beginning to get quite a sleek and well-conditioned look; it is as yet neither too hot nor too cold, though we have fires in the early morning and sometimes at night. No one, however, goes near them, and they only serve to remind us that it is not yet the spring. We drive a good deal, and sometimes ride, and the days seem to fly, but the snakes really *are* bad here. I saw a very large and deadly brown one coiled up in the fork of a tree under which I was painting, a few feet only from the ground. I went home as fast as I could and told Mr. R. to bring his gun and shoot it, but when we returned to the place where I had seen it, it was gone, and only a tiny grey lizard was walking up the tree. I never heard the end of that, and it remained a joke against me until I left. I never longed for anything more at Mackay than that the snake would come again. I watched one another day on the rocks below me. It went under a stone and Mr. R. went to turn it over, when two came from underneath, and how quickly we all made off! Though we see them so constantly there is very little fear, for they are much more afraid of human beings than we are of them, and get away as quickly as they can.

We are not quite in the wilds here, and the other evening

were invited out to dinner. The men were especially requested not to put on dress clothes, and they looked delightfully cool in their short, white shell jackets and cummerbunds. Mrs. D., our hostess, who was a good musician, played to us, and before the evening ended we had planned a visit to Habana, the next plantation. It is a dry and healthy heat at this time of the year, and not too cold to sit all the evening on the verandah. There I amuse myself often by catching night moths. Attracted by the light of the lamps, they come fluttering in against the window panes in dozens. Butterflies here, too, are most brilliant. One, a great, velvety black and green beauty, is six inches across, another blue, purple and green—in fact, every colour of the rainbow; but the variety here is endless. There, too, we count the wretched flying foxes as they pass by to rob the peach trees, and we listen to the songs of night-birds: and then to sleep to the sound of ever-rushing water.

Disagreeable Insects

Habana

We arrived at this plantation yesterday, lunching on the way with Mrs. P., who has the very perfection of a little bush house. She has also a wonderful collection of insects, and a larger selection of native orchids that I have yet seen anywhere.

The country all round is very like New Zealand, even to the Whares which the Kanakas have put up in preference to wooden houses. All day long we hear the crushing of the sugar-mill and the sing-song cry of the natives, who possess that peculiar knack which all dark races have of being able to throw their voices out to a great distance. They have a very happy time of it on these plantations, and all seem very jolly with their wives, children, and those belongings most precious to them, including fowls and pigs. We used to hear most harrowing tales of their ill-treatment—don't believe a word of it. They have an agent who looks well after them, and the most trivial complaint is inquired into. They are all recruited from the South Sea Islands, and they contract to work for three years in the plantations for £6 a year in wages. Everything else is provided for them, food, houses, and clothes for themselves, their wives and children, and at the end of their time they are returned, free of expense, to their homes, but most of them prefer remaining, and many return again after a time. Their food consists of a pound and a half of meat and bread, and three pounds of sweet potatoes, a day. Besides these, they are supplied with soap, tobacco, and fruits. Each man generally grows his own bananas, mangoes, water-melons, and pineapples. Their wives are sometimes employed as servants on the plantations, but as a rule only for a short time. They are clean and often make very good servants.

A few Malays are also employed, but these have the disadvantage of occasionally running amok. I had, as you remember, the misfortune twice to be in places where was developed this peculiar madness, and three men were killed, and

I have always felt nervous about it since, but then Mrs. R. says I am nervous at everything, most of all at her driving! She is very short-sighted, and took me across country once as hard as the horses would go, through thick undergrowth with hidden stumps in every direction. It was almost a satisfaction to me when we crashed into one, a horse on either side; but she always managed to get out of her difficulties, and I hadn't even the satisfaction of saying, "I told you so," for we were always on the outside edge of a smash which never quite came off, excepting on this one occasion, which she insists was a bitter disappointment to me.

We made excursions from Habana to the different places of interest. One day picnicking on a mountain—Black-gin's Leap, so called from this native having thrown herself over—Mr. L., our host, climbed down the face of the cliff for some orchids for me; and coming home one of the party shot down some of the large pods of a creeping vine from whose seeds they make the favourite match-boxes. It was a stiff climb to the top of this mountain, but the summit once reached the view well repaid

us. We looked down upon the whole of the sugar-cane district, with each homestead standing clearly defined in the network of green plantations.

Just below us was a dense jungle of tall tree-tops: shining on one we saw what we thought was a large orange and blue flower; next day a native was sent out to bring it in—it was a spider's nest, and the sun's rays midst the silken threads had dyed it these colours. These creatures grow to a very large size here, and some of their silken dwellings are marvels of beauty, not made for the purpose of trapping, but simply for luxury, with a platform in front which is braced to the nearest support. They live only on insects, and it is, I think, a mistake to suppose that they eat birds, though their strong webs may sometimes trap them so firmly that they cannot extricate themselves. They are most useful scavengers, clearing the room of every fly, and are not so poisonous as one would imagine; I have constantly taken tarantulas in my hands without being harmed.

Three hundred Kanakas are employed on this plantation, and leaving on Sunday morning (their holiday) we met them in different directions going out with their bows and arrows to shoot fish and birds.

Queensland has its thorns as well as its roses, and I came home with two big black ticks which had fastened themselves between my shoulders. They take good care to attack you where you cannot reach them. A great many dogs are killed by these pests, and sometimes horses and cattle, but if animals can once become acclimatised to the bite it does not affect them. The ticks in me were first covered with kerosene and then taken out with pincers, but I felt the bites for many days afterwards.

Another most insinuating creature is the little thin needle-like land leech; he very soon makes himself acquainted with you in the long lank grass or in shady places. I couldn't imagine at first what was wrong with my legs, but I soon discovered that their bite makes a most irritating sore. They move along by semicircular strides with bodies poised ready to lay hold at a moment's notice, and they are particularly energetic and familiar after a shower of rain. As for spiders, their name is legion; but I am partial to them, as you know, and think they are more sinned against than sinning; a good-sized one will clear the room of an amazing number of flies.

Caterpillars are the things my soul abhors. In some of the gum trees they form a great, black, crawling, creeping ball, wriggling and twisting round each other in such numbers that they cannot any longer sustain their own weight, and come flopping on to the ground, still never leaving go their hold of each other. Some of the beetles are really fiendish-looking, others of dazzling beauty. Here, too, you find a great variety of leaf insects, marvels of hypocrisy. It is almost impossible to believe that they really do possess legs, and even these are so like stems that it is only when you touch them that you realise the imitation. Yesterday I caught the largest stick insect that I have yet seen. He is a much more modest creature, and generally hides in out-of-the-way places, avoiding anything like publicity.

I have already painted one or two very large Praying Mantis, but the finest specimen, a large green one with purple spots on his body, I lost by a bit of sentimentalism. The fact is, I thought I had chloroformed him out of existence, and I pegged his wings down and fastened him in an air-tight box. But next morning I heard a scraping, and on opening the lid my prisoner turned his head round and looked at me so pathetically with his great eyes that I felt conscience-stricken at my cruelty and gave him his liberty. After all, my compunctions were misplaced, for the Mantis is a terrible fellow. He does not, as I had imagined, live on grass, but devours his own species, and I think if I had known this I should have added him to my collection.

I had my first experience here of a regular tropical shower, a veritable waterspout, and such thunder! it rained an inch and three-quarters in one hour, the hailstones being larger than a pigeon's egg. Mr. R., who was out in it all, hid himself under the sheaf of a palm tree, and the horses and cows rushed in wild confusion round the paddocks with their tails straight in the air, wondering who was pelting them.

We went to spend two days with the Ks. down the river, where we had a large boating party next day. We started in three different boats early in the morning with the tide; we had our lunch some miles up the river, and, while the men fished, we boiled potatoes, fried the chops, and made "billy" tea. We came home in the cool of the evening, with a boat-load of fish, and after high tea finished up the evening with a dance. They are most hospitable people, and the whole of their guests stayed for several days, riding, fishing, driving, and playing tennis by turns.

It was beginning to get much warmer, and in the few days that we were away from "The Rocks" the trailing plants in the verandah had all burst into blossom, the beaumontia, with its beautiful large trumpet-shaped white flowers, and blue thunbergia, the scarlet *Poinciana regia*, and the blue jacaranda. Some of those pests, the flying-foxes, had stripped the trees of all the fruit, and Mr. R. spent his evening shooting them as they went by. Hundreds of parrots are now sucking the honey from the blossoms of the gums, and the shrill cry of cockatoos is everywhere to be heard. The laughing jackass here is a bright-plumaged bird, with beautiful blue in its wings and back, and many of the birds, which are sombre-coloured in the South, here put on brighter plumage.

Macnade House

From Mackay I made another start on to Townsville. While waiting for the steamer, the pilot from Flat Top Island came off in his little boat and took me ashore. He had been all through the New Zealand war, and was one of those who helped to carry you after you had been wounded; you may imagine how delighted he was to meet some one with whom he could go over the old fights again. His wife gave me a lunch of beef-steak and "apple-pie", the latter made out of pumpkins, and afterwards some tea and cake, which lasted me till I got to the next port. They gave me also some seaweeds, corals, shells, and a carpet snake's skin. They had killed some snakes of this kind nine nights in succession as they came to eat the chickens.

We had a splendid trip along the coast to Townsville, but unfortunately we passed Whitsunday Passage by moonlight. It was very beautiful even by night, and the coast scenery here is very grand, with high cliffs and many islands, rocky or covered with timber. The inevitable tender came to meet us at Townsville, and in twenty minutes we were in the town. Next day I took a trip to Charters Towers, the principal gold-field of Queensland, where is a ceaseless din of many hundreds of stampers, pounding away day and night. The journey on to Hughenden was a most monotonous one, and I was glad to get out of the dusty train.

After three days' rest, I went back to Townsville, and to the Queen's Hotel, where I had telegraphed for rooms. The town looked hot and parched, but in the wide verandah overlooking the sea, we had the benefit of what air there was. Mrs. C. had filled my room with flowers, and gave me tea and real Scotch scones afterwards in her own cool little sitting-room; she had added a great many new birds to her already large aviary, and the rest of the evening I spent in sketching some of them.

From Townsville I went on to the Herbert River in the well-known little s.s. *Palmer*, the larger steamers not being able to accomplish this inside route. I was introduced to the Bishop of Northern Queensland, who was going up to Croyden, one of the gold-fields, where no one seems to have a "past", or if they have, it is one which is best forgotten. He was most amusing, and told us Irish stories, and the doctor who was with him talked snakes and flowers.

The heat in the small cabin was so suffocating that I went on deck and sat on a bench until broad daylight. Sleep was out of the question, for we had anchored in the night at the mouth of the Herbert River, and the mosquitoes were unbearable (they played with me for sleep and won). I say nothing of the cockroaches and other insects! The night seemed horribly long, and even the glorious tropical sunrise did not compensate me for its discomfort. Steaming along, under the shadow of Hinchinbrooke Island, the coast scenery cannot be equalled in Australia. We landed in a small tender at Dungeness on the mainland at the mouth of the Herbert River. It is a miserable, low-lying, dead-and-alive place; and here we sat and broiled in the sun for five hours, waiting for the tide to take us up in the tender.

The hotel was so unprepossessing, and the people about looked such rough customers, that I preferred to keep as far away from it and them as possible, and sat melting slowly under a scorching sun until we were ready to start. The low banks of the river here were covered for six or seven miles up with mangrove trees. As we got higher it narrowed and the vegetation became very tropical; here were large palms and wild native

chestnut trees as large as any English ones, their branches covered with orange and yellow coloured pea-shaped blossoms; beautiful blue and white Ipomeas were trailing in masses along the banks, and there were numberless other flowers that I did not know.

    I was landed at a pier close to the Macnade Sugar-Mill, and I walked from there up to the house with one of the clerks. They had neither had my letters nor telegrams (another piece of carelessness on the part of the post-office), but they gave me a most warm welcome. The house is a perfect one for this climate, built high up on the banks of the river, with a very fine garden all round it. I recognised many old Colombo and Indian friends in it. *I was glad* to get under the shade of that long verandah; it had been the hottest day they had known that season, and never did cup of five-o'clock tea taste sweeter than mine that evening. Mrs. N. next day showed my flower-drawings to some of the Kanakas, and they were delighted at being able to recognise them, though they insisted on looking at them upside down; they went off at once to get me others, and before evening I had work enough to keep me going for a good many days.

The air here is heavy with the scent of tropical flowers, and a bush of gardenias outside my bedroom window is one dense mass of ivory white blossom. Beside it is a jacaranda with its blue, tube-like flowers, while beyond is the bhel tree, sacred to the gods, and a medley of brilliant colouring—poinsettias, alamandas, begonias, poincianas, thunbergias, stephanotis, hibiscus trees, erythrinas, ixoras, oleanders, and a host of others.

We breakfast on the verandah and almost live on fruits; in the garden there are mangoes, conquats, loquats, guavas, granadillas, oranges, and lemons, besides many Indian fruits. We spend our evenings on the verandah, lounging in our chairs, telling stories and listening to the songs of night birds. One, the "chopper" bird, comes to the same place each evening and keeps up his perpetual little hammer note until one's throat almost aches for him.

We made up a party and drove to some country races at a small town called Ingham a day or two ago; it was even a hotter day than that on which I arrived, being 103° on the verandah at eight in the morning. We drove for ten miles through clouds of dust. It is a clean, pretty-looking country town, and the races and "show" were very amusing, the latter consisting of a small stall of unripe-looking fruit, a bag of sugar from Macnade (there were no others to compete, so it won the prize of £3), a pen of fowls, a bull-dog tied to a post, looking like any kind of mongrel, a half-bred Newfoundland, three bunches of wild flowers, and a dozen samples of school children's work. The stand was filled mostly with children, eating buns and other sticky delicacies, and the mothers were nursing their babies in most delightful unconcern.

We sat waiting until three o'clock, when three horses jumped some hurdles in front of the stand, then an opposition "larrikins" jumping-race went on outside, and a Chinaman, with a stall of oranges, got mixed up in the excitement, and this filled up the time until half-past four, when the race of the day, a flat one, was run. Then we had a regular tropical storm, and such deluges of rain came down that the crowd, as if by magic, dispersed;

every leaf and plant sobbed with heavy drops, and the dust was turned into lakes of water for us to drive through on the way home.

Another day we had a most sumptuous lunch at the Victoria Sugar Company's Works. It was given by a number of young bachelors, and after being shown over the workings of the mill we drove home in the cool of the evening by moonlight.

How strange it was that at the very time you were restless and uneasy in your mind about me, I was really ill. I telegraphed that I missed the post, not wanting to give you the anxiety of knowing that I had fever. Mr. and Mrs. N. were called unexpectedly to Townsville, and during their absence I brought it on by my own imprudence in wading across a river which at low tide one can run across with a hop, skip and a jump. I had crossed this river and miscalculated the time of my return. I found on coming to it that the tide was running strongly in, and as there was no time to be lost, in I went, and it was just as much as I could do to stand against the current. It was an intensely hot day—my clothes had all dried on me before I reached home; but in these tropical climates one cannot play tricks, as I found when the fever developed itself. The Kanaka woman who was with me used to pay me one visit a day and, in pitying accents, say each time, "Poor missee, me so sorry, missee die to-day," which was not reassuring. In my delirium the second night, I got up and went down to the river, but I cheated death again; she was just in time to see me and bring me back and prevent me (as I said) from "swimming home".

How it would have ended I do not know, had not Mr. and Mrs. N. come home, when the usual remedies were used and all that was possible was done for me, but I felt limp and weak for many a long day afterwards.

A Dangerous Voyage

Goondi

My six weeks' visit to Macnade came all too soon to an end, but Mr. N. had to attend a land case, and I to catch a steamer at the mouth of the river (the Herbert) to take us to the Johnstone River 80 miles away. We had to make an early start at three in the morning. Already, on the night before, heavy black clouds were gathering, and there was a still sultriness in the air with flashes of lightning and the distant rumbling of thunder; the big frogs croaked in the tanks (a sure sign of rain), lumbering beetles boomed their wings against wall and floor in a dazed way, thousands of winged insects filled the air and flew in through the open doors and windows; flying ants dropped their ill-secured wings, and a lovely pale green moth fluttered against the window and was quickly caught, chloroformed, and pinned out.

At six o'clock the storm burst on us with all its fury, beating everything to the ground as only a tropical storm can; the pattering of rain on the roof was deafening, and in a few minutes every path down the garden was a running stream. From the verandah we stood and watched the river gradually widening, and the howling winds and distant roar of the rising water sounded very ominous for our journey next day. It was much worse when we had really to face it, and with lanterns in hand (at that early hour in the morning) we waded and slipped down to the bank. The river had risen thirty feet in the night and looked very black and angry; neither threats nor persuasions would induce the Kanakas to launch the big boat, and the only other one was a cockle-shell of a thing that would barely hold the three of us—a black boy (the only staunch one among them) and our two selves.

At the first push out from the shore, a fallen tree nearly swamped us, and while Mr. N. steered I baled out the water; in a few minutes we had not a dry article on us, and the rain from my bent hat was running in a stream down my back. Our

Kanaka was firmly convinced that his last hour had come, and roared lustily, "Me no want sit along below a river"—which being interpreted means that he didn't like being drowned. Every now and then we were lifted on the crest of a wave (which meant logs underneath) then swung down again into a small whirpool, the force of the leaping waters nearly swamping us.

I do not think we had realised until then the utter helplessness of that tiny boat in the rushing force of the swollen river. Each fresh wave seemed to send a shiver through it, and, like a living thing, it trembled with the fear of impending dissolution; wind, water, and clouds seemed to sweep past in a wild race, and the thought of alligators (who in flood times are most enterprising) did not add to our comfort. Now the current swept us round a sharp corner, and we found ourselves close under the bank. There was a nasty grating sound underneath, and in a second the boat swung round, and we knew we were caught on a snag.

It seemed inevitable now that a hole must be driven through the thin planks, for the force of the current sent us spinning round in a most uncanny way; for a moment we wrestled with fate, suddenly our boat seemed to sink, then we were tilted up again and the jerk fortunately emptied out some of the water, otherwise we must have gone under. In the dim light we could just distinguish the great black trunk of an uprooted tree, in whose branches we had been caught, and we were carried some distance down stream before we could extricate ourselves. Now in a bend of the river there was a horrible roar and bubbling as another swollen stream, with a violent rush, joined it. Stunned by the shock, the meeting waters leaped into arches and were thrown heavily back.

We were caught on the outside edge of the torrent and there were tossed like a leaf, now helplessly swept forwards, then eddying round corners and darting on again with the swiftness of horses in a race, and suddenly we found ourselves in smoother water, but only to find that we had sprung a leak, and we had to bale out the water with our hats to keep ourselves afloat. A break in the clouds showed us the faint outline of the black belt of mangrove trees which meant "land"; only two points now were left to pass, if we could manage to keep from sinking. The welcome sight of a steamer was the next thing I remember in the excitement; we knew then that help was at hand, and in a few moments our little boat, which had borne us so bravely through the perils of the swollen waters, was beside it, only to sink as we were hoisted, just in time, into the friendly vessel.

By daylight the storm was over, and between Hinchinbrooke Island and the mainland there was not a ripple on the water. The little steamer steamed as close to shore as the swampy ground and tangled and distorted wind-beaten branches of the mangrove trees would allow. Fifty feet of water ebbs and flows here from the tide, leaving the sloping mud-banks covered with crabs and shell-fish. Hundreds of sea birds (patiently waiting for a meal) with heavy wings rose in a deafening uproar at the sound of the engines, and resumed their watch from the trees above, where numbers of pelicans were hatching their eggs on the very roughest of stick-nests. There was a constant plash in the water as the climbing perch dropped from the forks of the branches in every direction; I had often heard of them, but had never, until now, seen them; they were from three to six inches long. The tall dark trees of the jungle rose in the background, and threw their long shadows across the still waters, and away from the lee of the land there wasn't a sound or a ripple on these mirror-like waters:

they say they teem with fish, and that there is good shooting in the country all round.

This strait between the mainland and the islands was like a chain of inland lakes, each without apparent outlet for 25 miles. We passed Cardwell, then a deserted-looking town, for, some years ago, a storm passed over it and swept away half the pier. The steamer was delayed here for an hour, and we went on shore and spent this time under the shade of two magnificent trees, whose roots almost grew into the water. We went also into Mourilyan Harbour, a narrow, awkward-looking passage with high rocks on both sides, and one, very large and threatening-looking, standing in the centre of the bar. The harbour inside is lovely, and the beautiful hills are clothed to the water's edge with vividly green foliage, and a living network of creepers and palms.

Fifteen miles farther, on the Johnstone River, we came to the small, picturesque town of Geraldton. Here we seemed to be in the very heart of tropical Queensland. I spent the night at the little hotel, which was crowded; the manager, with most boundless hospitality, placed all his belongings, such as they were, at my entire disposal. Then, having breakfasted there next morning, I paid my small bill and walked down to the steam launch, which was to take me to Goondi Sugar Plantation. While I was waiting, Captain Clarke of the *Palmer* climbed a very high tree that was hanging over the bank of the river to get me a beautiful Eugenia that was in blossom.

It was now very warm, and, as we had to tow a barge laden with sugar-cane behind us, we went along at a crawling pace. Thus, though we had started at ten, it was past one before we reached the house, although only five or six miles up. The river is very beautiful, and the thick, tangled vegetation comes down to the water's edge. It is so dense that it would be impossible to get through it except by cutting your way. From the tall palms above, trailing creepers crossed and intertwined their graceful plumes among fan-like branches, great bunches of scarlet berries drooped from a dark-leafed tree to the ground in heavy plumes. Here and there a bean tree (native chestnut) thrust a crimson-flowered branch through the dense foliage to catch the sunlight from above; large water hibiscus trees were everywhere shedding their blossoms, and the eddy of the current swept the crimson

The Flower Hunter

Flowers, Bloomfield Queensland, watercolour, 54.8 x 38 cm
Reproduced by permission of the National Library of Australia

heaps in dozens under the banks, while ipomeas, white, purple, blue and pink, wild ginger and endless trailing plants formed a thick undergrowth everywhere below.

We steamed under the shadow of an overhanging tree, and I pulled myself up by a branch and landed to get some flowers. I was caught by a trailing sucker of a native vine, a deadly obstacle to encounter. It has sharp barbs along the stem, and forms an almost impenetrable network of thick cords from tree to tree; it is, I believe, a kind of "lawyer", an even worse variety than that which grows in New Zealand, and it is well named, for when once you get into its clutches it is difficult to free yourself again.

The natives are not very civilised here, and a few days ago killed and ate a Chinaman; they seem to have an aversion to (or perhaps I should call it a fancy for) this particular race. They are perfectly unclothed, and along the banks were their miamias—neat, snug-looking huts, made of grass and palm leaves, with one small opening. During the dry weather they live on the river-bank, occasionally making raids on the sugar-cane, but during the rains they all disappear to the mountains. There were more than a hundred of them here a week ago, but Mr. A. drove them all away; only a few are now left solitary. Their weapons are very neatly made, and their fishing-nets, of the inner fibre of the couragee tree, are marvellous.

Goondi is a very large plantation, with 700 souls on it; the dense scrub is still being cut down. This work is generally done by Chinamen. The heaviest rainfall in Queensland is here, and ten inches in a night is not an unusual thing. I am too late here for the flowers, but the native fruits are quite worth painting. I cannot wander about here alone, as the natives are not to be trusted. The heat is intense, and the atmosphere so moist that my paints in pans have become quite liquid. It is impossible to go out in the middle of the day, and we generally take a stroll in the evening; once into the Chinese settlment on the plantation. They, the Chinese, almost all seem to smoke opium, and when their work is done, they give themselves up to it. Once only I went into the scrub by a bush path (I had always looked upon it before as a sort of promised land, never to be reached), and here I saw my first wild cassowary; they are very strong birds, and but seldom seen.

It seems sacrilege to cut down the beautiful timber; some of it, the red cedar, is floated down the river. The birds have wonderfully bright plumage here, and I have seen several different kinds of kingfishers. Many of the fruit-eating pigeons too are beautiful, especially the king pigeon, *Megaloprepia magnifica.* Of the 700 species of birds in Australia, 500 come from Queensland, while there are 50 species of snakes, all the water snakes being venomous.

There is found here a frog that contains a wineglassful of water; it buries itself in the mud, and in dry weather remains in a state of torpor; the natives dig them up and squeeze the water from them, when they can get no other in dry seasons. A pair of honey-eaters have built their nest under the verandah here, and it is a great amusement watching these bright-coloured birds as they flit from flower to flower, burying their little beaks in the scarlet blossoms of the hibiscus. The natives brought in a small ant-eating porcupine. This funny little round ball of a creature feeds on nuts and insects, which it picks up on its long, slender, sticky tongue; the natives eat it, and look upon it as a great delicacy. These mammals lay eggs like the Platypus, and the young are suckled by the mother after they are hatched. There are numbers of the native pheasant in the scrub—in Victoria it is called the Lowan, in West Australia the Ghow—both are native names; it lives almost entirely without water.

The other night I felt too hot to sleep, and the singing buzz of the mosquitoes outside the curtains got on my nerves to such an extent that I put on my dressing-gown and slipped out into the moonlight. I went for some way along the river-bank, then down a pathway with dense jungle on both sides. Nature was all wrapped in sleep; here and there through the foliage the moon cast strange shadows across the path. I startled some animal feeding on the fallen nuts, and it went off with a bound into the inky blackness of the shadows, some unseen night-bird uttered shrill cries, and the still air was heavy with the scent of spice trees and orchids. Nature has been almost too lavish in her gifts here.

Then out of the belt of jungle again I went into a small space of more open ground. The soft gray dawn was just stealing along the horizon, and the gaunt skeletons of ringed trees, where fresh sugar-cane fields are being formed, stood out against the steely sky like grim sentinels at their post. Some of the birds were just beginning to waken, and a large cassowary bounded away in front of me, the long-bladed grass was bent double with heavy dew, and remembering that I had already had a sharp warning against trifling with this tropical climate, I turned my face homewards again. No one was as yet astir here, and I crept into my room, fell alseep, and never woke or moved again until the sun was high above the tree-tops.

It was a restless kind of day, too hot even to paint, and the atmosphere so moist that the very paints themselves wouldn't dry. From my window I made a sketch of the bend of the river, for we were close on its banks here; two large green and black butterflies floated lazily by as if they had only just been born into the sunshine; they rested on a poinsettia, and the temptation to go after them, despite the steaming heat, was so great that I went ouside; then a blue and red one danced in front of me, but though it was tantalising to let them go, such a vapour bath was beyond endurance, and I handed my net over to a small black boy, who, instead of butterflies, brought me a fat green grasshopper, well squashed in his moist little hands! Under the shade of the trees on the river-bank a boat was fastened. Here the rippling of the water sounded at least cooler, and a blue and white kingfisher seated on the end of a log was just what I wanted to sketch; his mate on her nest in a hollow of the tree above I found later on, and he sat and guarded her, occasionally darting across or into the water after some dainty morsel of food.

Under the shadow of the large Caladium leaves, gliding in and out among the stems, fish went by, pressing their noses along them in quest of food, and snapping here and there at a stray fly or water-beetle. A snail, with a thin transparent shell, crept from under a leaf, and, quick as thought, a great green frog swallowed it—these snails are in great request; I have often watched the water-fowls turning over the leaves looking for them—a pink and green fruit-eating pigeon cooed in the tree above me as he sent a shower of small yellow figs into the boat, sweet but tasteless to eat. A water-wagtail danced in the air after a dragonfly, and I heard the twitter of young birds as she came back to them with her winged meal. I sat so still in my resting-place that after a time she almost touched me with her wings, and in her nest close beside me I could count the five featherless necks of her nestlings as they feebly craned them up and gaped for food. A woodpecker climbed up the trunk of the tree, tapping here and there for a likely sound as he went jauntily on; a bright green lizard basked in the sunshine, and through the moist warm air was diffused an indefinable scent of sweetness that you never seemed wholly to catch. A branch of pale mauve flowers with long white stamens hung almost into the water, and above them in the long-bladed grass countless webs, so daintily spun that it seemed sacrilege to break one silken thread, glistened in the sunlight. The harsh sound of a bell brought me back to earth again.

Mrs. A. and I pulled a short distance up the river, and landing, made our way through a thick wood of native banana palms to the shade of a weeping fig-tree. Here we drowsed until the sun went down and it was cool enough to walk out into the more open country; we startled a bird, like a plover, off her nest, and with a plaintive cry she ran from right to left, then with a sweep upwards went out of sight, still uttering her cries in the distance. Not even the sound of an axe was to be heard, although this ruthless weapon is always at work on new-formed sugar plantations. Before we went home again, Mother Earth was beginning to fold her night wings round her—a bat flew out from the gray shadows of the trees, and a cool, sweet air brushed our faces as we rowed down the river against it. It was sultry enough inside with the lighted lamps, and we sat in our lounge chairs until well into the morning.

For two or three days I was very lazy over my work, and felt almost too listless to do anything. There was no use fighting any longer against it; it was another attack of fever, and I had to give in—this is the penalty one has to pay for living on these beautiful tropical rivers, especially while the forests are being cleared.

A Midnight Corroboree

Hambleton

The day before I left Goondi, I spent hours in hunting butterflies, which are found there in wonderful variety; some of the moths are most beautiful, one that I caught I have since heard is a new variety; it is over six inches across: the upper gray wings are finely marked with threads of white, and the head is of a paler shade, the under wings have one large, bright, rose-coloured, irregular spot on them. But hunting butterflies in this steaming heat is not pleasure, and enthusiasm is apt to lead one sometimes into uncomfortably near quarters with snakes, as I found to my cost.

From the Johnstone I had to go back to Townsville, where it was intensely hot and parched. We left it in one of the large steamers, and it lay all in a golden haze as the sun was setting. Distance lent enchantment to the view; the shore, all dotted with houses in the foreground, grew fainter and fainter, leaving at last only the outline of Castle Hill, and away in the far distance the purple ranges which form the usual background to Queensland coast scenery.

At Cairns the steamer came close to the shore, and on landing we walked along the pier between an avenue of banana bunches waiting to be shipped South; 14,000 bunches went by the last steamer, and the supply seems endless. They are grown principally by Chinamen, and hundreds of acres, I should think, are under cultivation around and about the town, which lies very low and is quite rural. In the evening I walked along the beach under the shade of an avenue of handsome trees. I did not know any of them, and I fancy the seed must have originally been washed there from some distant islands. John Chinaman is, as usual, to the fore here; he grows all the vegetables and most of the fruit, which comes to perfection in this climate; you can buy one dozen and a half grenadillas for a shilling, and other fruit is just as cheap.

Mr. Walton drove me straight to the Railway Hotel, of which he is the proprietor, and, late at night as it was, they had tea prepared for me, with a comfortable bedroom and sitting-room, and they were altogether so good to me both here and later at their hotel up at Myola on the railway line, that I shall always remember them with gratitude. My next drive was rather an exciting one, for when almost four miles out of the town, a Chinaman with his baskets meeting us on a bridge proved too much for the horses, and off they started as hard as their legs would carry them. Over the stones, through the mangroves, on to the road again, and over the little rickety bridges the light buggy was dragged, jumping from side to side as if it entered into the spirit of the moment. With a mixed feeling of terror and excitement I wondered what and where the end would be, and noting quickly as we passed some beautiful white convolvuli, I hoped it might not be far from there; and it was not either, for bang we came almost at that moment against a tree, a horse on either side of it; away went the pole and what a smash-up we had! I had to ride ignominiously back to the hotel sideways on a Chinaman's broken-kneed horse, only too thankful that things were not worse.

Hambleton Sugar Plantation, ten miles from Cairns, from which I now write, is one of the most beautiful places I have seen in Queensland. The house, which is very pretty and comfortable, is in an almost perfect situation at the foot of high mountains, with a magnificent view of them all round. The plantation itself lies in a valley below, and one can see Cairns by the sea ten miles away in front. The wild, rich, tropical vegetation is all around, and it is tantalising to see the Bellenden Ker ranges so close without being able to go up and explore them. I can only send you sketches and give you a rough outline of what this lovely country is like. There are oranges, lemons, bananas, tamarinds, pine-apples, melons, grenadillas, and custard apples, ripe in the garden; the latter fruit I have only now tasted for the first time. It was a large one. I ate it all, and the rich, creamy flavour satisfied me so much that I have never managed a second. It is much cooler here than in Cairns, and for the first time since I left Brisbane I have been able to take quite long walks. I have spent a lazy fortnight enjoying the peaceful quiet, the happy home life, and listening to the prattle of four of the sweetest little children I ever met. They never bore one and, like their fair mother, grow more winning day by day.

Before going further, however, I must not forget to tell you of a rather insane midnight ride I had to see a corroboree of really wild natives. Would I be tired? Would I be frightened? Would I mind a rough journey? and numerous other thoughtful inquiries were made, but you know well enough what my answers were. Would I say no to a trip to the moon if I thought I could get there? So off I started at seven in the evening with one of the overseers from the plantation, to ride eight miles to an hotel where we were to pick up the rest of our party.

It did not look an inviting evening for an excursion, for it was drizzling with rain the whole way, and now and then a muffled rumble of thunder came to our ears, as if it had not quite made up its mind to approve of our proceedings. My host and hostess, who were to have come with us, changed their minds at the last moment, and wisely too, for the expected corroboree was no novelty to them; neither would it have been to them, as it was to me, a new sensation to get wet through; so away we went with an escort of three gentlemen and two blacks, Sammy and Jacky. Presently the moon came out through the clouds, and we were able to enjoy, even by that light, the beauty of the tropical bush.

We crossed a very swift river by none the smoothest of crossings, and it was no easy matter to make our way by the light of the moon round and over huge stones hurled one on top of the other in terrific confusion from the perpendicular cliffs above, and then on we went through an old sugar plantation at the foot of the Pyramid Hill; such a splendid mill there was, all going to ruin, and the cane that we rode through, high above our horses' heads, was being trodden down and eaten by hundreds of cattle. Some of these were very wild, and seemed to object to our encroaching on their quarters. It seemed cruel that so much enterprise and money (over £200,000) should be wasted and lost because of the doing away with black labour. This is now my second visit to Queensland, and the more I see of this Northern coast climate, the more impossible it seems to be that white labour can ever be much utilised or relied on to do physical work amid such moisture and under such a sun.

But where was the camp we were seeking? We rode on and

on, and still no sign; on through another plantation and into scrub with not the faintest trace of a track, then out again and over an old wooden bridge, several planks of which gave way, and my horse's hind leg went through. It seemed that Sammy and Jacky were out in their reckoning, and by way of an experiment we all halted and cooeed together, but only the weird echoes came back to us; so we took another turn of exploring. The clouds were now growing blacker and blacker, and the road becoming rougher at each step that we took, so at last Jacky was put on one of our horses and sent off to try if he could find the camp. We all waited, while, to pass the time, one after the other told ghost and snake stories, bush tales of long ago, of creeping horrors, or of hairbreadth escapes from natives and bushrangers. Under the shadow of the moonlight every bough and tree seemed woven into human form, and the soughing of the passing wind as it swept through the tall tree tops sounded like the sigh of a weary spirit let loose, as it sank away into the darkness beyond.

I shivered and wished myself back. Presently, away in the distance, we heard the peculiar long cooeeing of our black boys, and the still more distant answer from many others, and before long our two black envoys returned. They had seen the natives who were afraid of us. "What did the white men want?" "Had they come to frighten them away?" and so on. When they were assured that we only wanted to see them as friends, and had brought them tobacco, two of them were persuaded to return as heralds with our black boys, and presently out came the two black unclothed, shiny bodies to guide us. How active they were; with mercurial swiftness they ran in front, laughing and chattering like two monkeys.

Suddenly we came to a place too dangerous for riding, and we had to get off. I, for a moment, was only too delighted to find myself on my own feet again, but what a walk it was! Now clambering up a steep rise, now sliding down a slippery gully, now into the open where the moon again came out casting strange shadows all round us, and I wondered once or twice what you would have said could you have seen me. Now we are going to be bogged altogether surely! They say I must be carried or get on to my horse again, but no! I would not do either, and by a succession of long jumps I came off unaided and better than some of them. How dark the scrub was, and at every step the horses kept getting entangled in the "lawyers" and long creeping vines. Presently mine stumbled and quivered all over, for he had been caught in a barbed wire fence, which the natives had stolen from the plantation and put round their camp, but beyond a few scratches he was none the worse.

After another two minutes, we found ourselves on the bank of the river with "gunyahs"[1] all about, while a crowd of chattering unclothed natives pressed all round us. They were much amused at the sight of a "white Mary", and they brought out their piccaninnies for me to admire. We had a peep into all the gunyahs. In each was a fire at the entrance, and close beside many of them lay the gins and old men asleep. They gave me two tiny babies to hold; they were only a day old and did not seem to mind being disturbed. The women were none of them five feet high, and for the first time in my life I felt tall. The men, too, are very short, but very active.

They were some time in commencing their corroboree, which was perfectly different from those we saw at Cape York. They danced less, but grunted more, and the peculiar sneezing noise they make all together is almost identical with that of the natives of Western Australia. With brandished spears and painted bodies, the men trod with stealthy measured footsteps, cautiously peering from side to side into the darkness in search of some supposed foe. Then suddenly a miniature battle ensured, the gins, sitting apart by themselves, beat splendid time with their boomerangs, and clapped their hands together, while the men, with hideous gestures and a monotonous chorus of grunts, madly stamped the ground with rhythmic motion, swaying their bodies backwards and forwards. Then with infuriated yells they advanced and retreated in and out of the fires, dancing faster and faster, and shouting "Ough! ough!" as each footstep went with a thud on the ground, until, fairly exhausted and streaming with the heat, they suddenly all retired into the darkness of the surrounding bush.

After the dancing was over, we gave them tobacco all round,

---

[1] Huts.

the women begging for some for the piccaninnies. We then said good-bye and started for home, which for us was not reached until broad daylight. The cocks were crowing, and the birds were already commencing to sing.

Myola

I left Hambleton a few days ago, the very morning of my return from our expedition to see the corroboree. I only had time to get some breakfast and pack up my things before starting, in a real tropical shower, to catch the train at Cairns. As we drove off, I felt a genuine regret at having to say good-bye to such kind friends, and to so much that was novel and beautiful, but I began to feel that I would never come to my journey's end if I loitered longer on the way.

This is a typical Australian Bush hotel, at the head of the Barron Falls, and I wished twenty times to-day that you had been with me to enjoy the magnificent scenery along the railway line.

I have now travelled on the engine, on a navvy's trolly, on a railway bicycle, and lastly on the cowcatcher of an express engine, so that I have had every locomotive sensation obtainable. You will say, "And how did you like this latter mode of progression?" And I will promptly reply that I wouldn't have missed it as a novel experience, but have no wish to try it again. Such a quick flight through mid-air in this position, holding on like grim death with heels and hands, brings rather too great a sense of exultation, your heart seems to fill your throat, your blood tears through your veins, and the speed through the air sounds in your ears like the whizz of a hundred spinning-wheels, while everything beside you runs into a watered ribbon of jumbled colours, and it is with a feeling of relief that the mountain bridges and sharp corners are turned, and the engine slackens speed on the level ground as she hisses into the station terminus.

The line by which I travelled has only been opened for four months, and it is by far the most beautiful, they say, in Australia. Besides being a good specimen of engineering skill in mountain railroad making, the beauty of each fresh turn becomes more and more impressive as it mounts the higher. In many places the train seems almost to hang over the precipices 600 and 900 feet deep, while still towering above are masses of granite rock and of wild tropical vegetation, sometimes palms, vines, bananas, or fairy draperies of hanging ferns; sometimes clusters of orchids, with scarlet flame-trees here and there, giving light and brilliant colour to the dense masses of vivid greens, which range from the palest apple and russet to the deepest olive.

There are waterfalls in every direction, and presently below, far down in the depths of vegetation, one sees the Barron River, and away in the distance, between the mountains, like another world below, the valley dotted with houses, with the blue sea beyond and the faint outlines of other distant mountains and the little indistinct town of Cairns almost buried amongst them. One longs for a few minutes to enjoy it all, but the merciless train keeps on, while here and there below one catches glimpses of the river dashing over great rocks; or of passing gleams of white foam at the foot of the falls, and finally, for one speechless moment, the falls themselves. I could only hold my breath and gasp "Oh!" for I was on the engine, but the driver gave no response, excepting to heap more coals on the fire. Another second and the vision was gone, and we found the river high up beside us, breaking and eddying round great rocks, or else, without a ripple, gliding along over sandy bars.

Gradually the train slackened its pace and we were at our journey's end; a three minutes' walk brought us to this hotel, which consists of two separate houses; our bedrooms and general sitting-room in one, the dining-room, kitchens, and other quarters in the other; a little space in the forest only is cleared, and all round us is the wild bush; it is decidedly cooler and I sleep for a second time with a blanket over me. Our bedrooms are made like loose boxes, a partition running only half-way up the wall, and as there are two large families of children here together, one does not have a chance of enjoying one's early morning's rest.

There is an old Scotch couple too, in the next room to mine, who never open their lips to each other during the day, but, unfortunately, reserve all their conversation for "Caudle Lectures" at bedtime, when, in despite of myself, I listen until wearied out to their incessant bickerings. I feel inclined to call out, as that American did in the story, "For goodness' sake kiss and make friends, and let us all get some sleep." We have heard their whole family history so often repeated that we know it by heart now. Yesterday the wife was hemming table napkins, and her husband told her she would have no use for that senseless rubbish where she was going—which sounded ominous. After five years' waiting, he had, we heard, built her a house, and she had under these conditions alone consented at last to join him. Once they left the hotel, but they returned; it was only a tent he had taken her to, and the discussions now became so vehement that in a body we all protested and begged that they might "have it out" elsewhere. He rather puts me in mind of my Irishman in Western Australia, whose language was unique, and who after pouring out his griefs and troubles to me, half of which were unintelligible, ended up with "Says I to my wife, says I, it don't dignify consputing, you better divide yourself with another person." I leave the literal translation to you. The same old gentleman sent me to look for a peppermint spring. After fruitless endeavours to discover its whereabouts, I found out that it was intended for a permanent one. But I am spinning out my letter, and your eyes must be wearied already trying to decipher my not too plain handwriting, so for the present good-night.

A Tedious Journey

Myola

I started at daylight this morning for a two-mile walk up to the natives' camp to get some sketches before the men had left for their day's hunt. A few yards from the hotel I came face to face in the middle of the path with a fresh-water crocodile. He was an unwieldy-looking creature, but a small and harmless variety. I do not know which of the two of us was the more astonished at the meeting, and he took himself off no quicker than I did. In these first hours of daylight nature teems with life and motion, the simmering hum and flutter of insect life fills the air, dragonflies dart over the surface of the water in search of their tiny prey, gay butterflies in perpetual motion circle in the sunlight with uncertain glitter, crickets chirp with might and main, birds swell the chorus with joyful song to greet the day, brilliant red lauries and green paroquets incessantly chatter among the branches, wild ducks splash and plume themselves in the river, the restless sound of the woodpecker re-echoes as each blow of his beak strikes the bark, wagtails dart to and fro, bright green lizards peer curiously from chinks of rock, and spiders run along their lacework of countless silken ropes well filled with legs and wings.

A chorus of barking curs greeted me as I reached the camp, which consisted of a few bark humpies on the bank of the river, from which a thin curl of smoke was rising. A woman of monstrous ugliness, whose mouth alone would have placed her in the category of ogress, threw down her bundle of sticks and greeted me with a sudden access of enthusiasm, and I was instantly surrounded by a gaping crowd of scantily-clothed natives. A loving husband on the conjugal threshold was administering a wholesome rebuke to his spouse, who did not in any way seem to resent it, a shower of blows now and then flatters their *amour propre*, and in dutiful obedience she instantly gave up a roasted delicacy that had evidently been the cause of their quarrel. The debris of their morning feast was being devoured by the starved-looking dogs.

It was a very picturesque scene; the rich, dark brown of the natives and their huts, the reds of the dying fires and films of blue smoke as they curled upwards against the dark background of forest jungle, and in the foreground the sheen of sunlight on the river, where the lithe figure of a native boy was dexterously paddling a little canoe to the opposite side, all combined to form a picture. Wild beautiful nature shut me in on every side. How could I caricature her? In utter despair I shut up my sketch-book and made my way back under the shade of the forest trees with their network of branches above all hung and festooned with thickets of clematis, convolvulus, and flowering bignonias, erythrinas, tossing acacias, feathery palms—but I have not the gift of words to describe half their beauty. Now in the sunlight the river-banks are green with sedges and tall white lilies, and beyond are masses of great moss-grown rocks, and the river tosses and tumbles round and over them, falling in countless cascades into the deep, dark pools below.

Then back at the hotel in time for a nine-o'clock breakfast, and off I started for a day's excursion with Mr. G., the engineer of this railway, and several of his men on a trolly down to the Barron Falls. There they fell in grand magnificence, 600 feet of rushing, roaring waters, swirling, crashing down a scarred and fissured face of rock into a wild turmoil of foam and spray below; hence the river flows for another few yards only to cast itself over a second precipice down 200 feet more into a deep basin of foaming water; when the last rocks are passed it flows away smoothly by sandy banks, past gardens and farms until it is lost in the great sea beyond.

I had come here to make a sketch of the falls from a ledge far down the cliff, and the men had brought a rope with them in case I needed it. It was not so easy a climb as I had imagined, slipping first over the dry, dead leaves of the gums, scrambling down boulders of rock, writhing through crannies with a swing from a great tree-root here, and a climb from a branch there, then on hands and knees groping my way cautiously from ledge to ledge until I reached my goal at last, where, with feet dangling in mid-air over the precipitous shelving rock, I looked down hundreds of feet below upon the brawling river. I made a rough sketch of the falls from here. There were clusters of delicate orchids below in the clefts of the rocks, mosses and lichens and a lovely sundew on a ragged ledge—"that weed", they afterwards slightingly called it, that I had risked my life to get, proved to be the rarest of its kind.

We had our lunch under another waterfall about eight miles away and then started off on a flower-hunting expedition. The heat had become intense, and under the thick cover and shade of these woods there was a death-like silence in these mid-day hours. On one of the steepest slopes of the cliffs one of our men found a rare coral-tree blossom and he afterwards climbed to the top of a tall forest tree for a beautiful yellow Cassia that hung in drooping yellow sprays and thin brown pods fourteen inches long. We came home laden with treasures; but I am too early here, they say, as I was, they told me, too late everywhere else for the flowers. As we came home with the setting sun nature was beginning her nightly revels: birds overhead were retracing their way home, and as darkness descended flying-foxes launched themselves from where during the day they hung suspended from branches, owls with soft, downy wings flitted silently across the pale sky. Moths issuing from dark retreats take the place of butterflies, bats wheel from right to left in rapid circles, booming beetles with jerking strength of will dart recklessly against the trees, and crickets add their shrill voices to swell the din. Under the deep shadows we trod over things of sickening softness, and the inexplicable rustle of mysterious beings is so little reassuring that it was with a feeling of satisfaction that we struck the cleared pathway leading home.

And now, with happy appetites satisfied, we settled ourselves comfortably in our lounge chairs on the verandah for the evening, and they told me that, that very afternoon, high revelry had been going on in the native camp, as they feasted off the roasted remains of an old woman who had been allowed, against their usual custom, to die a natural death the day before. Just as we were on our way to bed we heard the cackle of a fowl close beside the house, the unmistakable cry, growing fainter and fainter, of one being crushed to death by a snake. We all rushed frantically off with candles alight to the edge of the jungle; but the creature had gone off out of sight with its prey.

A cow in the grounds here has now and then given us a little excitement in the shape of a run; I am not the only one she has "bailed up", and one old lady one day took refuge in a barrel that fortunately was near at hand. But one takes these trifles as all in the day's fun. Everything here, for a country hotel, is most comfortable; being clean, with excellent cooking, plenty of milk, cream and eggs, and ice, fresh fish, and fruit every day.

Herberton

Here I am, on my way to the celebrated Muldiva silver mines and the Chillagoe Caves, and if this historical document is unusually stupid, I won't take any responsibility for its feebleness, for my energies have been almost spent on our two days' journey to reach this place. To-night it is quite cold enough for a fire, although the heat in the middle of the day was almost unbearable. The noise and bustle in the street give one the idea of quite a large town; but it is only a small straggling mining village among hills, not unlike the township at Mount Morgan. At present it has a dry and barren look, and we are back among the gum-trees again; poor stunted-looking ones, however, with a painfully gray, monotonous appearance.

I left Myola yesterday, at two o'clock, to catch the coach to this place; the country that we drove through for many miles was beautiful. We passed over the Cairns range and through tropical scrub, with here and there glimpses of the sea shining below us, and, in the far distance, the dim, blue mountains; but once over the coastal ranges, a feature of these northern latitudes, the belts of jungle become less frequent, and the country assumes a dull and uninteresting aspect, mile after mile of shadeless, gray, sombre-looking gum-trees, poor and scantily clothed, stretch away in indefinite monotony. Here and there along the roads we passed teams of bullocks carrying stores, and the inevitable swagman, with all his earthly possessions on his back, tramping away to the land of silver and of gold. The road was a very up-and-down one, but "Joe," the driver, a regular Australian bush boy, was such a splendid whip that even I was not nervous; not even when night came on, and we got off the track, and the seven horses went as hard as they could through the gum-trees, crashing down young saplings, and grazing stumps by a hair's breadth, but never once coming in contact with anything.

As the night became darker and the road rougher, we could sometimes, through the dust, barely distinguish even the wheelers, and I held on more and more tightly, and wondered if it was instinct or sight that guided Joe. Suddenly, crash went one of the bars; everyone had to get down, and it was an hour before it was patched up and we went on. We crossed the Barron River, where the fording place is a rocky ledge, so narrow, that an inch one way or the other would set the horses swimming. "It was just here," said Joe, by way of encouraging me, "that the coach went over into deep water not many months ago, and we had a rare old swim." However, we splashed through with a dash, and up the bank, at the top of which we heard the welcome sound of dogs barking, while here and there the lights of the township showed up. In the pitch darkness it seemed to consist only of two hotels.

Here I had my first experience of what is called an up-country inn; we all had our supper together in one long room. Joe sat at the head of the table, the cloth of which bore traces of many meals; the other *convives* were a miscellaneous collection—diggers

The Flower Hunter

Leptospermum lanigerum Smith, *var.* grandiflorum, Leptospermum myrsinoides Schlechtendal, *watercolour, 53.8 x 37.2 cm Reproduced by permission of the National Library of Australia*

in their shirt-sleeves, mothers with their babies, etc. There was a furious click of knives and forks, resolutely bent on making up for lost time, and scrimmaging their best for the unsavoury-looking compounds on the table. I was very hungry, but I could not stand these "fag ends"; and the pangs of hunger were only a secondary consideration to those of my bed. The house was so full that I could not get a room to myself; but at last they consented to make me up a bed on an upstairs verandah. Here I fought until daylight with mosquitoes, and, finally, submitting myself to circumstances, hailed dawn with inexpressible relief.

By five o'clock we were well on our way again: it was a most uninteresting drive; here and there we passed through a shady bit of jungle, but the rest of the journey lay through dry and stunted gum-trees. We passed many piled-up stacks of magnificent cedar logs which have been lying there for some years, waiting for the railway to be finished. The road for the last few miles before reaching Herberton was a great pull for the horses, and the heat was almost unbearable; indeed, even on the verandah of the hotel, I had to sit with an umbrella up, for there was no protection from the sun under the corrugated iron roof.

I went off at once to the Post Office where I had ordered my letters to be sent, but some one (they did not know who) had called for them the day before, and taken them away. Then I felt furious, and told them that they had no right to have given them up without an order from me; the man only smiled, and was so profuse in his apologies that I couldn't say anything more. They all turned up in the evening, papers, magazines, and all.

Was ever there a man more thoughtful?—the pages were even cut for me, and I especially noted the chapter on "dutiful wives", and will take great care, as you always say, of "your wife for you", and the fat port-folios that I shall send home from time to time will compensate for the months without her.

I had visitors all the afternoon, all doing their utmost to persuade me not to attempt the rough journey to the Caves. But how could I turn back after coming so far, notwithstanding that I have met with a great disappointment, as I had a half-promise that a lady companion would go on with me from here, and I found that the idea of the journey had frightened her. The prospect does not look promising; a coach drive to-morrow (for

I have determined to go on at once) from five in the morning until half-past eleven at night, when we ought to reach Muldiva, and then a rather indefinite Beyond. How I am to get to the Caves from there I have yet to find out, but I am armed with three or four letters which will help me on the way.

Muldiva

I am gradually nearing the Caves, but what a journey it has been! In spite of the many warnings I received I was determined to come, and here I am, sitting now, as I write in, a corrugated iron house in the principal street of this newly-formed mining town of Muldiva. I am only too glad to have been lent this retreat to come to for the day, away from the noise of the hotel, which is only a few doors off. Opposite me is the police station, which fact is painted in red letters on a piece of canvas. This place consists of two diggers' tents and a sort of verandah made out of branches of gum-trees. The general store is a tent on forked sticks with a wall of branches on all sides, the proprietor's name is written in huge letters upon it, and a counter with glasses and array of tins proclaim his calling. The thermometer is 120° in the shade.

Next comes a real bush bark hut, of which many are studded about in every direction, then another tent, a bakehouse, one or two more stores, and two shelters that call themselves hotels. A man sits under an awning in the principal street (which is still full of felled trees and stumps) with the air of an Indian potentate, guarding a keg of beer, tumblers, matches, tobacco, pipes, etc. Here and there a native goes by, more or less in a state of intoxication. The butcher's shop is a green arbour of boughs. Stores just now are "out", and a pound of flour for the time costs a shilling.

Everything is full of life and activity. The new chum that you met is reticent, the old hand communicative. Above, below, and around, are miners with thews and sinews, wresting the precious metal from beds of rock, burrows in hill-sides, and along the beds of an apology for a stream, whose waters are so full of lime that everything becomes encrusted with it, and even your clothes from the wash are powdered. John Chinaman goes by with his pack-horse, for already he is pioneering with his garden stuff; where his garden is I do not know: everything seems baked and parched up, and the poor miserable gum-trees do not look as if they could cast a yard of shade. All around are the bare rocky hills, and just behind the town is the great Muldiva mine which at present shows every sign of a prosperous future. A bullock-team goes by, and more natives' gins carrying water, about the only thing they are good for.

It is Sunday, and the day seems as if it would never come to an end, not a breath of cool air anywhere, not a book to read; bottling up my self-imprisoned thoughts, I sat on the doorstep, I sat on the table, then under it, but still I could not get away from that fierce heat; then I went back to the hotel and into a little hut next door, where I sat and fanned a child dying of fever; there it was slightly cooler, and I had something besides my own worries to think of. Evening came at last, and I went for a walk with the housemaid from the hotel up to a hill overlooking the town. She gave me a most ghastly description of life in a mining town, and already I long for the night to be over, though the thought of that journey back hangs over me like a hideous nightmare.

I have had many rough drives, but they all pale in comparison with that which brought me here; the five horses had literally to climb up and down hills and rough tracks for miles after leaving Herberton (they say it is the roughest road in Australia), dragging that great heavy Cobb's coach behind them. It needs to be strong, and so must, I suppose, be heavy; here and there, where the track was unusually steep, and the coach going down literally had to drop from one boulder to another, all the passengers excepting myself got out. I begged leave to remain, not because I was not a coward, but because I preferred terror to that walk over the hot stones.

In the gray dawn of the morning the temperature was just bearable, but as the day wore on the heat and dust became intolerable, and by ten A.M. we were only too glad to stop while they changed our horses, and get a quarter of an hour's rest and a cup of tea at Montalbion, one of the barest and most miserable-looking places I have ever seen. Thence we went on in what they called a "Buckboard", a four-wheeled, low, hoodless sort of buggy, in which we got the full benefit of the sunshine and dust; such clouds of the latter there were that no one could possibly have distinguished the colour of anything we had on. From Montalbion to our destination we passed over the same endless, rocky, gum-tree-dotted hills, one of which they call the "Feather-bed", because it consists of huge round boulders, of which a few only have been removed from the track, and here again everyone had to get out.

We changed horses once more, thirty miles from Montalbion, at a little hut, rough but very clean, where I quenched my thirst with some lime-juice and water, the only drinkable liquid I could get. Here we changed into a coach again. At the next stopping I asked, "Had they any soda-water, or lemonade, or gingerbeer, etc.?" "No, they had none of them fancy drinks; but would I like some sarsaparilla?" When we started again night was coming on, and we had only one lamp available, the heat of the sun having melted the candle in the other, and, too tired, at last to keep awake any longer, and the coachman having put a strap round me and fastened me to the coach, I fell asleep; for how long I don't know, but I was suddenly awakened by a bump and a crash: we were off the track, the leader was over a log, and the others trying to follow; they were all hopelessly mixed up together among broken harness; I have only an indistinct recollection of their bolting, but it is all so hazy that I cannot tell you more. We were patched up somehow or other.

A second time, when we picked up a log in the wheel, they bolted, but this time I did not care what happened. Finally, to my unspeakable joy, at two in the morning we reached this hotel. I was taken to my room where I fell asleep while undressing, and awoke at four A.M. to find myself sitting on the floor, resting my head against the bed. The whole house shook at six that morning with the tread of heavy feet, so that there was no more rest to be had, and indeed, in any case, the heat of the sun would soon have driven me out, so I got up, scooped the dust out of my bag, and finally had the luxury of a bath (though it was about the colour of pea-soup) and breakfast in my own room.

A few days ago the journey to the Caves was described word for work in a letter to me thus: "It is almost an impossible journey for a lady unless you camp out. The whole way the heat and flies are unbearable, the country lies very low, and on account of the heavy thunderstorms just now you are liable to be flooded out. The whole district is totally uninhabited," and so on; but now good-bye for the present. I cannot take you through the Caves in this letter, for a post goes to-morrow, and, as they are not an every-day occurrence here, I cannot afford to miss this chance.

Chillagoe Caves

Myola

Before leaving Muldiva I was anxious to see the much-talked-of mine which promises (so many people say) to be hardly second to Broken Hill.[1] I cannot, I fear, give you very clear account of it; but it consists of a number of contiguous "claims", extending over a considerable area of hilly ground at the back of the little settlement. Rocks crop up here and there through the barren soil, and there is nothing that I could see to distinguish it from any other hill about. In some places drives go into the side of the hill, in others shafts are sunk right down. The morning before we left, the manager took us all through most of the different claims of the Company. Every tunnel we went into had rich silver-bearing stone, some of it giving over 500 ounces to the ton.

At one shaft, the "Paisley", we went down a perpendicular ladder 180 feet, which I did not quite enjoy, though at first it looked as if it would be so cool down that narrow black hole, that I thought, here at any rate we will get away from the heat and glare. We did get away from the glare certainly, but the heat was stifling, and the men below, little expecting to see a lady come down, were working in the very scantiest of clothing.

The reef here was thirty-seven feet through and very rich all the way, indeed the whole place seemed a mountain of silver, and as, in a few months' time, the machinery will be up and they will start crushing, great things are foretold. There are tin, copper, and silver mines in every direction in this part of the country, but everything is as yet in its infancy.

After seeing the mine, we started at two o'clock for Chillagoe Cattle Station, to the owner of which, Mr. A., I had a letter.

I was driven there by Mr. C. in a small one-horse trap, the material of which needed to be of the strongest, for the road was an exceedingly rough one, for the most part over broad beds

---

[1] It has since that time not realised such high expectations.

of rock and pebbly ground. The whole country is a vast undulating plain, dotted with rugged masses of curiously-outlined limestone ridges, rising to many hundreds of feet, straight out of the ground, giving the landscape a stern and oppressive grandeur; the deep fissures of these towering walls are filled with gnarled and hoary trunks of trees striking and grasping the massive fragments with their rootlets and creeping and twisting in and out of crevices. Below, the huge blocks of stone are overgrown with an intricate wilderness of shrubs and creeping plants; while high above, these dark and towering walls are destitute of any living thing, and their stricken, shattered-looking peaks, networks of sharp pinnacles with needle-like points, stand gray and arid-looking against the intense blue of the sky.

They say the vegetation here is most beautiful after the rains, a blaze of colour from the flowers which cover the rocks, while the ground is clothed with large white lilies; now, excepting for the vivid green of the coral-trees and the brilliant pink leaves of a budding Banksia, the landscape has a dry and withered look, and the only living thing that we saw was a little yellow and black wallaby, that scuttled away like lightning when it caught sight of us. Climbing kangaroos are found in the jungle scrub. Not far away from here a man whom we met at Muldiva had for a pet one that ran up trees as well as an opossum.

The sun had been intensely hot all day, and great dark shadows of cloud, boding rain, were gathering for a downpour. We reached the station at six o'clock in the evening, and, oh! the heartfelt satisfaction and sweet sense of rest in being in a home again and away from hotels. We arrived only just in time. With a tremendous gust of wind everything took to itself wings; crash went the thunder, then died away into a dull roar; then, for a few seconds, continuous flashes of lightning, and down poured the rain in one great waterspout on the iron roof with the most deafening noise; the sound of water was everywhere, above and below, spouting, dripping, and soaking, leaping and rushing over everything, forming rivers and miniature cascades in every direction, and I thought of my warning letter. Things did not look promising for the morning; but when it came a bright sun was shining, and there was not even a puddle to be seen.

After a comfortable night's rest and an early breakfast, we started in two buggies for the caves, Mr. A. coming himself with us the first day, and taking us through them. We were some little time in reaching the first entrance. The rocks were piled up in such magnificent confusion that we had some difficulty in making our way over them and between the tangled tree roots; then, higher up, the broken path descends along jagged cliffs and deep chasms; black shadows fell from the closing walls of rock above and wild plants trailed and almost blocked the roadway, and now the black yawning entrance to these caves lay at our feet, and we went crawling on hands and knees into the opening in delightful uncertainty as to the depth below. We went from one lofty cavern into another, sometimes burrowing, sometimes wriggling full-length through narrow crevices, for, as yet, nothing has been done in the way of opening them up, and occasionally we had to drop from rock to rock, where a false step would have sent us many feet into the darkness below. Taking them individually, they struck me as larger, grander, and more imposing than any of the Jenolan caves in New South Wales, but the stalactites and stalagmites here are not so varied, nor are they to be compared in beauty with those in the Jenolan caves.

It is not yet known for how far the caves extend. I believe about thirty miles have been explored, and through the Cimmerian darkness of these Mr. A. conducted me for hours, until I could believe myself the denizen of another world, as weird and wonderful as the imaginings of Dante. When Mr. A. burnt red lights, as he did now and again, the glow, catching glistening masses of snow-white crystal, turned them into walls of sparkling diamonds. These lined the chambers, the floors of which were strewn with round white or gray pebbles, lime-incrusted in places and interspersed with the skeletons of kangaroos and rats, and with old land shells, and fossils of shells, as well as with leaves and wood. Here and there, across an entrance, transparent curtains had been formed by the drip of countless ages, the greater or less amount of iron in the water forming delicately-traced patterns on them from ruddy brown to shades of yellow and white. Tall stalagmites, nine, twelve, and twenty feet high, looked like monuments carved into every shape and form.

Leaving these behind, we came into more lofty, black, and gloomy chambers, their spacious floors paved with small gray pebbles. There seemed no end to them, one succeeding another. Here and there a ray of sunlight would come through a crevice in the rock above, and slanting downwards would catch a projecting rock, striking it with a brilliant lustre and making the darkness below more horribly intense. It was always under such crevices that bones were found. Here, too, dangled down masses of rope-like roots forming columns weird and snake-like in their writhings. After some hours, we came out into daylight again, and how scorching the rays of the sun felt as we made our way scrambling and tripping over and under rocks and bushes to where the two buggies had been left!

After lunch we started off to some other caves, at the entrance of which were hanging bright, green bunches of so-called native grapes, tempting-looking, but probably very poisonous and nasty. Here by accident I put my hand on the largest centipede I had ever seen. There is a considerable descent into the caves; courage is easily produced in theory but it was no joke scrambling down this small and very rickety ladder of rope-like roots, amongst loose and rugged rocks, which required something more than nerves and careful handling. These caves were even more beautiful than the others, some being more than 160 feet in diameter. The earth here seemed to have been rent by internal convulsions, for it was split up into deep fissures and gloomy-looking caverns of inky blackness. Those nearest the surface had some fine stalactites. In several places there were long straight tunnels leading from one chamber to another, and here we went through a good deal of burrowing; farther on there was a sound of muffled thunder and the distant roar of a mighty underground cataract; these subterranean rivers are found in most of the caves in this dry country, they bar the passage to other caves beyond and seem to terminate in the depths below.

Those of the party who had long backs and legs found them a good deal in the way and were considerably bruised, as well as shaken. Once we found ourselves on the edge of a vast precipice where our lights threw no shadow, and where no gleam caught the rock across the black abyss. Now on hands and knees we squeezed our bodies through tunnel-like holes and emerged at the other end sometimes to find ourselves imprisoned against a precipitous wall of rock, at others in lofty chambers again, where countless ages of time and capricious Nature had fashioned and chiselled the rocks into such fairy-like wonders that we felt tempted to bite a little finger to convince ourselves that we still lived in a substantial world of men. Making our way back was hard work, it needed a strong arm and a firm step and head to crawl up some of the rocky projections, and our hands and knees for many days after bore painful evidence of sharp pinnacles and rocky edges in the struggles to get over and under them, but the fascinations of these wonders are so strong that curiosity compels you to go forward.

I spent one day with a little native boy on a flower-hunting expedition. We went in search of a particular plant that grows only on a certain ridge of these limestone rocks. He had such a delightfully vague idea of its whereabouts that we never reached the spot. There was a painful melancholy in the bush here, an unspeakable solitude among these masses of wheather-beaten peaks, and an utter absence of external signs of life—"So lonely 'tis that God himself scarce seemeth there to be." High up in the crevice of a rock above us I saw a tempting bunch of large pink flowers; it required all my stoical resolution to attempt the feat of reaching it, but at the peril of slipping, I did my best. The higher I went, the more the cliffs seemed to rear themselves. After going through all the antique labours of Hercules to no purpose, I found it was inaccessible to all but an eagle, and ignominiously owned myself beaten, and contented myself with lower subjects.

Round the base of the rocks I found innumerable pods, berries, and flowers that were new to me. My little guide with his bare feet skipping over the rocks like a goat, familiar with every feature, while I, left behind, toiled wearily over, half-baked with the scorching heat of the sun, and wrestling against a wind that threatened to carry me off my legs and appeared well able to bear us over the rocks on to the plains below. The view in front of us was very grand, a sea of peaks falling away in the remotest distance across the lonely expanse, but the intensity of the solitude gave me a feeling of melancholy and a chilly sense of isolation from all that I loved.

The drive back to Muldiva was again made up of a series of climbs over rocks, and the buggy needed to be a strong one. Under the hanging rock where I made my sketch, we had lunch, and hitched up the buggy to rest the horse, who was the pluckiest of his kind. No obstacles seemed to daunt his courage, and the difficulties of bogs, logs, swamps or rocks (over which he climbed like a goat) were to him mere trifles.

The hotel was in a state of rabble when I got back, every room overflowed, and rest was impossible. They gave me my tea in my bedroom and I spent the rest of the evening in the manager's tent, then back to the hotel, and at seven the next morning mounted on the box seat of the coach, on the return journey to Herberton. The five horses started off with a gallop, breaking the drive once only at a small wayside hotel, where I stayed the night. Oh dear! how hot it was! There was no putting it on one side, and animal life in every shape abounded. Mosquitoes, revelling in fresh society, completely took possession of me on this occasion, out-manoeuvred me, for I had brought no net with me, and got up next morning a sorry-looking object. The iron sides and roof of the room I was in were literally scorching; so hot that I pressed a piece of paper against the wall and in a second it turned brown, but unlike most of the places I have come across, it was clean, and the sheets of my bed, though they were of the coarsest description of unbleached and unwashed calico, looked at any rate as if they had not been slept in more than half a dozen times before.

Next day we made another early start, and by half-past five we were many miles on our road; it was not quite so hot at first as on the day before, and the way did not in consequence seem so long, but towards Herberton the heat became excessive and, as a climax, at our last stopping and changing place the new team of horses smashed the pole. It was a consolation to find that other passengers besides myself were nervous, and several times they insisted on getting off the coach. Jack, our driver, had drawn the winner in the Melbourne Cup sweepstake, and all along the road he was greeted with congratulations and offers to "shout"—a most universal custom in this thirsty country.

I came back with my arm round Jack's very substantial waist most of the way, for I had the middle box seat, so that my feet could not touch the splashboard, and going down these hills I would otherwise have been more than a dozen times on the horses' heels. The three drivers on this line are splendid whips, Bob, Jack, and Joe; the first named has been driving Cobbs's coaches for twenty-one years. It is a terribly hard life, and how they manage to grow stout on it is a wonder.

It was five o'clock in the evening when we reached Herberton, and the landlady, unlike the last time I arrived, bustled out into the street to meet me, and had prepared (so she told me) the bridal rooms for my benefit. It was midnight before I went to bed, but not to sleep, alas! for a little dying child was in the next room, and the poor mother, worn out with constant nursing, appealed to me, and I took her place while she got some sleep. There is an hour between the night and the morning, when it grows colder and the darkness becomes more intense; then the tiny face grew paler and more pinched, her little fingers tightened on mine, and the breath grew fainter and fainter until it died away altogether. When the glory of the morning sun came in, it fell on the tiny hands folded together for ever, and the peaceful face of a last long sleep.

I had intended going on by the ordinary coach next day to Georgetown, but as I could not get the box seat, and would probably have had to share an inside one with a tipsy miner or two, I decided to get a trap of my own and to loiter by the way, as I was in search of flowers. There was no difficulty in doing this, and by two that day, I was off on my travels again, with three good-looking horses, and an extra pair in case of need, one of which Jackey, a black boy, rode, while he led the other (all black boys seemed to be called Jackey). I had also engaged the services of Mrs. S.—a treasure they told me, a woman of ample and masterly proportions, and a motherly sort of old body—to help me on the way, for this journey is not noted for its ease or luxury. At Mount Albion we stayed the night.

From here, we next morning made an early start for Watsonville. This is all a great tin-bearing district, and we were shown some wonderful specimens of the metal, some of which were given to me. The only available hotel was full, and we had to make our way to a settler's house some distance off. Everyone was most civil and couldn't do enough for us. One of the men here brought me in a new and beautiful variety of bauhinia, and a handsome grevillea, which I at once set to work to paint, and though our quarters were of the roughest description (for we were quite off the track of civilisation), and the heat and flies rather distracting, I put up smilingly with every discomfort for the sake of this flower.

My bedroom looked out on a foreground of cabbages and turnips, and a prosaic clothes-line with a portion of the family linen in a more or less tattered condition; the hope of the family had just been warmly chastised by his sister, and with the strength of his robust lungs he filled the air with wholesome sound; a fat man, with a bit of looking-glass on a bench where he had been performing his ablutions, was undergoing the operation of shaving, and there was a charming aspect of homeliness about the whole scene.

We had supper in broad daylight. I watched the bread being taken out of the camp oven in the backyard, it was at any rate hot and fresh, and the loaf the size of an ordinary footstool. The tea is better not described, there was no milk and the sugar was almost black. Hens strayed in and unceremoniously picked up the crumbs that fell from the table, and the landlord sat at the head with his sleeves rolled up, carving us junks of meat and occupying the time in between by taking shots with the knife at the countless flies. I tried to look unconcerned through it all, and I think I succeeded.

When night came on and with it crowds of mosquitoes, the landlady further harassed my pent-up feelings by relating to me stories of blood-curdling murders committed by the natives here, and ghastly tales of miners who had mysteriously disappeared, never to be heard of more. Finally I went to my room, and after taking a good look in my bed and under, to satisfy myself that no snakes were concealing themselves there, I fell into a restless kind of sleep, and woke up with a nameless sort of nightmare, in my start knocking over the candle on the chair beside me and scattering the matches broadcast. At the risk of being, as I thought, bitten, I had to get up and grope until I found them.

I distinctly now heard a creature making its way to the door, and it sounded in the darkness like yards of snake dragging along the bare boards. I strained my eyes to catch a glimpse of it. Now with a lighted match I was all right; for a moment I thought it was a death adder as the light fell with a metallic gleam on its shiny body, and my heart literally thumped. Then it slowly moved away and I recognised the smooth mottled back of a sleeping lizard about two feet long, a perfectly harmless creature that put its tongue at me and showed me the distinctive mark of nobility of its race in the blue lining to its mouth. He had quite spoilt the remainder of my night's rest for me, and I poked him out of the door with my umbrella and savagely sent him flying as far as I could into the darkness.

I was in such a fever of heat that rest was impossible, so I sat on the doorstep for the remainder of the time, waiting for the first streaks of daylight to appear, which seemed hours in coming. Then a horseman rode up, hung up his bridle, and walked unceremoniously into the "best parlour", and I had to make myself scarce. What odd types of humanity you come across here—all sorts and conditions of men. It was a delight to hear the sound of an educated voice again in this rough mining district, for he turned out to be an old brother-officer of yours in the 43rd, who was on his way to a station not far from the Croyden gold-fields. He had many a long, weary mile to ride before he reached that delightful place of abode.

At five next morning when we started from Watsonville the horses were fresh from their day's rest, and the leader would try to turn round and look at us. When our driver, another Joe, persuaded him gently with the whip he started kicking and got one leg over the trace, which set him off. Up went his heels; the two wheelers resented this, and in less than no time we had a nice smash-up. Joe was as cool as a cucumber, and, as the boys would say, "never turned a hair". I was so intent on watching the horses that I had forgotten all about Mrs. S., and turning round I saw her portly figure in the distance surveying us. How she slipped out I don't know, as on other occasions she required the help generally of two people. I jumped out over the wheel and landed in the dust on my knees; several men ran up from the hotel and helped to get the horses out, but the harness was broken, the pole smashed, and it was impossible to go on until it was mended. Here was another delay.

Oh dear, what a day of heat and flies! What the thermometer stood at under those four iron walls, I am afraid to think, and I quite believe the man who said he had cooked his dinner many a time on the roof. I felt that if I remained there much longer I would have been in the same condition, so, taking out my paints, I went on with my work lying full length under the shade of a tree trying to imagine myself cooler. The mosquitoes drove me inside again.

In the evening, much against Mrs. S.'s will, I took her into the bush for a walk, and a most monotonous one it was, too; her powers of conversation were limited, and she spoke of our delay in such an injured tone that I felt at last that I alone was entirely to blame for the horses' pranks. Gum-trees were thick all round us, and the fallen leaves, dry and crisp, crackled under our feet as we walked over them. The sound of the cicadas beating their tiny transparent wings against their sides made the most deafening noise in the trees above. An ancient poet writes—"Happy are cicadas' lives, for they all have voiceless wives," the preceding lines having been written from the fact that only the male insect can produce this noise. There was not a breath of air, the lurid sky was without a cloud, even the birds hadn't the heart to sing, and the silence was oppressive. I had milk for my tea, an unheard-of luxury. Some one had sent me a small bottle of goat's milk, and with that and a fresh-laid egg, I felt that I had had a sumptuous meal.

Towards night the heat became unbearable, and a dull lurid glare lit up the horizon. Away in the distance came a low continuous sound like the roar of rushing wind, and a dense pillar of smoke curled upwards with a dull yellow glare. Below, some terrified cattle rushed aimlessly forward and sure-footed kangaroos bounded away, ten feet each spring, the horses whinnied and stamped in the yards, and the air was filled with the shrill cries of cockatoos as they wheeled and swayed backwards and forwards in floating clouds in the blackening sky. Now with fearful rapidity came the menacing sound of crashing and crackling of timbers, and, leaping and blazing, the flames shot forward, sending blinding showers of drift and fragments of leaves across the road, the only bar now between us and a horrible death. The fierce scream of the blast rushed upwards, the flames leaping at their prey, and wave upon wave rolled onward. Below, the fiery tongues hissing, toppling, and hurling over each other as they spluttered, gripped, twisted, and grasped the tree-trunks, then defiantly hurled a fiery stream to the resinous leaves of the foliage above.

And now a fresh horror seized us; the panting flames had leapt the gap and crossed the road. A huge tree that was burnt through at its base now tottered and fell with a crashing sound, scattering a sea of burning fragments whose quick tongues clutched with relentless grasp the dry tufts of grass and the light saplings round the fenced-in yard. The smoke grew denser each moment. With sinews and muscles strained to their utmost, and with hands grimy and scorched, we wrestled and struggled in frantic efforts, beating and stamping it out. How the reds and the yellows struggled for mastery. The whole force of the fire was upon us, and we fought for dear lives' sake. Our throats were dry and swollen as we gasped for breath, a legion of devils was on us; for a moment we seemed to wrestle with the powers of Hell.

In the thickened smoke a man's figure staggered for a moment and fell with the cry, "O God, we are done!" Indeed, his words seemed too terribly true, and would have been so had not the wind been suddenly met by a stronger one from the south, which forced the fire backward. It was a wonderful deliverance, and a wonderful sight when the flaring torches that lit the heavens turned and swept on for miles until spent on a distant lagoon. The atmosphere was choking with the dust of charred embers, our swollen eyes pricked and smarted, our skins were scorched and our clothes burnt into countless holes, and when the morning light came what a scene of blackened desolation lay smoking and smouldering before us! The ground was still too hot with burning debris to start that day, and indeed we felt that our exhausted faculties and bruised anatomies needed the rest. My brain felt all on fire and the night seemed three years long, with a hundred snatches of nightmare dreams.

Once or twice my heart misgave me as I thought of the long journey before me, for the first time in my life with no friends at the end. I spent a day with my paints, then read a pastoral review two years old, and a treatise on lunatics, darned stockings, and gained much information from Jackey, which I did not at the time quite piece properly together. "Old woman big one go too much along a public house an baal him alonga Georgetown, mine think it too much drinkum grog, mine bin fetchum twice, me tellum Missus." It wasn't quite as lucid as it might have been, but sufficient for a warning.

Next morning we made another start, this time successfully, with the "Speaker" as a leader. I notice that a good many of the coach-horses bear the names of Members of Parliament, and you hear the coachman call out the familiar name of "Lumley H." in a way that isn't flattering to man or beast. I laughingly told

Chillagoe Caves

Flowers and fruit, Bloomfield Queensland, watercolour, 54.7 x 38 cm
Reproduced by permission of the National Library of Australia

Mr. H. of his namesake on my return. He didn't seem to appreciate the joke. The horse was a handsome one and good, though at times he was rather stubborn.

From Watsonville we left the Muldiva road and branched off on to another, where we came into a land of ant-hills. There was an ominous stillness in the air as we drove along, and a bank of heavy, black clouds hung low on the horizon, then came a low murmuring sound which grew to a roar, and the wind came howling and shrieking through the trees. We were enveloped in a shower of sticks, leaves, and dust: such a whirlwind of leaping, rattling and crashing sounds. No wonder the horses stopped short, and we clung with might and main to the seats and held on to our flapping garments which threatened to whirl us also in mid-air. The trees bent their boughs to the gale, rolling and tossing their limbs against one another, and now the distant growling of the thunder changed to an ear-cracking cannonade: peal after peal rolled in rapid succession, and the blue glare of the lightning flashed with blinding flame through the dense black clouds—and down came the rain! Such a waterspout! We hid ourselves as best we could under waterproof rugs and every available covering, and the water swished and splashed into a thousand miniature channels. Along our doubtful amphibious track the pitiless storm raged for hours, and it was a weary plough for the horses through the mud and lake-like water.

"This looks bad for the river," Joe said; and when we *did* reach it, it was running a "banker". Jackey tried to measure the depth of the crossing on one of the horses, but he could not stand against the strong current, and it was impossible to attempt to cross before the water went down. It was useless to return to Watsonville at that hour, so we had to make up our minds to do the best we could, and camp until the water went down.

No shelter, no fire, no food; it was not a pleasant outlook, and I felt that I alone was responsible for the weather. Mrs. S., I am sure, thought so too. She had maintained a stolid silence up to the present time, but I felt that something was brewing for me. She gave vent at last to her pent-up feelings, and burst into floods of tears over our "cruel surroundings"; she was more angry still when I had an uncontrollable fit of laughter: I felt that it was absolutely brutal of me, but the situation was so comical as we sat under that buggy, and the expression of her face was a study. I gave her both the seats to sit upon, and tried to make amends by wrapping my waterproof round her (there were still some dry places left in it). I gave her, too, the remainder of my goat-milk; it was partly sour, but she didn't seem to notice that, and the attention appeared to console her. I even took the deepest interest in the dire tales of woe she told me of terrible things that had happened to various members of her family who had been overtaken by misfortunes similar to ours.

Then Jackey got on one of the horses and rode some distance up the river to look at another crossing. He came back after a short absence and told us that a party of natives was camped about a mile away. This suggested food and shelter to Mrs. S.'s practical mine, and anything was better than sitting still in our damp clothes. I was bush-woman enough to know this, so we held a council of war and decided to risk the reception we might get from the natives, and went to their camp. We were greeted by the howling and barking of their dogs. "Both mongrel, puppy, whelp, and hound, And cur of low degree" were there. They sniffed and snapped unpleasantly close to our heels, but at a shout from the natives, the wretched-looking creatures slunk back into the warmth of the Gunyas, which master and animal share alike.

Some of the fires at the entrance to the huts were still smouldering. The blacks never let them go wholly out, as they keep away the "debil debil", so they say. I looked into one of them, but the closeness was overpowering. The natives, who seemed half afraid of us, were sulky and sleepy. The expression of their faces was far from satisfactory, and they sniffed at us with much misgiving, though one old woman *did* give Mrs. S. some sort of roasted root out of her dilly bag, and a portion of flesh that suggested opossum, which Mrs. S. said was not "tasty". I did not like to suggest that it might have been a portion of the remains of a cannibal feast, for many who died here find a resting-place inside the bodies of their sorrowing friends. It had ceased raining and the night turned out fine with a bright moon.

Mrs. S. slept, making a pillow of me. To me the hours seemed endless from the strange, weird, unaccountable night sounds; the stumps of trees took human form in the dim light, and the changing shadows of the clouds seemed to give them life. Then, across the night, came the dismal howl of a dingo, and he knows how to howl to perfection; the hoot of the night owl, and, towards early dawn, the sad cry of a curlew came familiar, the voice of a friend that I knew. I don't know where poor Joe had been, he was most uncomplaining as he came up with the horses. It was not the first time by a good many, he told me, that he had spent a night in the bush without food or shelter. The river had gone down so much that we could see the crossing; but now another difficulty arose, nothing would induce Mrs. S. to ford it. *She* was not going to have her body washed away to "goodness knows where; no, she would rather be killed and eaten by natives than that," she said; and all our persuasions were useless. As a rule most Australians of her class are accustomed to "roughing it", and having to take the good with the evil, seldom fail you in a time of emergency; but on her words were all wasted. "No, she'd walk every mile of the way back," etc. Joe lost his temper at last and used strong language.

Then again I held out what I thought a sufficient inducement, which had the desired effect, and finally, after an hour and a half, when our patience (an indispensable quality in these wilds) was almost exhausted, she consented to go. At each halt and each fresh dip into a hole bigger than the last, she gave a good wholesome scream. It wasn't altogether pleasant, for when in mid-stream we felt the buggy for a moment float, the half swing round suggested that we might be carried down the river. Even Joe didn't like the look of things, and standing on his feet, with one lash of his long whip and a shout to the horses, he let them have it: they bounded forward, snorting and splashing, and in another few minutes—oh, happiness!—we were over, and the perilous transit accomplished.

The sun came out very warm, and there was a fresh scent in the air from the gum-trees; flocks of bright-coloured parrots went by, and white, gray, and black cockatoos, painted pigeons, and a pretty little zebra-dove, a most trustful little bird that soon becomes tame when caught. A wagtail almost touched us, it came so near; they are most inquisitive, and will rest on your horse's back as he feeds: they sit on the backs of the cattle catching flies, and are most interested in everything that goes on. Jackasses were everywhere, chuckling and laughing to themselves as if they were enjoying great jokes at our expense, and no doubt we were a ludicrous sight, for peal after peal of merriment broke from them at each fresh push that the horses gave: there is no better barometer than this same merry old bird, as when wet weather comes his spirits immediately fall below zero. We also saw a pair of scrub turkeys; their nest is a mound of leaves and twigs, sometimes three and four feet high; the eggs are laid in tiers, two and three birds sharing the same mound; they partially cover the nest with sand, and leave the eggs to be hatched by the sun. The ordinary wild turkey hatches its eggs in a flat nest on the ground.

The country now became very rough and broken, with high pinnacles and large blocks of rock in heaped-up confusion, interspersed with patches of scrub, and flowering banksias. We jogged along picking our way for miles under dazzling sunshine. With a weary solitary slowness, Joe, never at any time communicative, smoked his pipe of peace. Mrs. S. also for hours maintained a stoical silence. Our appetites sharpened in advance as we caught sight of the rough bush hut, where with a sigh of relief the tired breakfastless animals hailed our halt for the night. Our evening repast finished, we felt substantially happy, and I stretched my poor machine of a body in blessed thankfulness for rest on that homeliest of canvas bunks.

At four next morning we started, for it is a very heavy day's journey from here on to Springfield. We crossed a branch of the Lynd river and next day the wide sand-beds of the Einnesleigh by mid-day, and at the foot of a rocky range of hills halted for lunch and an hour's rest for the horses. It was a good stiff climb to the top, and we all walked up. On the other side of the range we passed a coach and exchanged greetings. At Cassidy Creek we stayed the night, and after a very early start reached Georgetown next day as the sun went down.

This town is the centre of a large mining district. I thought the hotel a palace after the roughness of those we had passed, our dinner tasted good, and my late misfortunes vanished like mist. With the luxury of bath, clean sheets, and a real spring bed, I was soon lulled in a dreamy sleep and never stirred until nine next morning. Mrs. S. was quite genial as she brought me my breakfast, and could afford now to laugh over our past grievances.

There was a funeral that day, and a "wake" which she looked upon as a holy sort of enjoyment. She had found a congenial friend too, in the landlady, so her cup of happiness was full, and beyond bringing me my breakfast in the morning, I saw nothing more of her.

My only friends were two little children, boy and girl, who used to come to the window and watch me painting. They introduced themselves to me the first morning by asking "if I was the lady that was bringed there by the other lady?—then was I the lady what Daddy said warn't much to look at?" I took all the compliments to myself. They asked every imaginable question, most of them unanswerable. I took them for a drive one day on the edge of the lagoon; the little girl, who looked about four, told me that "Daddy shot er angel here once." "What did he do with it?" I asked. "Oh," replied the child, "we ate its body, and Mother put its tail in her hat"; I concluded from this that it was some sort of bird, probably a white crane. I had one other friend, Billy, a black man, who wore one garment, more tatters than shirt. Billy was a man of humour, and used to beg for sixpence for his wife. He was not quite himself one day, and I told him he was tipsy again, and I wouldn't give him one. "Never mind, Missus," he said, "if I are tipsy, 'taint at your expense."

Off the Track of Civilisation

Myola

After four days I had had enough of Georgetown, and its "distractions" began to pall on me. I was quite homesick too. "Every dog," they say, "has its day," and I am sure every cat her night, for they used to congregate on the roof and kept me from getting any sleep. As they played Romeo and Juliet crescendos came very much into their love-making. Unfortunately also, we were there on Saturday and Sunday, when miners in this thirsty country come in and "knock down" their weekly earnings. I had seen, too, what little there was of interest all around. Indeed, the natives were the chief attraction to me, as I liked noting the points of difference between them and those other tribes I had so far encountered. These were a wretched-looking, misshapen and repulsive race. Away from the outskirts of civilisation, they live on roots which they dig up with pointed clubs called nulla-nullas. When the yellow cones of the Bunya tree (a kind of pine) are ripe, they congregate together in great numbers and have feasting and corroboreeing. Snakes, lizards, kangaroos, bandicoots, and opossums also come into their diet, and the grub of a very large moth, which is roasted, and they say tastes like marrow, is considered a great delicacy.

Then, when animal food becomes scarce, they kill and eat a fat gin or piccaninny. They also make raids on the settlers' sheep and cattle, which the latter naturally object to. Their greatest ceremony, about which they are most reticent, is one called "Bora", when boys passing into manhood are made "Kippers". It is supposed to have something of a masonic nature about it, and the explorer Leichhardt may have referred to this ceremony when he spoke of having met men who exchanged masonic signs with him. "Kippers" have to conform to certain rules, and live on an exclusive diet, and for some time before the ceremony they have to go through a period of great abstinence and self-denial. No women are allowed, under penalty of death, to witness it. All young men, before they become warriors, are supposed to go through it. If a youth has grown into manhood before going through their ceremony, and wishes to become a "Kipper", he has to go through severe ordeals to test his strength. If he shrinks, or is in any way cowardly, he is unfit for his "Kipperhood", but if in battle he has the good fortune to kill an enemy, his claims are recognised, and he is admitted to the ranks of a warrior, and is at once at liberty to marry.

I was shown a musical instrument that was used on these occasions, of which no woman was allowed even to hear the sound. It was nothing but a shaped stick with a stone attached to it by plaited reeds, which was spun in the air and made a soft whirring sound as it went round.

The Bora ground is a small enclosure hidden away in some quiet spot. I once looked into one which was slightly dug out; there was a low wall a few inches high, of earth all round it, and two small openings. Although the natives will tell you of other customs, no persuasion will induce them to say one word on this subject, and no European, to my knowledge, has ever witnessed this rite, which is practised, I believe, in all parts of Australia.

The Australian natives are the keenest trackers in existence, and even on horseback will follow the indications at a gallop, where a white man walking would distinguish nothing. They will track the hoof of one beast among a hundred others; their sense of hearing and sight is extraordinary, and they are very quick to hear and carry news; nothing escapes them. They have no particular homes, and wander where their food is most plentiful. If there is a death among them they generally, for a time, leave that part of the district. Like all dark races, they are very superstitious, and if a strong man, or chief, dies, they think that by eating a portion of his flesh they partake of some of his strength. The temptation to kill is so strong in them, that a black boy that my father once had for a good many years begged him not to walk in front of him alone, as the wish to knock him on the head was too great for him. They cannot be trusted, and the idea of gratitude is unknown to them. These last sentences apply to all the Australian races.

At certain times of the year, about here the lagoons, they say, teem with wild duck, cranes, geese, pelicans, and other birds. In the heart of the town the flies and mosquitoes were unbearable, everything was smothered with flies, and my arms got tired with flicking them off, and my patience became exhausted with the swarms of them that followed us even when we drove out. The country around looked very burnt up, the grass was scanty, and the dust so great that I am sure we must have already swallowed more than the proverbial peck on this journey. In the early spring the country is very different: yellow wattles mark the line of most of the rivers, the earth is carpeted with patches of bright-coloured everlastings; here and there, through the long vistas of Eucalyptus stands a coral-tree, and the brilliant yellow blossoms of the cotton bush and tufted grass trees send up their tall, sentinel-like spears.

Now towards the end of a long, dry summer everything languished, and only the deafening whirr of locusts, whose perpetual voices seem to carry a sound of heat and headache with them, filled the sultry silence. We had not yet come to our journey's end. The flowers that I had come in search of were not to be found near Georgetown, but many miles out towards the Gregory Range, which was off the track of civilisation, and this meant camping out. There was no time to be lost in making our preparations; an extra man must be found, two pack-horses, stores, etc. Two small tents were soon procured from a man on the outskirts of the town; Joe got the horses, and we repaired to a store where I laid in the usual provisions. These housekeeping details consisted of two cooking utensils, blankets, tea, sugar, biscuits, rice, flour, salt, butter, matches, water-bags, sardines, tinned meats, condensed milk (for I can't manage tea without it), soap, and candles; the other odds and ends we hired from the hotel. It was a great start, as we left at two next day, with an open-mouthed crowd to witness our departure, and make foreboding remarks on probable misfortunes which awaited us.

I must say that the joys of planning my first campaign were considerably marred by the fact that Mrs. S. was the only companion to share those joys, which to her material soul were most questionable; but then *she* had not the joys of a hobby, and my specimens to her were nothing but "rubbidge". I had not even the shake of a hand at parting, or a "God b'w'ye" to cheer the way, but there was something ineffably delightful in the thought of this wild away-into-the-mountain-to-shoot-tigers feeling about it all, and the halting when and where we liked to raise a temporary home without let or hindrance from man or beast.

We crossed a branch of the Gilbert River, and then went westward through a dull and monotonous country of low scrub, not a sound to be heard but the screech of a black cockatoo as he soared in solitary flight overhead, and the deafening whirr of grasshoppers as they flew in thousands from under the wheels, and towards evening, the plaintive cry of a curlew and whoop of the more-pork.

We made our first halt by the side of an old watercourse. There were green sedges here, marking the spot where a small spring bubbled up, and in the fertile deposits of sand swept down by a hundred torrents there were good nibblings for the horses. What better camping place could we find? Sticks and dry leaves were soon heaped together for our fire, and while we prepared the tea, the horses were unharnessed, saplings cut, pegs driven in, and our temporary home was rapidly established.

Mrs. S. made a capital damper which consisted of well-kneaded flour and water rolled out on a piece of bark, and baked in the ashes; my bag formed our table, with a clean towel as a cloth, and now, with our table spread and our water boiled and our feast prepared, Mrs. S. and I enjoyed with the greatest relish our first open-air meal. The men with their lighted pipes had rigged up their quarters some distance off; by nine o'clock the fires had gone out, and there was not a sound but the scrunch of grazing horses and the clank of their hobbles as they went to fresh feeding grounds.

There was something unspeakably sad in the silence of the night. The moon cast uncertain shadows round projecting rocks and the stems of the trees, weaving them into impish forms. Not a leaf was stirring and the silence was death-like. I tried to sleep, but my rest was as disturbed as my thoughts. Don't believe when told that sleep in the open air is so restful. My first experience here of it was not promising, and I was glad enough when morning came, and with daylight a thousand songs. Hordes of insects ran on the ground with important air, and flew through the shafts of sunlight; numbers of parrots bent the fragile boughs of the gums as they sucked the honey from the flowers, incessantly chattering the while, a kangaroo hopped to the water to drink, and bounded off in frantic haste as he caught sight of our caravan. What a sunrise it was! A ladder of golden shafts shot up through the sky, all barred with deep purple, and outlining the pink clouds above with threads of molten gold.

Joe went off at daylight and shot a fat jungle hen for the men's breakfast. Appetites satisfied, and our kits packed up, by nine o'clock we were off again, with nothing left behind as a memorial of our brief pilgrimage but two small black patches of ashes which the next wind would scatter. We now came into a land of bottle-trees, and had to steer our way most delicately between them and pinnacles of yellow clay four and five feet high, the homes of white ants. Leaving these we came into forest country, where from in front came the sound of distant lowing of cattle and the sharp crack of stock-whips. The barking of dogs and loud hallooing of stockmen rang out, while in and out through the trees came the mottled reds, whites, and blacks of the cattle, and we had quickly to rein in as the herd scattered in front of us, jostling each other, breaking the bounds and dodging the riders. Now one unruly beast goes off with a scamper, tail stuck straight in the air, but the cattle dogs round him up again. They snort and sniff, as they pass unpleasantly near us. The drivers stop for a moment to give us a word in passing; then all is silence again. The cattle, poor things, looked lean enough at this time of the year, and are probably on their way to some boiling-down works.

Now we were out of the forest again, and across a burnt-up-looking plain with a long stretch of rank grass, both yellow and dry, and we made our way very slowly, dodging the hidden black stumps that told their own tale, and with the sun overhead, through the hot misty haze, we saw the sparkle of light in the still waters of a miniature lake with deep shadows and reflections of trees and green sedges round its banks. Close to the shore they seemed to break in one long ripple of transparent wave, cheating our visions with an illusory supply of what we longed to have. As we came nearer, it all seemed to recede and take new forms, then slowly faded under the glow of the hot horizon. It was the first mirage that I had seen in Queensland. Towards evening we saw another; the film of heat giving it gigantic proportions.

We passed some magnificent bushes of yellow hibiscus, and on the edge of a low scrub a white bauhinia in full blossom. I was amply rewarded for what I had been through by these treasures. There was not a trickle of water at any spot where we could make our camping ground, and it was night before we came to the banks of a weary, shrunken river. The water was muddy and brackish, and had to be well boiled before we filled our water-bags. We passed a camp of natives who had directed us to this spot, not by any means an enticing set of human beings, with legs like compasses, and intentions evidently inhospitable. They had not an article of clothing covering their bodies, and were armed with spears and nulla-nullas. They were evidently out on a foraging expedition, hunting for deep-boring grubs, wild honey, and roots. No women were with them. As a rule, they spend the summer in the forest lands, and make their way up here in the winter, where, on the high ground, they hide their women and children and live in the caves of the rocks.

The country is all dotted with huge boulders of granite, with outcrops here and there of quartz: evidences of the terribly dry season were very apparent; the hidden watercourses had sunk, leaving hard, cracked fissures behind, where fish had buried themselves deep in the mud, and just here and there between the holes only a trickle of water was to be seen. The dry bark cracked and peeled from the trees, as the hot wind swept through them, withered leaves strewed the ground, moss peeled off the rocks, buds were killed before they had blossomed, and dried-up petals fell in showers each time a breath of wind stirred. Nothing remained of juicy creepers but a heap of withered arms clasping the trees. Here and there, at their feet, beasts too weak to force their way to fresh hunting grounds lay dead; the triumphant power of the sun had ruthlessly held his destructive sway over everything, and there was an unutterable look of desolation about the whole scene.

We pitched our tents beside a solitary acacia tree; its yellow blossoms had alone defied the fiery despot, and the sweet scent, so dear to an Australian, filled the whole of the surrounding air. The horses had to be hobbled some distance away for feed, as there was none here, and the rocks were too thick to take the buggy over, and I decided to go on riding next day with Joe and Jackey to the foot of the range.

We started next morning at daylight upon a very rough road, climbing with our horses over breakneck rocks, and hunting in crack and cranny for flowers. We tethered the horses after a time when the rocks became too steep, and it was now a four-footed climb for all of us. Like a game of football the echoes of our voices were kicked back from rock to rock until the breath was fairly beaten out, and Jackey cooeed and hallooed his loudest, enjoying the fun of the match. Gliding over one of the rocks we saw a carpet snake about twenty feet long, which fled with lightning speed when he caught sight of us, and so did we. I found several grevilleas, and one or two other flowering plants quite new to me, and, with all my anticipations realised, we commenced our descent to the horses again.

I don't know what the thermometer was on those rocks, but my skin felt literally scorched and toasted to a nicety. I was horribly thirsty, but my inability to swallow that river water left the others free to apply their lips and finish the contents of the water-bottle. Slipping, sliding, rolling, stumbling, we at last got to the horses, and made our way back to the camp, which we reached at two. I felt amply repaid for my labours. Alas! Mrs. S., with that cunning which literature attributes to the serpent, had extracted a bottle of brandy which we had brought in case of need, and which I had carefully hidden, and was now in a state of utter collapse, so we had to fasten her into the tent. It was no use worrying myself into a greater heat over it, so I took it as philosophically as I could, and spent the rest of the afternoon with my painting.

We were to have started early next morning on our homeward way, but Jackey's horse had incontinently taken to his heels and kept that darkie amused for three solid hours. I had given Mrs. S. a strong dose of salt and water to stem the tide of alcohol. She was passive enough to take it "if I insisted", and with a majestic sweep, finished it off, for the sake of the "sunstroke" from which she assured me she was suffering.

We took a different route on the return journey, crossing another branch of the Gilbert River, where the ground for miles was lumpy and stony, and we went along at a jog-trot, eggs-to-market pace. The horses (which I had hired in place of our prancing steeds) were solid and trustworthy, but years of backaches seemed concentrated into that one day's journey. I sat sideways, I leant backwards, then forwards, but all in vain, and at last had to resign myself to the monotony and perpetual see-saw, bone-dislocating motion. Joyfully I encamped for our last night's meal, with a sense of satisfaction difficult to describe hailed the lights of Georgetown next evening. As we crossed the river two men were being brought in by the police, handcuffed, for "duffing" cattle. This is rather a favourite and profitable amusement (as long as they don't get caught) among a certain class of men.

Another day of quiet and we started at sunrise on our way to Herberton, a journey that was not devoid of interest; our horses were, from the long rest, even Joe allowed, a bit fresh, but he assured me they would "steady down". They had, however, no such intention, and the first sharp crack of the double-thonged whip on the off leader was too much for "the Speaker": away they all went forward with a bound, bits between their teeth, legs and bodies stretched like greyhounds, every muscle strained to its utmost, rattling their hoofs on the stones, then on the hard baked ground, pounding through sand with such speed that before it could smother us it was a long gray cloud in our wake. Every joint and plank in our buckboard shivered and groaned as we swung to and fro, and I held on like grim death to the shaking seat. Mrs. S.'s solid weight steadied her, but her spasmodic screams gave fresh stimulus to the excited horses. Never in our lives before had we gone at such a pace, now almost on to a fallen log, now under a sweeping bough, and we had to duck our heads sharply to keep them from being taken off our bodies; the veins in Joe's face and arms stood out like cords in his desperate efforts to rein the horses in.

The cockatoos above screeched in derision to see us flying by. We started a kangaroo so suddenly that she threw her young out of her pouch and the horses crushed it to death with their heels as they went over it. What a gallop it was! Now we were jerked forward as the wheel caught the root of a tree, but we swung to again, and when once more in the open we breathed more freely, for the pace was beginning to tell on the horses. "Steady, boys, steady!" Joe kept persuasively calling to them, and our trouble seemed at an end, when suddenly a fresh difficulty occurred. We came upon a big dray in front blocking up the road, and in trying to pass between it and a tree, the heavy wheel came in contact with our light one. I have a dim recollection of a confused something, and a good womanly scream from behind, then a blank. Another moment and we were all sorting ourselves from under broken wheels and horses' hoofs and scattered harness. The buggy on its side was minus a wheel, the leader had picked himself free and gone off, the wheelers were doing their best to follow his example. We had to gather our scattered senses as best we could, and each one of us lend our help. They steadied the horses down, and got them free of the broken harness, and then we held a council of war.

I was on this occasion the imperative mood of the party, and no one arguing the point that further progress for us was impracticable that day, at least in the buggy, we made the best of a bad bargain and repaired to an old deserted miner's "numpy", which was a few paces off, with our bruised and shaken bodies and the tattered luggage that remained. The owner of the dray lent us a most willing hand, and it was settled that I was to ride one of Jackey's horses, using his saddle, and Mrs. S. to go in the dray; the men set to work and mended the wheel and patched things up sufficiently well for Joe to drive slowly on; and now, before starting, our waggon host produced that solace to all mankind, a packet of tea, tin billy, loaf of bread, and, O luxury! a tin of sardines.

At three o'clock all was ready again for a start. They lifted me on to the mare, but my ungallant steed seemed to object to this arrangement; back curled her ears, down went her head and shoulders, out flew her heels, and simultaneously over her head went I! I wasn't to be beaten and tried a second time, when she steadied down to a canter alternately with a brisk trot, but this means of locomotion—sitting sideways with no support—after some miles meant downright dislocation and was as trying to her as to me. After a short stoppage she refused to budge another inch, so, fastening her behind the dray, I got inside, and was not sorry to be able to lie full length on the straw, for I felt brusied and battered in every joint. There was an arched framework of stretched canvas over us and an opening in front where we could look over the horses' broad backs.

It was a heavy lumbering procession, not a pleasant means of locomotion, and a decidedly monotonous way of travelling, but withal one felt a solid sense of security. Our host rode on the shafts in front of the waggon, never vouchsafing a word, but content to smoke his pipe. Mrs. S., who had been secretly enjoying the contents of our flask though outwardly repudiating it, was drowned in oblivion. That woman's companionship was enough to cool the ardour of the most adventurous. Sunshine faded, stars blinked through the paling day, and we still jogged on, until the welcome sound of the barking of dogs proclaimed that our long day's journey had ended. At a small wayside inn we camped for the night, and from there on to Herberton we had no more adventures; and here, without one pang of regret but with a smile of relief, I returned Mrs. S. to the bosom of her family. With affectionate solicitude she tried to throw her expansive arms round me, but I waved her off, and I left her sobbing at our final parting. What food for reflection that journey would bring her, and over her neighbourly cups of tea I can imagine the heroine she would represent herself.

Another start and then another—my last at five in the morning, and in two days' time I was back in my own little room at Myola, thoroughly glad to have accomplished the journey. I had hoped to have slipped in unobserved, but several friends were there to meet me. I am bruised from head to foot, I am burnt nearly black, and my arms and shoulders, even through my jacket, are all blistered with the sun. As I had made the trip in defiance of all warnings, of course no one sympathised with me, and this made the remembrance of my sufferings harder to bear. At any other time of the year it might have been only a rough journey, but in this particular month it was something quite beyond a joke. In answer to the many questions I have been asked, I can only say that the caves were beautiful, but the road was rough, and, to anyone who is bent on a pleasure trip, I should say, take it in some opposite direction. From its having been an unusually dry season the heat all along was intolerable, everything was parched and burnt up. The land also in this direction is mostly poor country and only returns a bare existence. The dry ground had scarcely a blade of grass, and the thin, shadeless, scraggy gum-trees looked more weird and sad than usual under the fierce glare and heat of the cloudless semi-tropical sun and sky.

Most of the rich alluvial scrub lands of Queensland lie along the banks of creeks and rivers, and skirt the sea-coast. These are dense with forests of fig trees, with every shade of foliage, native sassafras, bunya and pine, red cedars, broad-leafed Leichhardt trees, beech, ash (nothing like our English ones),[1] and many others, all interspersed with feathery palms and creeping vines, forming such a thick canopy above that they shut out all sunlight, while their long trailing arms twisting and clasping stretch from one stem to another, and form such matted cords that it is impossible, except by cutting an entrance, to get through them. Below are smaller varieties again, twisting and bending to gain a passage to the light. In the early morning and sunset these scrubs are full of life, with flocks of pigeons eating the fruits, cockatoos and parrots of every colour, whipbirds and bellbirds, scrub turkeys, wallabys, bandicoots and a host of other living creatures. But in the heat of the day all is silent as a tomb.

---

[1] Though these trees have received from colonists the familiar names of trees in Europe, they have nothing in common with them.

Encounter with an Alligator

Cairns

I rested up at Myola for ten days, and on the eleventh morning I wished it all good-bye, staying one day more here in Cairns, where I have been spending my time among birds, butterflies, lizards, young alligators, and other reptiles at a naturalist's establishment, and where I painted a small, very lively black snake, with the figure 2 in white most perfectly shaped on the middle of its head. On the return journey I called to inquire after its welfare, and found it in spirits! it having the day before bitten the proprietor. To-night I catch the steamer up to Cooktown.

Cooktown

After leaving Cairns our next stopping place was Port Douglas, a small town built on a narrow promontory of land. The only feature of this deserted and grass-grown little town is the long stretch of beach which curves away for many a mile and forms the racecourse and principal highway to the town. There are tin mines on the ranges and good agricultural tracts inland.

Miss Bauer met me at the wharf at Cooktown at six in the morning and, after a rather hurried toilet, I drove up to her parents' pretty cottage to breakfast. Here I intended remaining for the next steamer on to Thursday Island, but the following day a regular crusher of a telegram came from there, upsetting all my plans; and yours in answer almost decided me for the moment to return; but, Micawber-like, on second thoughts I decided to await events, and after a delightfully quiet fortnight in Cooktown,

Encounter with an Alligator

Nelumbo nucifera Gaertner, Herbert River, watercolour, 54.8 x 38 cm
Reproduced by permission of the National Library of Australia

where I was allowed to paint and do just as I liked, I planned with the Bauers' help a trip to the Bloomfield River. The difficulty was in getting there, as nothing but a small schooner goes, and with the strong tradewinds on these coasts it sometimes takes five or six days to reach it, although it is only thirty miles down the coast. A large steamer, under the circumstances, would be bad enough, but nothing short of a paradise at the other end would induce me to run such a risk as that. However, the gunboats *Rapid* and *Lizard* have both come in just in the nick of time, and I am to go in the latter on her way to Samarai, as it will only take her a few miles out of her course.

Some of my very happiest times and recollections will always be associated with this happy little home of the Bauers. I came to them an absolute stranger. What a welcome they gave me, and how good they have been to me ever since!—always ready to help when I needed it, untiring in their efforts to get me flowers, and taking the keenest interest in my work. My eyes wore out sometimes painting from daylight till dark, for I couldn't keep pace with the flowers that came, and while I spent hours with wet bandages on them, Mrs. Bauer sat beside me and read aloud. There was nothing they couldn't do, what they did was well done, and with all their busy life they had time for everything.

How I did enjoy our bush scrambles in the evening, and our afternoon tea out of those dainty cups, the delicious home-made cakes and the fruit (my appetite notwithstanding the heat was always voracious there); then the long talks in the cool verandah (with its trellis-work of creepers and baskets of orchids), lazily rocking ourselves in our easy chairs, with the glorious sun setting before us, bathing those rugged, volcanic slopes of Mt. Sands in purples and golds, and the distant mountains of indefinite heights in every shade of pink and blue. The long stretches of the Endeavour River, with the town below, and the rugged framework of great rocks at the foot of the garden, all are before me—but here is the sketch!

Have I said too much? But how the wind blows here! And I can assure you that it takes a second thought and a strong effort of the will before one makes up one's mind to face the perpetual gale, and it takes all one's time to keep a hat on and an umbrella from blowing inside out. One day we paddled our own little Rob Roy canoes across the river—they were very light, weighing only six or seven pounds, and went like the wind, and from the other side I took a sketch of the town from the same spot where Captain Cook made his, one hundred years ago.

A black girl the Bauers are training for a maid affords us great amusement: she is a really wild untamed being from one of the native camps; only ten years old, and wonderfully intelligent, painfully inquisitive, and very honest, though, I daresay, she already knows the contents of every box and drawer in this house; but is utterly without affection or gratitude, like all her race, and yet there is something very winning in her soft gentle manner and voice. When the flag goes up and the steamer comes in, she runs in saying, "Yankercher (flag) one fellow sit down alonga pole." When the butcher comes and leaves the meat she says, "Bullocky sit down alonga box," everything *sits down* in their language. The other day her mistress Miss Jennie Bauer was ill. Maggie was in high glee, and with her face beaming said, "Bymeby, Miss Jennie die, Maggie plenty hat plenty dress belonga her." But Jennie got well, and when she came in to dinner a sad look passed over Maggie's face, and with tears in her eyes she said, "Jennie no die, Maggie no get hat, no get nothing belonga her."

Before leaving, I went to see the grave of Mr. M'Lauren, the missionary. It was so grown over with weeds that it was hard to recognise where it was. His was a noble life sacrificed, and had he lived he would have done more for the New Guinea natives than most of the so-called "good men" there, by teaching them first to till their ground, and also to learn from his good example that the white man wishes to be their friend. A very good German missionary in Northern Australia, not having properly learnt the language, was for more than a year teaching natives to give up their "livers" (instead of hearts) to God. As in cannibalism this is one of the tit-bits, the sacrifice must have seemed rather too great!

Cooktown is a very pretty place, and there were no wretched steam tenders. We overlooked the town, and the Endeavour River winding away in the distance until it is lost among the far-away hills. It was named the Endeavour after Captain Cook's vessel, which he brought into this port for repairs, and, in the School of Arts here, they say they have his original records.

Living with the Bauers on the outskirts of the town, I learnt more about the natives and their habits than I did anywhere else. Mrs. Bauer came here when this place was first settled, her husband then being manager of a large sugar plantation some miles down the coast, which has since been given up on account of heavy labour expenses. She had always kept a diary, which was most interesting, written as it was in the very early days of the colony.

Here the natives brought me spears and dilly bags in which they carry their food. They are, as elsewhere, very keen for money, and spend it at once on tobacco. They are a miserable-looking race, and are still, even close to the town, cannibals. Even when any of them die a natural death, the temptation is frequently too strong, and when they are burning the dead bodies, as they often do with their deceased relatives, they will snatch at portions of the flesh and eat it.

When young babies die, they double them up between two pieces of bark and carry them about from camp to camp, often using them as a pillow. It is quite unbearable to go near them at such times, but they do not seem to notice it themselves. They pierce their noses and tattoo themselves across the chest, raising up a great ridge of flesh with the deep cutting, which is done with sharp shells and then filled up with clay. They also cover bad wounds with this clay, and the children are particularly fond of eating it. Two white children died here not long ago from eating the same stuff. Black children eat and grow stout on what would kill a white child, just as poor little white gutter children thrive amid drains which to a country child would mean certain sickness or death. I tasted this edible clay, but found it far too nasty to swallow. The women do not wash their babies in water until they are sometimes two years old, but they rub them all over with their own milk, which gives them a polish, and the more shiny their little bodies become, the greater is considered the beauty.

While I was here a great many inland natives came down to the coast for ripe berries and turtles' eggs. Most of their dainties in the way of food—for instance, the wild turkey's eggs—the old men only are allowed to eat; they tell the others that they would die if they touched them, and thus secure the best of everything.

Bloomfield River

I left Cooktown on the 21st for this river, starting at seven in the morning in H.M.S. *Lizard*. It was blowing very freshly as we left the harbour; the waves gradually got wilder and wilder and the wind drove more furiously every moment, and I made my way very quickly to the cabin, where I lay, not daring to raise my head, feeling unutterable things. It was not long before we were in the teeth of a regular gale; its full force was upon us and we were pitched and tossed from side to side with the snow-crested mountains behind and around. The steamer shivered and groaned as the overwhelming strength of the waves and wind together heeled her over, almost swamping her before she had time to right herself again; now we were high up on the crest of a wave, and now down in the trough of the sea; the wind howled and shrieked through the rigging.

Captain P. came down to me, and said, "I am very sorry, but with such a sea and wind it would be impossible to enter the river. What had I better do?" Here was a nice fix! They had to meet the *Rapid* on a certain date, and the navigating lieutenant said, "Even if we returned to Cooktown we could not get in there with such a sea." I knew this coast well, and suggested running into shelter until the wind went down, which it generally does at six in the evening. This we did, and in an hour or two the storm had spent itself and the sweeping waves were quieting down.

Meanwhile the day was drawing to a close, and we had no time to waste, so away we steamed to the entrance of the river. "Heave out the line," I heard them call. The anchor caught fast and brought us to with a jerk. The sea looked still an angry, tumbled waste, and white lines of breakers chased each other along the stretch of yellow sands. The boat with some difficulty was launched, and between the rise and fall of the waves, I had to drop into it as best I could, but not before I had made sure that the officer of the boat (Mr. Gurner) was a good sailor. "Admiral Fairfax," the captain said, "used to say he was the smartest midshipman he had on this station." So I was content, and even the sound of his great honest voice above the storm reassured me. Notwithstanding that, several waves went clean over us, and I buried my head under the tarpaulin, feeling deadly sea-sick, and thinking of what an utter fool I was to go on such a wild-goose chase in search of "probable" flowers. Seabirds and pelicans were backing against the wind, and with flapping wings screeched overhead. The muddy banks of the river were lined with scrubby, wind-beaten trees and low mangrove swamps, and the thickly-wooded country behind rose high up one hill behind the other.

As we rowed up through the interspaces of the mangroves we could see flat stretches of swampy ground and a thick vapour was already rising from the stagnant waters. There was a sickly scent now as we rowed past the twisted, snake-like roots of the water-plants and the oozing mud was stirred from the sides, as the sailors dipped their oars, and water rats scampered here and there up the deadly slime.

It was the first time a boat of its kind had come up this river and the natives on the bank were very much excited. I had arranged to lodge with a woman here whose husband owned the little cutter which runs backwards and forwards with stores. We had been told that he had already gone home and prepared her for my coming. We landed and filed up the narrow pathway to the house, Mr. Gurner and I leading, three blue-jackets in the rear carrying my portfolio, Gladstone and dressing-bag; and no wonder Mrs. D. looked scared when she saw us.

Here I suffered some surprise and many disappointments. The husband had not arrived, and I had to explain my mission as best I could, for she was a Norwegian and didn't understand much English. She told me afterwards that her brothers had been drowned here and a boat-load of people came to break the news to her, and she thought that we had come to say her husband would never return. Nor did he return for three weeks after, by which time all provisions had run short, and everyone had given him up for lost. From all accounts I do not think he would have been very much missed.

It was a very fevery-looking spot in a hollow on the bank of the river; oily, greenish, stagnant water lay beside it, and, as the night came on, there was a strong smell of rank vegetation and mangrove swamp combined. I felt as if already I had swallowed whole syndicates of germs. The Crotons were growing 12 and 16 feet high, and everything else was equally luxuriant. I sat on the top log of the three steps leading up to the house, with a very dirty, chattering crowd of natives round me, until it grew dark. A thin half-ring of crescent moon shone coldly down on us, the stars came out one by one, a chilly, cold gray mist crept along the river blotting them out, while perfect clouds of insects dinned war-cries into our ears and drove us inside, and I would at that moment have given all I possessed to have turned back, had it been possible.

I said nothing when I wished Mr. Gurner good-bye, but, like Paddy's parrot, I "thought a dale", and I had an intense feeling of loneliness I couldn't shake off. Mould and cockroaches were everywhere. We had tea without sugar or milk, pumpkin, and junks of some sort of flesh—I had watched the natives preparing the tea with most unclean hands, the meat would have drawn out any teeth other than canine. In the early days of Australia, I have heard of tea that they designated "Jack the painter"; the men liked something (they said) "that was strong and took a good grip of the stomach," and to ensure this the dry leaves were given a dash of green oil paint. I think that what we had must have been handed down from those same times.

Then the children were put to bed; the youngest, a grandchild, cried lustily all night, and poor Mrs. D. groaned with fever. She did look utterly broken down, and hopeless despair was always written on her face. Sleep was out of the question, for the pigs under the house (which, like all those in Queensland, is on piles) kept up such a perpetual squeaking and grunting in their search for food, that rest was impossible, and the mosquitoes were in countless numbers.

I tried next morning to get the natives to take a note for me over to Mr. H.'s to whom I had a letter of introduction, but neither for love, pipes, tobacco, nor even a scarlet print with white bull-dog heads upon it, would they be bribed; they were afraid of the tribe of natives there. Then I tried to get a letter to the Mission Station, five miles up the river, but there was no boat, and even had there been, the two dear, good Moravian Missionaries who inhabited the Station, I feel sure, would have been too strict in their ideas to shelter a lone white woman for some days, with no means of getting rid of her.

As a last hope, I wrote to the Constable, asking him to send a black boy up to the H.s'; but, alas! he was away. I could not get through the tall, blady grass to hunt for flowers, and it suggested also every kind of snake; but along the river-bank, later on, I picked a large yellow blossom of the tree hibiscus and painted it in with a bilious-looking setting-sun background, which even now gives me a pain when I look at it, bringing back the same sensation I had then.

Another day went by, and still no sign of anyone coming. I felt like a Bluebeard's wife as the day declined; still no one came, and I was really getting so hungry that I determined I would at any rate make an effort to cross the river and get some message sent to Mr. H.'s station some distance up. Some trees falling across the water had made a partial bridge, and on these I tried my luck. By climbing on to the big root, and with the aid of an overhanging tree, I balanced myself on the log and found the first few yards easy walking, but in midstream there was a big fork in the tree to get round, and thus I lost my hold of the branches overhead and had to go very gingerly down on my hands and knees. It was horribly slippery and the river looked very black below me; I turned myself round and slid so quickly down the other side that I only saved taking a header into the river by catching at a small twig, which however broke away in my hand; but I managed to balance myself sufficiently to get on to the next log.

After going a short distance I discovered to my horror that the tide was fast coming in, not going out as I had thought, and between me and the bank, the water, instead of being wadeable, was high enough to be over my head, and the sloping banks were of soft mud. It was not a pleasant lookout, and I began to wonder how long a time I would take in drowning in this position. It was impossible to turn, so I commenced a backwards movement, but my skirt got in the way and jammed me; I was never, I think, in such a fix before. The branch behind me sloped upwards, and there was that fork of the tree to pass again, there was no creeping backwards up *that*. The water now had reached the top of the log. If I dropped my feet I knew that the current would suck me under, and in desperation I drew myself up and threw my body backwards against the log and twisted round on my face. I could never had performed this acrobatic feat at any other time, but life at that moment seemed very sweet! When once I had my arms round the fork I pulled myself up on to the main branch.

Between the root of the tree and bank there was now a great gap where the tide was rushing through with tremendous force, and close alongside of me there rose something that, for the moment, I thought was another half-sunken tree. Then it fell, a gray, loathsome creature that almost paralysed me with fear as I marked the long line of its greedy-looking jaws. I knew that the river teemed with alligators, but, somehow or other, I had never given them a thought. Its horny back was not more than a foot below me, and I hardly dared to breathe, much less to move. It slid along under the log and I felt the vibration of its body rubbing as it came up on the other side, then it turned with its head up stream again, its snout just above water as if it smelt game. Uncertain as to its movements, it sluggishly played round and round. My eyes were riveted on it, and in the horror of the moment I forgot the river, tide, and everything else, as with the rising water it came so close again that my feet almost touched it as it stirred the slimy ooze and mud from the bank with its tail. For a few seconds the voracious monster lay apparently insensible to everything, but with its ears open to the slightest sound; I hardly dared to draw breath. Now, as if waiting for the supreme moment, its opportunity to spring, it rose the full length of its body and menacingly clashed its jaws, then with snout down stream, it went under, leaving nothing in its wake but a long ripple on the surface of the water.

The tide had reached my feet when I caught sight of a native girl in the distance, and a loud cooee brought her to me. In a few minutes there were half a dozen more natives round me, who threw a log across the gap, but the current swept it away; then they launched a large one, and a black boy, climbing out on to an overhanging branch, reached me his hand and guided me to within a few feet of the bank; a step or two alone from him and I caught an outstretched hand, and oh, the joy of standing on the ground again! Just for an instant something rose in my throat, but I quickly pulled myself together again.

The natives, with an imperturbable look on their faces, expressed no surprise in finding me in this position, nor did they offer any sympathy. It would have been probably a little pleasurable excitement to have watched me go down, for just at first they reluctantly gave me help. I shall never again think that an alligator, unless under the influence of hunger, will attack a human being, or that they are anything otherwise than cowards; but I hope sincerely I may never be put to the test again.

I spent an anxious and restless night after my hideous adventure, waking up each time I fell asleep with a nameless horror that only comes in a nightmare, the darkness seemed so terribly black, and the oppressive silence was only broken by the singing din of countless bands of mosquitoes fighting outside my net to gain an entrance; the sense of loneliness stifled me, there was a breathless and oppressive heat in the small close room, my head throbbed as if it would burst, every bone ached, and I felt as if that demon fever had got hold of me again, and this added a fresh horror to the night. I got up then and chewed the leaves of a plant that the natives say will take this fever away. Whether it was this or not, I don't know, but after a time nature triumphed over misery and I fell asleep.

When daylight grim and gray filtered in at my window, my pains were gone, and, with a longing for a breath of fresh air, I got up, dressed and went out. Everything was still asleep and a misty gauze of smoky blue was just rising from the low grounds and river-bank. With the rising sun came life in every shape and form, the hum in the air of insect wings, butterflies with every rainbow colour. Birds sang and fluttered above and below, and now and then I was startled from my musings by the grunts and squeaks of common, lean, hungry-looking and preternaturally long-snouted pigs.

After a painfully frugal meal I took my clothes down to the river to wash the salt water out of them, for the contents of my Gladstone bag had been saturated the day we landed, and everything had become sticky. The river was low and the mud bank so slippery that this was not such an easy amusement as I had thought, and, moreover, I rubbed all the skin off my two thumbs, which, combined with the heat and unwholesome food, made them very sore for several days. My laundry work, however, had all been to no purpose, for a little later I heard shouts of laughter coming from the natives, and I found them walking about in great pride in my dried garments, quite irrespective of fit or order. For a moment I felt very cross, but they looked such grotesque figures that it was impossible not to laugh. I could have forgiven them more readily had they not been so horribly lazy; they would not be bribed to do anything.

A brilliant red mistletoe was growing in a tall tree close to the house, and it I longed to have. In tempting accents ("mine give budgery plenty tobacco,") I tried to persuade a black gin to climb up for it, but she only laughed and shook her head. Then a sudden inspiration struck her and she made the modest demand for all the clothes I had on me, particularly the hat and boots! They will often be quite content with one boot, and in the north of Western Australia will look upon themselves as fully clothed when they are wearing a battered old hat and nothing else.

I went into their camp to see if I could find anything more palatable to eat than in our own. Something with an unwholesome look crackled and sputtered on the red ashes, and some fur suggested native cat. Then a happy thought struck me, I would fish; and, proportionately delighted with my line, which I found—an old native one with an oyster fish-hook—I set off for the river. Here, from a most fascinating seat on a rock, I had no sooner cast my line than I found it anchored to a log. With a little skilful manipulation I freed it again—another throw, a short expectant silence, and with a sudden jerk that nearly unseated me, my rod for a moment was bent double, then snapped at the point, and under my very nose I saw the fish go by. Now up, now under the water, the line went down, and I after it, scrambling along the bank under the bushes into the mud. It caught on a snag, and, in another moment, I hooked it with my rod.

But now my fun commenced. The fish—for he was a very big one—was off again, and he tugged and dashed as I tried to play him, but dared not pull him up; I might as well have tried to play an alligator, for he played me, as, streaming with heat and panting for breath, I still held on. Then a hidden stump, a stumble, a plunge and a jerk, and my fish and line had gone!

Darkness, when it came, was most welcome, but the evening, spent in battling with heat, and mosquitoes and other insects, seemed to have no end. I caught some beautiful moths, which were attracted by the light inside the house, but by morning the cockroaches had eaten off their bodies. I cooked and prepared a pumpkin for breakfast next morning, and the natives ran down a lean, scraggy hen, which, roasted, gave us a most sumptuous meal, and I felt so well fortified that I had made up my mind that day to cross the river by other means, and make my way up to Mr. H.'s station. I was just starting on an improvised raft when he himself appeared—what a joy it was; he had accidentally heard of my arrival, and in five minutes my things were packed, and Timothy Cox, a regular Paddy from Cork, was ready to take us over the river in the smallest and ricketiest of punts with a pair of decrepit oars. "Now don't fear, Missus, I'll land yez safe," he said, and so he did, but on a sandbank in the middle of the river.

From that bank we escaped only to run, lower down, on to another, where the stream and strong tide together caught us and we went up and down in a most unsatisfactory manner, but we were finally landed on a muddy bank, from which we made our way along a pretty pathway all overgrown on both sides with a tangled mass of tropical undergrowth, to a little horse-tramway, belonging to the old fast-going-to-ruin Sugar Plantation, which was formed here eight years ago when this river was first opened up, and of which Mr. Bauer had had the management. The enormous expenses, and the doing away with black labour, ruined it, and nothing now remains but a small village of empty houses, rusty machinery, and dilapidation everywhere. A caretaker only now lives there with his wife.

There were big bushes here covered with limes all going to waste, and masses of grenadillas, yellow with ripeness, hanging temptingly from the verandah; there were goats too, and what didn't this suggest? "Would I have some milk?" I felt that I could drink a bucketful! and there was cake too, plain, homely, and currantless, but how delicious it tasted, and how luxurious that real white cloth looked, all spread on a table under the shade of the trees! My appetite was insatiable, and even when we reached Mr. H.'s pretty bungalow house at Wyalla Station I was quite ready for the second lunch that awaited me there, and never in my life before had any home seemed more welcome, or any bread and butter better; my bedroom too, the grandeur of an upstair one with a dainty curtained bed, and everything looking so sweet and fresh, and all the dearness of home over everything even to the heartiest welcome.

In the dining-room there were shelves of books and a piano. I seemed to see everything now in a new light, as if I had been out of the world for ages, and yet how short a time it really was. The view was lovely; the long valley waving with grass, now vividly green, lay below the hill where this house stands; beyond the valley there is a thick belt of rich tropical jungle, and towering above the dense range of thickly-wooded mountain, and clothed to the very summit with foliage of every shade of green and russet, rose the highest peak, 4000 feet. This garden forms the foreground with a fringe of cocoa-nut palms, mango trees, tall hibiscus, and other flowering shrubs. It was like entering paradise after leaving that low-lying fever-stricken bit of ground on the other side of the river.

It was so cold last night that I sat with my coat on; one can hardly realise that there could be such a difference in the temperature between this place and Cooktown. We sit all day in the room in which I am writing, which is quite open at both ends, and through a trellis-work of grenadillas we look at the mountains beyond. To-night, as I write, we hear far away in the distance the peculiar cry of the natives mourning over one of their members who has died; then the wild, sad cry of the curlew and the homely tinkling of cowbells reminds us that we are still in a land of civilisation. This is a cattle station now, but when the plantation was formed they grew sugar-cane along the valley, then tobacco, which grows splendidly and took a first prize at the last Melbourne Exhibition. Rice, too, grows well, as also do tea, coffee, and all kinds of tropical fruits.

To-night Mr. H.'s two sons brought home over a hundred pounds weight of fish which they had caught in nets at the mouth of the river—trevalli (a fish not unlike a cod), John Dory, mullet, fresh and salt water bream, flat-heads, skate, flounders, and several others. Bread, butter, everything they use is made on the place; the only help they have is from the native girls who take it in turns to come up on different days. Very little amuses these dusky maidens and all day long they are laughing. I do not wonder now that the native to whom I gave the note to deliver refused, as his "gin" (who lives here) preferred another husband and went off with him. The deserted one made his way here one night and creeping into the camp speared his faithless wife in two places, then ran for his life. Everyone was awakened by wild shrieks from the natives, but the disappointed husband was off like the wind.

Flesh wounds these natives don't seem to mind, treating them with a kind of healing clay which is smeared over them, but measles and other diseases carry them off at once. It is sad to see the numbers who have been wounded by guns, and here, at any rate, they have been shamefully treated by the white people. One missionary here even sold them for £5 a head to a well-known *bêche de mer* trader in Cooktown. This model missionary was afterwards, however, sent away and made to return the money. At the present time the native women have been kidnapped for these *bêche de mer* and pearling boats, and the young boys, too, for servants.

Mr. H., who has always been a friend to the natives, can do anything with them, though he came here in the "good old cannibal days", when they were not pleasant customers to meet. We paid the camp a visit this afternoon and watched them throwing their boomerangs. The natives are wonderfully dexterous in using them, and it is a pretty sight to see them skimming along the ground, rising and falling in a circuitous curved flight through the air, and finally swiftly coming back and falling at the thrower's feet. At night they sometimes, during their corroborees, throw them with lighted torches fastened to one end. Their spears, nullahs, hatchets, and shields are all made of the same hard wood (partly hardened by the action of the fire).

I once saw a fight in Western Australia among the natives. I stood with the non-combatants at a respectful distance. Their flesh, which heals with the greatest rapidity, was horribly gashed and cut about, and I was so horrified at the sight that my legs couldn't carry me fast enough from the ghastly scene. They show their scars with warrior-like pride. Their battles are mere questions of strength, and the weaker side leave, and thus intimate that they are beaten. Women never join in the battles, though they will sometimes grow so excited in looking on that they will seize their yam sticks (made for digging up roots) and with wild shrieks and gesticulatons will fall on each other, hacking and hitting in the most barbarous way, finally scratching and tearing at each other's hair. They seldom take part in the corroboree, but sitting on their crossed legs in rows they form an orchestra, "most melancholy" if not "most musical". Their great performances take place during the full moon.

It is very hard to find out what their religion is, and they are generally reticent about it. Thunderstorms are caused, in their belief, by departed spirits; the last man who has died is supposed to influence the elements, and the chief of the tribe will sometimes in a most vehement way expostulate with the unseen spirit.

They kill many of their female children as being inferior to the male, especially if they are cross, when they knock them on the head with their nullahs. "Piccaninny no good, too much cry," they will tell you. They fasten their dead babies (when they don't eat them) between tightly-bandaged pieces of bark with banana leaves. One that had been used as a pillow, and which I made a sketch of, nearly drove me out of the camp. The mother was still in mourning, and had her forehead and body plastered over with white clay. Her husband, who was a fine-looking man, had two bullets in his body, which, however, did not seem to inconvenience him. They generally, in their love-making, seize upon and carry off their wives, if from another tribe, and the young "Lochinvar" generally commences operations by stunning her on the head to prevent her from screaming: this generally is an excuse for declaring war, which is a sort of pastime to them.

The belief of this particular tribe is that death is caused by a small round smooth pebble, the size of a pigeon's egg, being placed in the affected spot by some hostile black. The patient sometimes recovers, or thinks he does, by a similar stone, which is called "Mudlo", being rubbed over the affected part.

This evening we watched the "gins" preparing their food of zamia nuts, which they pound into a soft, pulpy-looking stuff. This is put into bits of bark and water run through it to extract some kind of poison. It was like thick pea-soup when strained afterwards through their dilly bags. I ate some of the nasty, unwholesome-looking stuff, and found it utterly tasteless. I also took some pounded root, which I might have chewed for hours without producing any impression on it: it was like india-rubber. They were cooking yams in the ashes, and long, thin roots too, which were not so bad.

We crossed the river after leaving the camp, and made our way along the bank under the shade of the beautiful jungle all hung and matted together with ferns and creeping vines. The curiously-shaped and coloured fungi here would have delighted the hearts of enthusiasts who collect these unwholesome-looking delicacies. The natives, I believe, cook several of the edible ones, but I should be sorry for the experimenting white individual who attempted to eat them, after my own painful experiences. Some, of the most delicately-coloured pink variety, are found under logs and over-hanging, rocky ledges, where not a gleam of sunshine penetrates; under damp ferns and mosses are others of a most deadly-looking blue colour, or flaunting in scarlet spotted with yellow, and with purple gills. Again, there are delicate parasol-shaped, green ones with the thinnest stems, big brown monstrosities, and huge puff-balls, some filled with yellow dust and others soft, pulpy, and black, all looking equally poisonous. I was glad to get away from them into a beaten track, and, through the long grass, home.

On the way home we came face to face with an ugly-looking cow, who wished to dispute our right to trespass on her territory, so we quickly retreated and wisely left her in possession. Here the cattle are really wild, and though they say that if the herds close round you or follow you, there is no reason to feel afraid, as it only means curiosity, I call it prolonged agony. Snakes of various kinds abound here, carpet ones occasionally make a home in the rafters above, so they say, and a cat brought a small and venomous one in the other evening and played with it under the table, while we, in delightful ignorance, ate our dinner; but these are trifles that are in a moment forgotten.

An Abundance of Flowers

Wyalla

I have been going through all the sensations of a new enterprise, and have made and baked the three last batches of bread for the family. You will say I might have spared their digestions, but it was really just "done to a turn", not "as light as a feather", but just as bread ought to look. I get up at five in the morning too, which is another advantage, though I never believe the old adage of the early bird and the worm. Here one must learn to do everything oneself, for your fickle Mary Jane is a creature of impulse, and never consults your wishes; but when the fancy takes her, and when the solitudes of the bush pall on her, she packs up her bag and walks.

I have now been here for a fortnight, and my visit is drawing to a close, though as yet it is rather a puzzle to know how I am to get back to Cooktown, and as D.'s boat was so long in arriving, I do not fancy the idea of trusting myself in her. We have led, I suppose, a rather monotonous life, though to me it is so new that it has endless interests in the native camps and blacks alone, who all day long sing, laugh, and play. Yesterday, we jogged merrily along in a springless dray to the old Bloomfield Mill, which has just been bought and is being removed, so the last hope is gone that this place will ever be alive again. Even at the tin mines, five miles away, very little metal is coming in, and at Lion's Den, farther away, still less.

We had a good scramble to the top of the hill, where the Bauers lived when the mill was working. It was a warm day, and a tedious walk, but we were well repaid. Stretching away in front of us were miles of seashore, the entrance to the river, and a long perspective of headlands fading away in the dim distance. Behind us, hundreds of feet below, lay the long valley, now waving with green grass instead of cane; and towering above again, mountain after mountain of thickly-wooded jungle. The lights were rich and beautiful in the setting sun. Eash fresh step disclosed another picture, and if our Australian artists only knew what rich and endless subjects they would find in Northern Queensland, they would surely make up their minds to endure a little roughing and camping out, and take a three or four months' holiday at this time of year. It would well repay them.

To-day we climbed to the top of the mountain (Macmillan) near the house, and a nice scramble we had; we started early, Mrs. H.'s brother, her son, and six native women on foot, carrying lunch baskets, etc., and Miss H., Gina H., and I on ponies as far as the foot of the hill where the climbing commenced. Following for some distance through the jungle a rocky track made by pack-horses and mules from the mines, we emerged into the open, where the grass was green and smooth-looking, but on closer inspection we found it was so high as to be over our heads; completely hidden underneath were big rocks over which we slipped and fell every minute.

It was indeed very hard work, and we stopped a good many times to admire the view. The native women, who are like kangaroos on their feet, enjoyed our discomfiture, and thought it great fun each time we fell. Past this we again came into the scrub, where the real climbing commenced, and where every few yards we were caught in tangled masses of creepers and vines which throw their arms from tree to tree. Our gentlemen guides had to cut the way before us as we went along. The luxuriant vegetation was dense and smothered; overhead tall palms stretched their leaves heavenward through it all. Far up in the branches, well out of reach, we saw a rare and lovely white orchid. In these northern tropical wilds the flowers grow high where they can catch the sunlight above, that fringes the edge of the jungle.

It is tantalising to see the ground strewn with fallen blossoms and not to know which leaf owns them; while on the opposite side, in Western Australia, it is low on the ground that we see the overgrown garden. The dreary sand plains, which in winter are desolate and withered, are then one blaze of colour with flowers of every form and hue, some like feathers, others deep-fringed, blinding to paint; wonderful shades of hibiscus, patches of crimson desert pea, with here and there a white variety; others again more like insects, bee and butterfly ground orchids, black anigazanthus or kangaroo's foot, with its five sooty fingers lined with lemon colour; the bright green variety with its scarlet calyx; pink, yellow, white, and crimson verticordias; sweet-scented veronicas and heaths—but their name is legion, and if I wander off to endless colouring I shall never get to the top of the mountain and you will never hear the end of that climb, so we will go back to the palms again. Lycopodiums were trailing along the ground, and ferns and mosses everywhere, with more bright-coloured fungi.

Here and there through the trees we caught a glimpse of the world below us, but we had to hurry on. As we came nearer the top, thick clouds kept passing over us and left us unpleasantly moist, and at one rather lengthy halt we got covered with leeches, so we hurried on. It grew colder now and the road rougher; in front of us was a deep chasm between two great boulders of rock, and the only crossing over it was by a bridge of matted roots. Here we went on all fours. Then we found a porcupine, and the native women, who look upon these animals as a great delicacy, were some time in lifting it from the ground, it clung so tightly with its strong claws. They killed it by hitting it under the throat. On we went, slipping down rocks and dropping from one to the other, over most uncomfortably deep and black-looking chasms.

In some places it seemed impossible to get down, but at last we reached our final goal, the edge of a huge rock, and the only lookout from the top of this mountain. Away below us lay the valley and coast-line of the Bloomfield. Thick clouds kept passing over us, but now and then through the sunshine we had an uninterrupted sight of perhaps one of the finest views in all Queensland. We looked down on the valley 4000 feet below. We had been five hours on the way and were quite ready for our "billy tea" (which took a long time to boil at this altitude) and our turkey sandwiches, which never tasted better. The gins cooked their porcupine, which smelt very gamey in the ashes. I made my sketch as best I could through cloud and sunshine.

Growing in the ridges of the precipice was a pale, pink, waxy, tube-shaped flower, with close hard dark green leaves. We caught here a very large handsome gray moth, and both it and the new

THE FLOWER HUNTER

Fruit, northern Queensland, watercolour, 54.7 x 38 cm
Reproduced by permission of the National Library of Australia

flower I painted, on my return, after a good hour's rest. On the last part of our journey through the scrub, it was intensely dark; now and then a fire-fly or a phosporescent fungus gave us light, which made the blackness afterwards even denser; and as long as the matches lasted the natives lit them and guided us over the slippery rocks. Half-way down our horses met us, but neither Miss. H. nor I took advantage of them, as we preferred trusting our own legs, once or twice having found ourselves on the edge of a precipitous rock. We were exceedingly glad when we emerged on the plain, and more so when over the hill we saw the lights of home again.

Next day some of us started early and went up to the Mission Station. We took the horse-tramway from the old mill to the river, picking up six native men with their spears on the way; they were not a savoury addition, and we were not sorry to part with them. A favourite little dog belonging to the H.'s that we had with us got his head under the wheel of the tram, and a large portion of it was completely scalped, exposing the skull. We laid him under the shade of a tree thinking him dead, but in a few minutes he came running after us, looking a pitiable sight; we bandaged his head up, and a fortnight after a thick hairless skin had grown over the wound.

The Mission boat was at the river to meet us, and a crew of natives pulled us up to the Station; each twist and curve of the river disclosing some fresh beauty. Here a reach with low banks of bulrushes, yellow water lilies and huge caladium leaves, and wings and buds of bright things all flashing in the sunlight. Now between rocks or cliffs, all hung with ferns and fairy draperies, we rowed, and under arching trees in dense shade where feathery creepers dipped their heavily-laden blossoms, and gigantic tree roots formed such networks in the narrow passage, that we had to push and twist our way through them to gain an outlet, then with steady strokes we glided into glowing sunlight, over deep dark pools into a sound of falling waters, where the shallow under-bed gleamed red and yellow over pebble stones and where we had to be lifted bodily over the rapids.

A picturesque group of natives in single file went by, as they forded the river, going off on a hunt, with their spears and nullahs slung over their shoulders, and not a vestige of clothing covering their copper-coloured, shiny bodies. They pulled the boat here into the bank to pick me some bright scarlet, gourd-shaped fruit. A wood-pigeon broke from its cover and a big frilled lizard went off with an ungainly roll. Then swiftly again they rowed from under the drooping branches and across to the other side of the river, where we put in-shore and they moored the boat while we made our way up the bank to the cottages of the Moravian Missionary Station. Here we rested for lunch, and then walked a mile up to the foot of the falls.

Walls of rocks towered high on both sides of us, while huge boulders and stones below were thrown in heaped-up confusion, as if any army of Titans had played a game of pitch and toss. The water rushed in frantic haste in and out between them in its downward course, and with a roar of thunder from the heights above, in front of us, fell the mighty deluge, scattering clouds of mist and foam as it struck, swirled, then twisted, and leapt from one ledge to another, forming double rainbows in the sun-shafts, and then falling, a vivid transparent green, into purple shadows of the pools below, leaving behind every bough and leafage bent with the weight of glistening drops.

Growing from the sides of the steep cliffs were rare orchids, and the overhanging trees sent down showers of cream-coloured blossoms. They were far above reach and I sighed in vain for them. Gnarled roots and lycopodiums formed a network to the loose ground, and masses of crimson bottle-brush grew in the deep fissures of the rocks. We had tea at the Mission house before returning. The two missionaries were most kind in their welcome. We peeped into the natives' houses, inspected the copy-books in the schoolroom, and interviewed the black mothers and their piccaninnies before leaving. The men were all away on the march, hunting. Under the present management they all seemed happy enough, and their teachers seemed to be thoroughly in earnest over their work; sometimes there are between two and three hundred natives there; they come and go as the fancy takes them. A little black girl, who had run away from her husband at Mr. H.'s a few days ago, was there, and returned with us; her little mate, on hearing she had left, unmindful of the alligators, swam the river and came after us, but her husband caught her and took her back again; she did not look more than thirteen, while he was a wretched, blear-eyed old creatured of about fifty. They constantly run away from their husbands, who are always chosen for them from another tribe; but, as the men seem to have an unlimited supply of wives, it is only occasionally that they trouble themselves to go after them. I have grown to think the black girls pretty, and their mirth is infectious.

The familiar scent of gum-trees (just off the river-bank) was everywhere, but here again it is a different variety, smaller than those I am familiar with, and shadeless. They look upon them here as strangers, and later on I had to defend the much-abused eucalyptus; few even among Australians known its value, and that according to an eminent botanist, one species, *Eucalyptus regnanas*, represents the loftiest tree in the world. One of these trees on the Cape Otway ranges measures a little under 500 feet in height; another has a circumference of 69 feet at the base of the stem. In forest glens they run up sometimes for 100 feet before throwing out a single branch, while the oil from all of them is invaluable in cases of consumption, scarlet-fever, sprains, etc.

Colonel Warren quotes from Scripture in reference to the medicinal value of the eucalyptus—"The leaves of the tree shall be for the healing of the nations." Many, even of the bushmen, do not know that a small, weeping variety contains in its roots enough water to satisfy many a thirsty traveller. In some of the old watercourses in Western Australia you see a variant that is really beautiful, with vividly-green foliage and the purest white, curiously-twisted stems. Here too you see the lovely scarlet-flowering variety; but the names of these trees and the uses to which they may be put are endless.

The next evening I went to see the camp for the last time to wish the natives good-bye. Nature was folding her soft gray wings, and the bright moonlight played fantastic tricks as she guided us through the forest. The blacks had formed their camp on the banks of the river under the shadow of the tall jungle trees, and we were greeted on our arrival by a chorus of barking curs. It was a typical scene of wild native life—the rough gunyahs of leaves and boughs, the flickering light of the fires, and the weird forms of the natives as they passed to and fro. Here an old woman with apish jaws, wrapped in a rug, was crooning over the hot embers, roasting some roots; beside her a dog with a numerous litter of puppies. I asked her how many, and she held up her ten skinny fingers. "Blucher", a fine big man, came forward and shook hands. "Rosie", his wife, a young-looking girl, who we knew had been severely beaten that day, hung back in the hut; she had killed two of his wives, and that day had tried to kill number three.

Another old woman, more like a hideous witch than anything else, whose skeleton would have been a treasure to any museum, had her legs bent outwards and flattened like boomerangs. She was finishing a grass bag, splitting the canes with her teeth as she worked it. Two large wallabies were swung in a tree, and a plentiful supply of yams and zamia nuts were lying scattered about in dilly bags. Two mummified babies fastened up in bark were doing duty as pillows inside one of the huts, and the indefinable mixture of smells was too much for our olfactory nerves and soon drove us off. The dancing shadows from the fires played upon dark supple forms and burnished skins, while the imperturbable features of others, as they eyed us, did not entice us to stay. The crickets were chirping with might and main in a deafening competition with a chorus of frogs, as we turned our backs on the camp; bats whirled in and out of the moonlight, night owls whooped, moths flapped our faces, and a troop of mists softly chasing back others hurried us away from fever and ague, home to a fire.

Cooktown

I decided on Saturday to go on to Thursday Island by the next steamer, and as it was too late to arrange about riding into Cooktown, I had no alternative but to go by D.'s boat leaving next day. He had previously said that he was going on three different days in succession. At first he was to start on the 16th, but when the 16th came he put it off until next day, then again to another day, and he finally left yesterday. He was positively going at twelve; they gave him two hours' grace but he still would not say when he was starting. Hour after hour we were kept there, not daring to express our feelings, as we were entirely at his mercy. At last in despair, in the most humble manner I could put on (feeling all the time as if I could have hurled unlimited adjectives at him), I asked if he meant to leave at all that night, as I had to catch the steamer next day. "I'll leave when I *do* leave," was all the answer that I got.

The sun was now setting and the long purple shadows were turning to gray, we were miles from home and still the creature would give us no answer; finally, when our patience was almost exhausted, and irritated at last to desperation, after a diplomatic commercial transaction, we eventually started at seven, with a miscellaneous cargo of pigs, turkeys, fowls, pumpkins, tin from the mines, orchids, ferns, and goodness knows what besides. There was no moving room on board that boat, and a mere hole did duty for a cabin. I saw a woman's head poke up it, and I asked her if it was stuffy down there, to which she answered, "Awful, but you grows accustomed to it." I did not try it, but sat as best I could beside the man at the wheel for an hour, during all which time the boat lay like a log at the mouth of the river, as there was not a breath of wind stirring to take us forward.

A brilliant moon was rising and not a sound broke the silence, when suddenly from the depth of the water below there came a soft murmuring sound like the plaintive notes of an Æolian harp, which rose and fell in a gentle cadence. Some said it was a musical fish, others that the sounds came from a shell-fish. The sounds seemed stationary, but stopped at intervals.

If we suffered torments from mosquitoes in daylight, no language can describe what we endured from them here at night. They came like a legion of devils, a whirlwind of flying needles in countless thousands, and allowed us no truce. But a shift of wind scattered them at last, and a sudden breath of Æolus sent us bounding away from the shore, and the boat skimmed through the water like a slender sea swallow, dipping its bows, then scudding with outstretched wings over the silver-tipped waves.

The physical uneasiness of sitting bolt upright now became so absorbing that I had to try and sleep stretched on the top of the cabin. From a half-doze, half-dream, I started and gave such a spring that my companion the steersman only just caught me from going overboard. Poor fellow, he was himself drowned on the return journey by falling from the rigging into the water. A shark must have taken him, for he never rose again. He had an infinitude of quiet humour and old-world stories.

After my last escape I tried the top of the luggage, but a stone jar under my shoulder gave way, and I fell through space on top of a pig. Then I grew pathetic over my miseries, and lay sleepily there watching the shimmer and glint on the waves, the countless stars in the black vault above, the foam as it hissed from the sides of our boat, and, as the gray day broke, the birds that helter-skelter rose chattering from their roosts on the islands of rocks. It was half-past three in the morning when we anchored close to the shore. I climbed over four other boats to the pier. I had the felicity of feeling that I was the only living creature waking at that hour in Cooktown, as I made my way up to Mrs. Bauer's house and, through unlocked doors, crept silently into my room, where I soon fell asleep.

Brilliant Sea Flowers

Off Thursday Island

Two days later I went on board the s.s. *Jumna*, and for once I almost enjoyed the journey up to Thursday Island. We anchored near Channel Rock Lighthouse, to take a passenger on board from a *bêche-de-mer* and pearling boat, then on again to Clermont Lightship, where a boat comes alongside for letters, and another eighty miles on to Weymouth Bay, so well remembered for the noble exploits of the explorer Kennedy and his party, some fifty years ago. They lost seven of their number here, from fever and starvation, and the undaunted leader, with his faithful black boy "Jacky Jacky", left for Albany, where a ship was to wait for them, but Kennedy was speared by the natives, and Jacky alone reached the last camping ground. One of the grasses of this wild land has been named after his native name "Galmarra".

There was not a ripple on the water as we went through Albany Pass. We had just sat down to dinner, but I slipped away on deck to see what I could see. We could, however, only just distinguish the high ant-hills in the entrance, looking in the dusk like monuments, like Mr. Jardine's house perched up on the cliff, and the flag that ran up as we went by. It was close to this place that the ill-fated *Quetta* struck on a hidden rock and went down. All those who were saved were rescued by Mr. Jardine's boats excepting three. The men in those boats never rested day or night in their labours, and I afterwards heard here at Thursday Island how unceasingly they had worked.

We are to anchor not far from here, for it is a dangerous coast to travel by night, and our captain, who had commanded the *Quetta* at the time she was wrecked, and who was one of the few saved, was naturally cautious. The *Jumna* has now anchored eighty miles off Thursday Island, and the boats are coming alongside; the purser is asking for letters, and the steward, in anticipation of his "tip", has twice officiously pressed his services upon me; my port-manteaus must be strapped, good-byes must again be said, and my letter must abrupty come to an end.

Thursday Island

How glad I am that I did not allow myself to be guided by the impressions of others! "Do not go to Thursday Island, there is nothing to be seen or done there," I was told, but feminine perversity, as you would call it, just made me long all the more to go and see for myself. I would not choose it, perhaps, for a home for the rest of my life, but for the time being, to a stranger it offers many attractions. Why do we never hear of the beauty of its surroundings?

What a view lay before us, as we trooped on deck that morning to get the first glimpse of these last bits of Australian land! A cloudless sky and a sparkling sea of sapphire dappled with white waves met our view; island after island rose before us, and each turn of the pounding engines disclosed some fresh scene of beauty. In the distance we saw the shimmering light of early morning on the roofs of the houses in that little bay, which will soon, with King George's Sound, hold so important a place in the defence of our Empire. We find it already the rendezvous of eight ships of war; and with a rattling of chain, and a splashing of water, down goes our anchor close beside H.M.S. *Orlando*, our own flag-ship, which cannot venture close in.

Later on, I am allowed to go ashore in her steam launch, and most thankful I am, for a motley crowd welcomes us at the pier, and, but for the aid of the blue-jackets, I might be sitting on my baggage yet. The hotel is only two minutes' walk from the pier, and the landlady, who is both portly and gracious, takes me to my room, in front of which is a Cingalese, with delightful unconcern, engaged in washing two babies in a basin of water, though all along the wide verandah gentlemen are lounging and smoking in their long easy-chairs. There is a remarkable air of freedom and *sans gêne* about everything and everybody, but we must remember that it is holiday time. Knots of sailors in spotless white are to be seen in every direction. To-day there is a regatta, and as the winning boat passes the ships great cheering goes on almost constantly.

In the afternoon I go for a drive in the one cab on the island. The roads are limited, but I get a birds'-eye view of the territory, and we drive afterwards through the little town. What a medley of tongues and faces one hears and sees! Britons, Italians, Spaniards, Maltese, Hindus, Cingalese, Negroes, Malays, Kanakas; at least a dozen or more different nationalities. A Cingalese, who is on the verandah when we get back, comes and exhibits his wares outside my sitting-room window—twenty-guinea cats'-eyes, bad pearls, and Colombo-set rings. "Nothing so beautiful seen here before," he keeps on telling us. At last, in disgust he leaves us, with a parting shot, "This ship no good; no buy." It seems so strange in this far-away place to hear the bugle-calls.

Each morning I get up at daylight, and come back with a bunch of flowers which are worthy to form a gift for our queen. They are truly beautiful here, and all new to me. Mr. Savile Kent, the Inspector of Fisheries, is staying at this hotel, and each morning, at low tide, he goes out hunting on the reefs. The verandah is covered with the most beautiful living corals and sea anemones of every shape and colour; varying from deepest crimson to pale pink, as well as every shade of mauve, purple, blue, yellow, and green; I did not know, before, that such brilliant sea-flowers existed. I remember that a diver in Western Australia once made me long to go down with him, for he told me there were more beautiful gardens under the sea than above it.

I wish that the nights were days, for there is so much to be done. By this post I send you a sketch of a bird's-eye view of the town and the warships, taken from the site where they have commenced the fortifications. It blew a gale up there (it always does), and I was working under difficulties when I made my sketch; first my hat went, then my umbrella, and I was glad at last to turn my face homewards, for the sun was scorching, and I already begin to look like a half-caste.

To-day, the Governor, Sir Henry Norman, landed officially with the Admiral, Lord Charles Scott, and this house, and all the windows about, rattled again and again, as each gun went off. How they must have astonished the natives on the surrounding islands! To-night, Prince of Wales' Island is all alight with huge bush fires, whether in honour of the Squadron or not, we do not know; there are only natives living there, and a small settlement of *bêche-de-mer* fishers. These latter partly cook the *bêche-de-mer* (or sea-slugs), then dry them in the sun and smoke them. There are several different kinds of these slugs, and they are horrid-looking creatures when taken fresh from the water; I believe most of them go to China. These waters also send away, annually, £120,000 worth of pearl shell.

Thursday Island

My week is almost up, and I have intended leaving by the next boat, but I have tempting offers to visit the different islands, and, as a beginning, I have decided next week to go to Somerset on the mainland. Thus my plans are altered, and I am going again to let myself drift. Last night there was a children's fancy dress ball at the Residency, and we had a rather awkward accident, for, as we (the Governor, the Admiral, and I) were starting from the hotel for the ball, in the landlady's pony carriage, in the dark, we drove very quickly under a stretched clothes-line. It caught the Admiral, who was sitting in front, with such force under the chin, that it sent him flying on to his back in the road. Fortunately, the dust was inches in depth where he fell, and beyond a severe bruising, and a cut under the chin, he was not seriously injured. The Governor, who was sitting behind with me, escaped unhurt, but lost his helmet; while, with my usual ill luck, the line caught me violently across the eyelids and nose, quite stunning me for the moment.

The suggestion that I should be carried back to the hotel on a "lady's-chair", made by two pairs of hands, however, quickly brought me to my senses; so I managed to walk back, had my face bathed, and my nose all plastered up, and, thus repaired, went to the dance. You cannot accuse me of vanity, for in an hour's time, when I could no longer endure the pain, and had to come back, I was a hideous sight, and next morning had two of the blackest of black eyes, which will last for many days to come, to say nothing of a broken nose.

The last of the ships left next morning, and a good many of those who were at the dance came to the hotel at one in the morning to make their final adieux. They danced, they sang, and they made speeches; they hip-hip-horrayed, and sang "For they are jolly good fellows", and "We won't go home till morning" (they certainly did *not*), and finally, I think, they danced on the table, for in the morning its back was broken.

When they left, I went to stay for a week at the Residency, where Mr. Douglas has been untiring in his efforts to get me flowers, and whence we have made several excursions to the neighbouring islands. We spent one delightful day picnicking at Hammond Island, starting off early in the morning, and taking our lunch with us. We walked to an old mining claim which was almost deserted, one man alone believing in its fortune, and working steadily on alone. The day had become oppressively warm, and the walk there and back through the heavy sand was so tiring that (now don't laugh at me) I fell asleep while still walking! We boiled our kettle on the beach and had "Billy" tea, rowing back to Thursday Island in the cool of the evening. On our way back we passed a small island, where, several years ago, the bodies of eight natives were found completely mummified and fastened up in bark.

After dinner, we told stories; each one of us was called upon to tell one—most of them were thrilling tales of hairbreadth escapes. I told my story of the candle. You remember years ago, when we were travelling in Western Australia, we stopped to take shelter for the night from a thunderstorm at a shepherd's bark hut, the only one within thirty miles, and consisting of only two rooms. The man made us welcome, but told us that his mate, who was in the next room, had died only that afternoon. The storm was raging outside, and there was an oppressive gloom on the four of us as we sat round the table by the dim light of one tallow candle stuck in the broken neck of an old black bottle. Suddenly the flame lengthened, and shooting up, left the wick without a spark behind, and went up and up to the ceiling before it went out. I always tell the story just as we all saw it, in the hope that some day I may come across some one scientific enough to explain this curious phenomenon to me.

Then we had our bumps electro-biologised; my bump of firmness (no, not obstinacy) was well developed, my intellectual faculties were weak. I always knew this, but it was unfeeling to tell me so. It blew (as I thought) such a gale in the night that I expected at least to find the house roofless in the morning, but as no one remarked about it, I suppose it is no unusual thing here.

The next day I left Thursday Island to stay with Mr. and Mrs. Jardine at Somerset; the latter I had the pleasure of meeting here with her three charming children.

Somerset, Cape York

I have not written to you for a week, but posts are very irregular, and the residents here have to trust to the Government steamer, or their own boats (when they are here) to bring them. I was to have gone back to Thursday Island to-day, but I feel like a boy who has been granted extra holidays, because I remain now for another fortnight, and then, before turning my face homewards, I am to take another few weeks visiting the different islands in the Straits. This visit has been one long summer's day, and I shall never leave any place with more regret. The sketch I send you gives a very poor idea of the beauty of everything here. This little bay, with its wonderfully blue water, contrasts splendidly with the endless shades of colour in the jungle, where the leaves are sometimes almost as brilliant as the flowers themselves, and yet they tell me this is the worst time of the year to see it.

When we landed here, the little pathway up the cliff to the house was so full of interest, with all its new plants—new, at least, to me—that I made every excuse to loiter. I do not know if many botanists have been here already, but excepting three trees, there is absolutely not one plant that I have ever seen before, and at a little distance from the sea and sheltered from the wind, the jungle is even more beautiful than on the Johnstone River, which I thought nothing could surpass. There is a magnificent palm tree beside the Jardines' house, of a species which is not known anywhere else, except in one spot a few miles away, and the native fig trees, now covered with fruit, are magnificent-looking, with wonderful colouring, their young leaves of a delicate pink, shaded off to a vivid green in the older, while they are as large as most of our English trees. Another tree, with clusters of flowers like a jessamine, is a mass of starry blossoms, and the whole air is redolent with its scent.

Marcus Clarke in his beautifully-phrased introduction to the poems of Adam Lindsay Gordon, characterises Australia as "a land whose flowers are without scent, whose birds are without song, whose trees are without shade; a land where Nature was learning her A B C, and upon which she had scribbled her early thoughts in quaint and curious hieroglyphs, in savage and secret signs, laden with Sibylline oracles of Orphic potency; a land in which the deep-voiced wind that sweeps the broad bosom of the earth makes wild and mournful melody—a melody that moans in the leaves of the spectral gum, or whispers among the feathery foliage of the weird casuarina." Now, however eloquent such a description may undoubtedly be, the writer has allowed his wish for effect to mar his accuracy; and although our landscapes may frequently present only the sad or savage aspect of Nature, the flowers of the Australian bush are beautiful, and noted for delicacy of form and richness of colour to such an extent, that in external loveliness they may well challenge comparison with the tenderly-nurtured children of the gardens and conservatories of the older world.

To stigmatise them as without scent is, moreover, a grave injustice, for many of them emit freely a perfume which fills the surrounding air with fragrance. What can be more exquisite or more delicate than the scent of *Boronia megastigma* and *Boronia heterophylla*; of *Boronia serrulata*, Sydney native rose, of many of the acacias; of *Arthropodium strictum;* of *Alyxia buxifolia,* or of the beautiful so-called "rock-lily" of Sydney, *Dendrobium speciosum?* Surely Marcus Clarke was a little too sweeping in his condemnation.

The too short day is over here, before I realise it has commenced. I wish I had the privilege granted to Joshua of power to arrest the sun. I never want to go to bed, and I grudge the night hours that I waste. I am up at half-past six; when I have a big tumbler of milk, and commence my painting; otherwise I could do nothing, and even now I must leave dozens of flowers to wither. I work on till the cool of the evening, when kind hands take my painting from me, and we go for a scramble, or the horses are brought round and we ride. We spend the evenings in our lounge chairs on the verandah, and the children, who have beautiful voices, sing to us.

Sometimes we watch the natives at their corroborees, which are different from those I have seen; they wear masks representing birds of different species, or alligators. Last night they were pelicans, and they imitated all the movements of these birds in their dances, which were almost graceful, but it was on the whole a most grotesque sight to see the fire-light flickering on their huge beaks ornamented with feathers, while round their waists they wore the young white leaves of the cocoa-nut palm torn into shreds. Those who did not dance, sang or chanted and kept time, beating on a sort of drum.

Some strange natives from the Batavia River are here now, very much tattooed across the chest and on the arms. They also have one front tooth knocked out. One of their prettiest dances is a funeral one, when they carry the head of the dead and go through a sort of processional ceremony. They place the dead body at first on four high sticks and wait until the head falls off before they touch it again.

Dullness seems a thing unknown here; there is life and movement going on all round; steamers are constantly passing back and forwards, and some fire a gun as they go by. The flag is always hoisted on our flag-staff in return. Everything is wrapped in sunshine, and my friends here seem to live contentedly year after year away from all the cares and worries of the outside world. This is the only house (with the exception of a telegraph station about twenty-five miles off) in this northern part of Australia.

Mr. Jardine is the only settler here, a worthy monarch too, coming from Rockhampton in the first instance, with his brother, in 1864. They came all the way overland with stock, and were nearly a year on the journey, having many hairbreadth escapes from the natives, who never in a single instance let them pass without attacking or following them. They were not an amiable race in those days, and between Somerset and Cape York could muster 3500 fighting men; now there are only a hundred or so left. It was here that Kennedy, the explorer, years ago, almost within sight of home, was killed by the natives. At different times camps were formed here of white settlers who shared the same fate, and Mr. Jardine could tell some curious tales of long ago, but I only hear of his brave and daring deeds from outside sources. He has many a time had to fight hard for his life. He can arm a hundred men if necessary, and you would be amused to see the number of guns, pistols, and other weapons hanging against the walls, many of them being kept ready loaded in case of sudden attack.

A Mrs. Thomson here, years ago, was rescued by H.M.S. *Rattlesnake* from the natives (who had previously killed her husband, the master of a trading vessel, and his mates, and had compelled her to live with them). She had been with them for so long that she had forgotten her own language and could say nothing but "White Mary". In a few weeks, however, after her rescue her mother tongue came back to her, and some years afterwards she could barely remember a word of the language of the native tribe with whom she had lived.

This house, like other Queensland houses, is built on piles with a wide verandah all round, and the long and lofty rooms opening one into the other. Hanging against the wall in this room are a few little relics from the *Quetta*, waiting some day to be claimed. The flag, which is in the Memorial Church at Thursday Island, was picked up on Murray Island, a hundred miles away, where it had been carried by the strong currents.

There is plenty of good shooting here, wild-fowl and numbers of quail, and the most beautiful varieties of doves and pigeons. The birds have nearly all bright plumage. Rifle-birds are here in numbers; their feathers are like black velvet, and the head and neck look a dazzling, metallic green in one light, but blue and purple in another. There are mullet, whiting, schnapper, jinfish, herring, bream, and others, besides turtles, oysters, and crabs weighing sometimes six and seven pounds each, which the black gins catch among the mangrove trees.

In front of the house there is a Dugong stage erected. Now I am sure that you don't know what creature this is. It looks part pig, part seal, and part whale, and grows about seven or eight feet long; its hide is an inch or more thick; it is a graminivorous creature, and the natives hunt it with harpoons in shallow water where it comes to browse on the grass banks, and with its long protruding lips plucks off the long thin blades of grass which could not be kept in the mouth were it not that the roof is covered with short, bristly hairs. The male has two long front tusks, the female none, and the grinders are the same as those of an ox; it rises now and then like the porpoise to the surface to blow. The meat is very nourishing and tender, varying in taste according to the different portions; some parts are like veal, others like pork or fish, and the oil tastes like pure melted butter, and is most fattening: for this purpose they are boiled down and the oil exported.

An American writer has said, "It is a dish of which Apicius might have been proud, and which the discriminating palate of Heliogabalus would have thought entitled to the most distinguished reward"; it belongs, like the whale, to the family of mammals, and is most human in its grief when its young are caught, sometimes fearlessly following the boats for miles with the most appealing look in its eyes. The young calf in the same way will follow its mother, crying out in the most heartrending way.

There are alligators here too, but they are seldom seen. Mrs. Jardine talks calmly of killing a snake 16 feet long. They grow to a very large size; one that was killed had swallowed a wallaby weighing 57 lbs. and a wild pig 32 lbs. This is well vouched for and is no mere traveller's tale. The snakes are sometimes most troublesome, killing fowls, dogs, or indeed anything they come across. One, 14 feet long, wound itself round Mr. Jardine one night. They had to cut it off him in three places before they could unwind it. He killed a brown snake here the other day measuring 12 feet in length, the largest I have ever heard of.

The natives have remedies for the bites of different kinds. They are more afraid of the brown snakes than any other, and, when bitten, pound up the leaves of a plant, a specimen of which I have painted, putting some on the wound and drinking a concoction of them. When bitten by the death adders, which are numerous here, they rub a portion of the creature's inside on the wound, and this they say always cures it, though they are sick and weak for some days after. They think less of this bite, however, than of most others. Almost every flowering shrub is the home of colonies of green ants, and woe betide you if you shake down a shower of them upon yourself, as I did more than once. Leaves and flowers are spun together by spiders that the ants keep for this purpose, and inside these homes they lay their eggs. They are decidedly vicious and can give a very sharp nip.

The worst pest in insect life that Queensland possesses is the "white ant" or termite. Nothing comes amiss to them—books, pictures, clothes; anything but solid rock they will riddle to powder; everything is grist to their mill. This is why houses are build on piles coated with tar, because of their antipathy to this. They will build up towers and domes with an alarming rapidity. Penetrating down one of their mounds of earth, you will find spacious nurseries, galleries, and chambers of most elaborate construction, under the multitude of cupolas and pinnacles. The queen is a hideous, shapeless-looking, swollen termite, with disproportionate bulk. The perfect insect in due time becomes possessed of badly-fastened wings, which on the slightest provocation fall off, while others of poorer rank never acquire a fuller development than that of larvae. There are scorpions too; I found one in my bed at the Barron Falls, and wondered what the hard thing was that I was lying on, but it never bit me.

Another thing to be warned against is the nettle tree. A "gentleman", thinking he would play an *amusing* trick on me, gave me some of its branches in the dark with some other flowers, and I took it in my arms not knowing what it was; it brushed against my face, and next morning my whole head was swollen, and I could not see out of one of my eyes for some days. The pain was intense, and with this added to the great heat at the time, I suffered far more than I cared to acknowledge. Horses

The Flower Hunter

Clerodedron inerme R. Brown, Abutilon, Acanthus ilicifolius Linne, *watercolour, 54.6 x 38 cm*
Reproduced by permission of the National Library of Australia

have been known to die from the stings of this tree, and they are also sent mad sometimes with the pain; but, as a rule, they know its look and give it a wide berth. One of the most useful of all the Queensland plants which, though originally not indigenous to Australia, has become quite acclimatised now, is the pawpaw apple, which grows in the form of a palm tree.

Just now this little bay looks quite gay with the Government steamer the *Albatross*, the *Paluma* gunboat, and several pearling boats lying at anchor. Talking of these latter reminds me that I never told you of 8000 or more ounces of old Spanish coins that were found by one of Mr. Jardine's boats on a distant reef, together with an anchor and three guns. Mr. Jardine has given me several of the silver dollars, all cemented together with coral, which are a great curiosity, and which I intend to have made into a paperweight. They show different dates from 1725 to 1820. The natives say that the ship from which these relics came ran ashore on the reef; that they killed and ate the crew, and that the ship split in two and sank in deep water.

Now good-bye and good-night. Good-bye too to the happy hours here, and to the good kindly friends I leave behind; though not to all, for Mrs. Jardine leaves with me to-morrow for our trip to the neighbouring islands.

The Skeleton in the Tree

Marbiag

You probably won't know where Marbiag is, so I had better tell you that its English name is Jervis Island—the most northern of this Torres Strait group, and only thirty miles from New Guinea. I wish I thought that this fact would make your heart relent, but, alas! you extracted my promise not to go there, and I can only content myself by looking at the long array of dug-out canoes which come from New Guinea, where they make and ornament them better than these islanders, who trade there for them.

We left Thursday Island early yesterday morning with a strong head wind and the tide against us, and what a tide runs here! After struggling long in vain to make enough headway before it got dark, we decided to anchor for the night close to Banks Island, just off one of the native villages. We had quite made up our minds to sleep on shore there, but it was altogether too uninviting, and we broke through our first resolution after seeing the natives, who all seemed to have colds or sore eyes; the unwholesome-looking children being covered with horrid-looking sores. The women were perfect nightmares of hideousness, and each old hag seemed to be nursing a baby; they nearly all too looked like great-grandmothers. We wandered about until it was dark, and then came back to the steamer, which we reached in rather a moist condition, as the plug had come out of the boat, and before we discovered it she had filled considerably with water. It was an uninteresting island, with nothing much to see; there were a few native gardens with some potatoes, but beyond this no cultivation of any kind, and no native plants in blossom.

Before daylight next morning we were away. We passed several small islands on the way, little more than coral reefs formed by those assiduous working insect creatures. At low tide they are almost covered with water, and many an unwary vessel has come to grief on their sharp-edged, fringed reef walls. The sun was just rising as we steamed into Marbiag harbour, and as soon as our steamer came in sight, the shore like magic was suddenly peopled, and the splashing of paddles was soon all round us. We breakfasted, however, on board, and it was some little time before we had all our belongings packed into the boat, for Mrs. Jardine had brought bedding, blankets, towels, and every requisite to make us independent of the natives.

The shore was lined with native huts; these are formed of rafters and posts of bamboo, fastened together with split cane; the walls and roof are thatched with grass and lined with plaited cocoa-nut, and the floor covered with a coarse sort of matting; a hole in the wall does duty as a window, and the only other opening is the door.

Our house is most grand—a brand new one, with the luxury of a table and some chairs. The natives always squat on the floor. They were very different from those on Banks Island, and are not "Binghis" (natives of this part of Australia), but a colony of South Sea Islanders. The men are strong and well made, and the women are buxom. They seem very pleased to see us, and anxious to do what they can for us. They have the greatest respect and admiration for Mrs. Jardine, for at one time she and her husband lived not very far from this island, and they speak of him as the "Mamoose" (first chief). The men had had a great time of dugong-fishing the day before, and we had slices of this for our dinner, and exceedingly good it was too. We also had fish, yams, and cocoa-nut milk from the young green nuts, which last has a tart and sparkling taste, and is cool and refreshing. There were other delicacies that I looked upon with caution, and over which I exercised my own discretion.

You would have laughed to watch my efforts in writing to you this afternoon, as the inquisitive black girls leaned over my shoulders wondering what it all meant. Sometimes a piccaninny joined, and I couldn't keep him from sticking his fingers into the ink. When they become too troublesome I have to call for Mrs. Jardine's aid. In the evening we went for a tour of inspection round the village, which contains about 400 to 500 people. Here and there through the camp there were graves, each of which is ornamented with shells, bottles, clothes, pots, and everything belonging to the dead person who is buried there. The last one we saw had a most grotesque appearance with a slate, a comb, an old purse, and one boot, besides the usual shells and decorations, and over all an old mosquito net.

There is a large fire under the cocoa-nut palms at night, and men, women, and children all sit there and sing. Their voices are powerful, but most unmusical, and, as the noise is deafening, I prefer to look on from a distance, and from here as I write to you to-night I can watch the lights flickering on the ruddy-coloured faces, the bare arms and legs of the women, and the little, naked, shining bodies of the children, who look so round and tempting that I long to give them a smack, especially when they come round me in dozens each time I take out my sketch-book. I had twice to-day to give it up in despair.

Multitudinous life swarms in these sunlit islands, and I was introduced to my first tarantula here this afternoon, a great hairy-limbed fellow. To-night the mosquitoes are buzzing in myriads under these tawny roofs. It has rather a disturbing effect, but I suppose we shall get more accustomed to them by and by, and as we have nets with us, may hope to sleep soundly to-night after being tossed about last night in our little steamer. It has neither affected our spirits nor our appetites, and even now, late as it is, I am finishing my second cocoa-nut, which fact alone will go far to convince you of what Queensland has done for my powers of digestion.

Many of the natives here have almost golden hair, having bleached it to that colour with lime and the ashes of the Wongi tree, which bears one of the principal fruits of these islands, and this Northern Australian coast. It is a very handsome tree, about forty or fifty feet high, with shiny, oblong-shaped leaves, almost pure white at the back. The fruit is the size of a plum, and varies in colour from green to yellow, crimson, or black, according to its ripeness. It is something like a fresh date. I used to eat pounds of it. Some of the other indigenous fruits, which the natives seem to relish, are exceedingly nasty. All the Eugenias are fruit-bearing, and the fruit varies in size from that of a large apple to others the size of cherries. The leaves of one of the large varieties is an antidote to the bite of the brown snake.

The tide had just turned as we woke next morning, the sunny waves were tossing and tumbling their foam along the beach, and the sun rose on the dome of a vividly blue sky. Everything was dripping still with moisture from the heavy night dew, and we looked out on to a medley of brilliant colouring: such spring foliage of greens, strange plants everywhere; such a wealth of cocoa-nut palms with their nuts in every stage of ripeness, from green to yellow and brown. Papaw trees with great yellow melon-shaped fruits under the tuft of leaves above their tall stems, giant bamboos, and quantities of banana palms grow about, while the ground in places is blue with convolvulus and a kind of clitoria that creeps everywhere. The natives, waist-deep in the water, were making an early start with their canoes, and the sand was strewn with their fishing tackle, spears, and baskets; the mats of their sails for a moment flapped loudly in the wind as they hoisted them, spreading to the breeze. Away the whole flotilla sailed. A bath had been provided for me, and it was no easy matter taking this, for the natives, wishing, I suppose, to see if I was white all over, would keep peering through the small opening in the wall that did duty as a window. The natives all bath in the sea, and the children spent half their day splashing and playing about in the water.

Our creature comforts had now to be attended to. I watched our breakfast being prepared. It consisted of yams which they put into a banana leaf with the milk and fruit of the cocoa-nut scraped into it; it was then cooked by steam and served up in the same leaf, never once being touched by hands. I told Mrs. Jardine to impress upon them that any contact of a hand with my food was against my religion. The fried slice of dugong was almost exactly like veal, as was also the turtle, but the green tail (I think it is the fat) I could not make up my mind to try. The ovens of the natives here are similar to those used by the Maoris in New Zealand; heated stones with water poured on them and fish and yams wrapped in banana leaves or grass put all together on top.

They are all very curious about the painting; the children with wondering looks in their big brown eyes come constantly crowding round me, watching every move with great curiosity. I am a new sort of animal to them, I suppose, for they peep round the doorways at me and then rush off with shouts of laughter, to be again joined by a second lot; then, bolder still, they creep noiselessly in, looking over my shoulder, and at last, hemmed in on all sides, I have to call again for Mrs. Jardine. The chief sent them this morning to get me flowers, and they came back laden, about twenty of them, with bundles all of the same kind, one flower stuck inside another, and with the leaves all carefully stripped off.

Do you remember, long ago in New Zealand, promising a Maori sixpence each for specimens of a certain kind of walking-stick, and how twenty or thirty curious-looking red objects appeared some days after coming along the beach? As they came nearer we saw they were Maoris, each labouring along under the weight of a bundle of carefully-steamed and well-skinned sticks, and how angry they were at you because you wouldn't buy the lot, and how they chopped them all into bits so that the soldiers should not have them for nothing; though they afterwards laughed and appreciated the joke of being found out.

The natives here seem a very happy race, caring nothing for the past or the future; living only for the hour. The feeling is infectious; with no anxieties, no cares, nothing but a life of idleness, one almost forgets for the moment, while basking in that sunshine, that there is such a place as an outside world. They laugh and cry too in the same breath, and are the very embodiment of content.

At two o'clock the fishing boats came back laden with booty, one dugong—a great fat unwieldy-looking creature, which they rolled in on to the shore—three large turtles, a kingfish, and several crayfish, which are very brightly coloured and different from those in the south. In the open sea the natives harpoon the turtles, assailing the shoal with arrows and spears; but on shore, when they come to lay their eggs in the sand, they turn them on their backs, and with axes make their shells fly in splinters. The women collect the firm yellow fat from the intestines, then boil it down and skim it until it becomes colourless and light. The turtles lay from forty to seventy eggs in trenches in the sand, which they scrape out and fill up again by means of their hind legs. The natives are horribly cruel in the way that they kill them; they open them on the left side and scoop out the blood, and cut them up piecemeal while they are alive, exposing in full action all the internal organs; the poor things writhe in agony, snapping their mouths and opening and shutting their eyes for hours as they lie in the sun.

The "wit" of the village is a very old and hideous woman with one solitary front tooth and a mass of tangled gray hair.

The Skeleton in the Tree

She came and sang and danced by turns in front of us this evening, amid shouts of laughter from the others; the more noise they made the louder she yelled, and she looked like a veritable witch. As she still danced on, great beads of perspiration rolled down her face, and finally she sank down exhausted. We gave her some tobacco and she went away apparently satisfied. She and a man in camp are both said to be mad, and the latter is supposed to have been bewitched (they call it *purupuru*). He is horrible to look at and has no nose or upper lip. This evening there are a great many more canoes here, and a fresh crowd of men came into the camp laden with cocoa-nuts, yams, sweet potatoes, pumpkins, and one poor solitary fowl. These gifts they laid down at our door while we distributed tobacco in return.

There is a fig tree here with the skeleton of a man encased inside, the tree having grown completely round it. The story is that he was fastened to it alive, and the branches in time twisted and grew round the skeleton until now nothing more of it can be seen. It was a handsome tree and close to the shore, and I thought would make a pretty sketch, so went down to take it. I suddenly heard a splashing of oars and saw a canoe with eight natives in it, with merely the local airy costume of fringes on them; they had come from some of the islands off the New Guinea coast, and they looked as if they would not have been above giving me a quiet knock on the head if an occasion offered. I did not finish the sketch that day, and I did not even give them the chance of seeing me, as I quickly slid away under bushes and through the long grass, utterly regardless of snakes or any other kind of reptile in my quick endeavours to get away from them. I daresay they were perfectly harmless, but I cannot get over my fear of them.

Some of the young girls are very graceful, with beautifully-turned limbs, and all of them are plump, I fancy from living so much on dugong, the oil, of course, being very fattening. There are five white men's graves here under some large salmon-coloured flowering flame-trees, with the same old story, "Murdered by the natives." They show you these and point to the inscriptions on them with great pride.

Now, however, they are peaceful, and on Sunday they refused to climb the cocoa-nut trees because it *was* Sunday. I regret that they do not add to their Sabatarian reverence a due respect for matrimony; they will sell their wives to any trader for a trifle. On one of the reefs here there are two old Spanish cannons encrusted with coral; the natives say they ate the crew in the good old times.

Mr. Jardine, who came with the children unexpectedly last night, when shaking hands with some of the men said—"Hollo! you not dead yet! I thought you were hanged long ago!"—they smiled and looked as pleased as if he had paid them the greatest compliment. Some of the men have villainous-looking faces, and I would not care to trust myself too long in their company. A child died in camp last night, and it was buried this morning; they had cut its forehead and body to draw blood when the pain came on, and this seems to be their only remedy.

Thursday Island

We reached here, Thursday Island, to-day in a terrible storm of wind; the steamer tossed and rolled every way and the waves dashed sometimes clean over her. I was deadly sea-sick, and lay like a log in my little berth until we anchored. There was a most amusing procession as we left the island at daylight—every man, woman and child in the village following in the rear, as we walked to the boats, where there were great handshakings. The chief came off to the steamer to see the last of us and of our tobacco, while we were laden with mats, cocoa-nuts, and the usual offerings.

Torres Strait Islands

Somerset

After ten days at the Residency on Thursday Island, I went back in H.M. gunboat *Paluma*. They had lost one of their men in the bush, and had come up to the island for black trackers, who found him very quickly, not much worse for his outing.

I spent a lazy, happy three weeks at Somerset. It has been a very dry season, and most things that were in full blossom and fruit when I was there before, were only *now* in bud. I was to have left there for Port Darwin, but I missed the steamer, and had the pleasant satisfaction of seeing it go by with no means of catching it. Later on, I was amply rewarded, for H.M.S. *Albatross* was going to other islands, and, as I had had permission from headquarters to go where I wished in her, it was too good a chance to be lost.

We left Somerset at nine in the morning of the 25th, and after a day of such tossing about as only the *Albatross* is capable of performing, we anchored for the first night off Dove Island, and had a comparatively smooth time. Next morning we were off at five, a long sea chasing us, and after (to me) a weary day of more rough seas and depressing sea-sickness, we anchored at six in the evening off Murray Island. The friendly planets were merging into one, and the golden light of the setting sun behind the jagged outlines of the cocoa-nut palms was very beautiful, native huts lined the shore, which was strewn with dug-out canoes, while larger and more imposing-looking ones were at anchor in the little bay. The whole village had congregated on the beach and seemed in a state of great excitement, for white visitors here are of very rare occurrence.

We anchored a short distance off, and, not knowing if we could get quarters near, dined on board. Before we had finished our meal the steamer was surrounded with canoes, and Mr. Bruce, one of three brothers, the only white people on the island, came off in his boat to ask us to stay on shore. This was joy to me, and my pent-up spirits at once rebounded with energy at the thought of leaving that tiny, stuffy cabin which Mrs. Jardine and I had shared together. It was unbearably hot, and the *Albatross* rolled whatever the weather was. We were warmly greeted by the natives on landing, who insisted on shaking hands—men, women, and children. There was no getting out of it, and I was very glad that I had my gloves on.

Mr. Bruce's house was on the edge of the shore, and we sat on the sands until the moon had risen two hours above the horizon, enjoying what cool air there was. Then Mr. Bruce and his people lighted Mrs. Jardine and me up the hill to an empty house, which belonged at one time to the last Missionary. We had brought all requisites with us, bedding, towels, etc., and our beds had been made up on the floor for us. Here we were left in sole possession with the inevitable dog "Snap", which goes everywhere with his mistress.

It was too tempting a night to go to bed, and we sat in airy costumes listening to the roar of invisible breakers as they broke on the long line of coral reef, and I drank cocoa-nut milk, and, unmindful of nightmare, ate the nut itself afterwards. While the nuts are young and green they are soft and can be eaten with a spoon. How soundly we both slept! Even Snap had nothing to grumble at, and did not, as he usually does, whine softly to himself.

We were awakened at six next morning, when a buxom maiden came up the hill with gourds of water for our baths. I had mine in a very primitive dish. The sun had just risen, but the landscape was still drowned in vapours, while the heavens above were roofed with a sapphire blue; as the mists rolled away the view each moment grew more beautiful, and how often I wished that some fairy godmother, by reason of her wand, could have wafted you to me. Each leaf sparkled with dewdrops, the sea without a ripple lightly spreading over shallow sands was of that peculiar shade of green that is only seen in tropical waters.

The coast-line was fringed with cocoa-nut trees. In front of us was a species of india-rubber, a large tree with dense green foliage and a long plum-coloured fruit which the natives cut into strips and dry, and from which they make a splendid crimson dye. Beside it was a flame tree, one blaze of scarlet blossoms. Beyond that again stands a tree with the whole trunk and branches clothed with masses of white flowers. Out of the hot, moist ground I could almost fancy I saw the plants grow, all nature seemed to revel in the exquisite beauty that she unfolded in never-ending blooms of brightest hues and vivid contrasts. Dusky figures of women were busily going to and fro, under the bright green foliage, carrying water in yellow and brown gourds on their heads. With backs as straight as arrows, the men, waist-deep in water, were hauling their fishing-nets. There are days in our lives that we never forget, and I think that this was one of them. Perhaps it was that I felt so well, and so much alive, and that the world was a beautiful one. Every bird was singing, the air was full of scent and sound, a distant hum of bees was overhead, and butterflies danced in the sunlight.

I couldn't keep still, and, after breakfast, which consisted of fish, yam, curry, and fruits, I went with some of the native girls to the top of a hill to sketch. You would have been amused to see me trying to make myself understood by signs, and by drawing pictures on the sand. The mosquitoes bit my wrists and hands, and my companions were delighted when I pulled up my sleeve, and were much amused either at the thinness of my arms or the colour, for they laughed heartily and tried to make me understand that they were no good for food. One girl, less shy than the others, took my arm up and pretended to bite it, then, making a wry face and shaking her head, she put it down and laid her own sleek, brown one beside it, patting it impressively to let me see what a superior article it was.

I didn't get through much sketching; the wind had risen and my flapping hat and garments blew every way, and moreover I felt too much "out for a jaunt", so we all laughed on, and if there was a joke I must have appeared in their eyes to have enjoyed it as much as they did. Our mirth became infectious, for other natives now joined us, and a long procession wound its way up the hill to where we were sitting, but I was unaccustomed to being the centre of attention and it began to pall on me, and I took up my sketch-book and went.

Below me as I came down the hill I saw Mr. Tom Roberts, the well-known artist, who was with us, painting the head of a very Jewish-looking boy, surrounded the whole time by an admiring crowd. He made a splendid study of his model, who had an ornament of feathers stuck in his woolly head and a big scarlet hibiscus in his ear-ring. It is the men here who decorate themselves with flowers and make themselves beautiful, while the women carry the loads and do most of the hard work. Just as the forty-guinea finishing touches were being put on the picture, the whole thing fell, butter side downwards, into the sand. It looked hopeless, but next day the oils had dried, and we carefully wiped off the sand, after which it was retouched, and looked as well as ever.

The natives here are a fine-looking race, stout and well made, their sleek shiny bodies look well nourished, and, indeed, so they are, for on their fertile island they have not even the trouble of growing most of their food, which is in abundance everywhere, and consists of fish, yams of several kinds, dugong, turtle, pigs, fowls, bananas, melons, papaws, cocoa-nuts, and several other kinds of native fruits. We watched a young boy catching a gray sea-gull with a small fish-hook made of shell and stuck into a fish as a bait, which the bird greedily swallowed.

The sea along the shore every here and there was thick with sardines. Two men with long bamboos drove them together to a point, and at the right moment a third dived quickly down with a conical-shaped basket and filled it before they had time to get under the sticks. Several large sharks came swimming into the breakers after them, the fish jumping in hundreds out of the water as they came near, and we watched the chase going on until the black line was lost in the distance. The women were bathing close by quite heedless of one shark whose fins above water showed his great size. He seemed to be sniffing round them. They only splashed the water at him, and he thought better of it and went off. Once only was a shark known to attack a man and to bite him badly when he was diving for fish.

These islands teem with life, it is everywhere; every pore bursts with it, above and below—flying, burrowing, creeping, crawling, swimming—and yet how little we seem to know of the great mystic drama of it all. Out in the rocks, in the deep clear pools, over slippery seaweeds and countless barnacles, were wonderful sea-urchins and anemones of every shape and colour, like beautiful living flowers, and there are treasure-houses of shells, corallines, and sponges.

Crabs and lobsters, shrimps, and vividly-coloured fish darted in and out of the crevices of the rocks, a yellow water-snake slid away from close under my feet and hid himself under some green ribbon-like seaweed, and I jumped so quickly getting out of his way that I came backwards with a great splash into a deep pool behind me, to the intense amusement of my dusky friends, who never tumble, and are highly amused when you get pricked with the spines of sea-urchins, or stung by stinging creatures that you remember for many hours after. A bright blue crab scuttling away into a cave all lined with coral, the home of these countless boring creatures, attracted me, so did an old anchor half imbedded in the rock, scarred and rugged all over.

The natives ate shell-fish that they picked up, but I received them with caution, such digestive powers as they possess being denied to a white woman. Glossy-backed cormorants leisurely eyed us from the pinnacles above, and hundreds of sea-gulls flew over us uttering their shrill sad cries as they swooped, wheeled, and poised on their quivering wings.

The air was heavy with the echoes of a hundred songs. Every tree has its various inhabitant, every plant and flower its insect. One generation goes, another comes, nature is never still, and each season brings its own fresh world with it. We scrambled back to camp over the cliffs, toppling over stones and sliding over slippery grass. On the way we picked some papaw apples, and under the shade of a large eugenia tree we sat down cross-legged and made a feast off them and bananas.

The sun was just setting as we came back, and through the hazy vista of palm trees we could see the dusky figures of the natives moving to and fro in the flickering light of the fires, which burnished up the tall stems of the bamboos like shafts of molten metal, and in golden threads crept through and outlined the drooping fronds of palms and the thatched roofs. And now the boats are made fast in the landing places, and over the merry blaze of the fires the natives take their evening meal. Darkness closes over, fold upon fold, the gloomy world from above, shut out from behind the clouds, and over the night comes the drone-line sound of natives singing. One by one they steal away until only Mrs. Jardine and I are left; and now to rest, to the sounds of murmuring waves and sighing of winds in the palms above.

Not many years ago, this island boasted of being the principal among those inhabited by cannibals, and the old men and women still bear in their bodies the traces of their dreadful customs, being quite piebald; a horrible condition caused by eating the putrid flesh of their victims, the poison from which produces this discoloration. They are changed in their habits now, and, the day after we arrived being Sunday, they held their services in their church, one at six in the morning, another at eleven, and another in the afternoon, ending up with Sunday school for the children, who varied the entertainment by singing, "And this is the way we wash our hands", etc., and other kindergarten songs. They are a very happy race, but Mr. Bruce says by no means an amiable one, and they cannot be depended upon.

We came in for the tail end of their great annual feast, when they invite the natives from the other end of the island to their fair, which lasts six or seven weeks. During the best season for yams and fruit they fashion the form of a ship, or house, with bamboos (on this occasion it was a representation of the *Albatross*, our own steam launch), and then cover the framework with every kind of fruit and yams. In the centre of their ship were the engines, which consisted of the fire where they did their cooking. Next year the feast will be returned by their neighbours, and so on.

There were four marriages the first afternoon we were there,

Mr. Savage, the Chief Inspector of Police, who was with us, officiating as clergyman. One man cried hard the whole time because (his bride told us) he loved her too much. At seven in the evening they commenced their native dance, which they kept up until 3 A.M.; it was the best I had seen and quite different from the mainland corroboree, only the men danced on this occasion; they wore head-dresses like cocked hats, made out of white feathers, reed mats and coloured cloths round their waists, with anklets and armlets of flowers, and big bunches of croton leaves on their belts behind; most of them carried short clubs and carved spears in their hands. The women and those who did not take part in the dance sang and beat drums, while the others danced different figures representing fish-spearing, shooting with bows and arrows, and other sports.

The next night the women danced, and the men went through all the manoeuvres of sailing, with miniature boats set in full rig in their hands, singing the whole time. Then the South Sea Islanders danced, gesticulating very much the whole time, and singing part songs, the same words over and over again. It was quaint and musical, and we asked them the meaning of it; they did not know: "Long time ago same as belonga great-grandfather," was all they said.

Here it is a woman's privilege to propose to the man, and it is generally after these dances that she does it by first making a present to him or to his father and mother; if it is accepted the thing is settled. The men really are splendid-looking fellows in their native clothes; and so muscular and strongly made, that they danced as if on wires, so light and active were they.

One day before leaving, we rowed to the end of the island in one of their dug-out canoes. Landing, we made our way through a bit of wild tropical jungle, so dense above our heads with a tangled, matted mass of creeping plants that hardly a ray of sunlight peered through. Here we soon found ourselves on the edge of a strong spring, and, before we knew where we were, we were ankle-deep in mud. High up in the fork of a tree above us we saw the thick coil of a carpet snake lying asleep. He never stirred, notwithstanding the incessant chattering of the natives under him. From here on I walked with extreme caution, in anticipation of other smaller and more venomous snakes below.

Then we came into a steep, rugged gully with fern trees high above one's head, and here and there, on a more level slope of ground, small, cultivated patches of kumeras and taros (native potatoes). As we came into open ground again, there were two magnificent coral-trees (erythrina) in full blossom, with masses of salmon-coloured flowers of a shade that I had not seen before. I have added considerably here to my collection of flowers and sketches, but I find it no easy task keeping pace with the former as they are brought to me, and the heat at times makes it very hard to work, for you live in a perpetual state of Turkish bath.

There are Straits pigeons here in thousands. They wheel overhead sometimes in a black cloud, and along the shore there is a constant cawing and chattering of countless sea-birds, which are hatching their eggs. On one small promontory we had to pick our way through the nests, and the noise as the birds rose overhead was quite deafening. We had had a good scramble. The others went home while Mr. Bruce and I walked to the highest point of the island, 800 or 900 feet high, where we got a splendid view of the whole of its outline, and, away in the distance, saw the breakers here and there on the great Barrier Reef; and was not I tired and hot when I got to the top! It was getting dark, and I came down with a series of jumps, a black man holding tight on to my arm all the time in case I fell; the more I tried to shake him off, the more determinedly Mr. Bruce, in his native language, told him to hold on.

After tea, I went off again along the beach by moonlight, alone with a little black girl (this sounds rather Irish). We were afterwards joined by two not over pleasant-looking men. Visions of five graves I had seen, where, over the bones of white men, one may read the ominous words, "Killed and eaten by the natives of the island," rose up before me, and I suddenly had a longing to return. Poor things! I daresay my two friends were entertaining me to the best of their ability; they gesticulated wildly and grew very excited over something; but a walk under these conditions becomes monotonous when one can understand nothing, and it is trying to have to wear a perpetual smile.

When I got back I found a black girl dry-rubbing her teeth with my tooth-brush! It had evidently done duty as a hair-brush as well, judging from the look of it, but these are trifles, though the tooth-brush did happen to be the only one I had with me. The natives were dancing in front of the fires, the light playing

Torres Strait Islands

Unidentified flowers, Jervis Island, Torres Strait, watercolour, 85 x 38 cm
Reproduced by permission of the National Library of Australia

fantastically on the savage faces of the men, and it was long past three in the morning before I went to bed—most dissipated hours to keep in these out-of-the-way lands, but time is of no account to these people, and, even when I did go, I left an old native still tracing a pattern with a sharp-pointed piece of hot stick to work on a bamboo pipe—bau-baus they call them. These they pass from one to another in smoking as common property.

Our time at Murray Island too soon came to an end, and with the tide in our favour, we reached Darnley Island in four hours. "Jack the Mamoose", of royal descent, came off in his boat for us, and we went on shore in grand style, rowed by the black police, who get their uniform and a pound a year from Government, and look upon themselves as great swells; they keep order on the islands and are useful in many ways.

The only white man living here is one called "Dirty Johnstone", and well he deserves his name. It was to his house that we first went. A few days before, he had written to Mr. Bruce, saying that a mysterious stranger in the form of a male being had suddenly appeared in the island, and Chief-Inspector Savage had come to inquire into this, thinking it was an ill-treated black boy from a *bêche-de-mer* boat, or a man the police were looking for, who had stolen a cutter. The men on the native boat knew nothing, their faces were perfectly blank when questioned; then we went on to Johnstone's hut, who, when he saw us coming, ran to wash his face, probably the first time for a month. He could not understand Mr. Savage's inquiry, but, on going inside, the mystery was explained; on the bed sat his black gin, with a three or four day old baby in her arms; the joke will probably dawn upon Johnstone some time during the next week.

It was a very hot walk back through the heavy sand, and we were not sorry to reach the Court-house, where they gave us cocoa-nut milk and papaws. It was rather trying having to shake hands all round, especially as a good many of the natives were suffering from some kind of skin disease, and had horrid sores which we doctored with poultices of papaw leaves. "Jack" sat and talked to us for the rest of the morning, telling us in a sad "O tempora, O mores" tone stories of long ago, of shipwrecked sailors and cannibal feasts.

We went off to the *Albatross* to lunch, when the rest of our party came ashore, and Mrs. Jardine finally made up her mind that a bed on the floor of the Court-house was preferable to that stuffy little cabin on board. Snap did not like his quarters that night, and after trying every part of his bed and then mine, he finally made himself a bed on my clothes. A black puppy also joined him and set up a piteous howl, but we dispensed with his society in double-quick time. That night the natives danced until three in the morning, so we did not get much rest.

Mrs. Jardine and I had dinner on shore off yams and cocoa-nut milk, and then squatted inside one of the huts, chatting to the men and women, one of whom could speak good English. A black baby left its mother and crawled on to my knee, and they gave me three immense yams, and Mrs. Jardine explained to me that they liked me, and hoped I would come again because I wasn't "flash". I felt the honour. I didn't like taking the yams, as I could give nothing in return; they heard me telling this to Mrs. Jardine, and said, "We want nothing in return; it is our custom to give to strangers, and we like to see you sitting here as one of us."

We were up very early in the morning, and went off to the *Albatross* for breakfast. At eleven o'clock Court was held. Five or six charges were brought and proved against "Dirty Johnstone", who seems to be a very bad man, and has already been tried once for murder.

After Court we had another marriage; the bride this time was very grandly dressed in a square-patterned bright blue print; a green silk necktie tied behind with the points forming a bib in front, a sailor hat trimmed with pink ribbons and a scarlet feather, and a big scarlet pocket-handkerchief completed her costume.

We dined in one of the South Sea Island houses, and then went off to see "Old Ben", a well-known man here, with a most benevolent face, who takes and cares for all the motherless children on these two islands. He had a very large and well-built house, and while Mr. Savage and Mr. Roberts smoked with him, I ate sugar bananas, and made a sketch of the inside surroundings, which were of a miscellaneous character.

Coming back, I was taken possession of by a band of mothers, and I afterwards went with two native girls in a little canoe to a small island, the home of thousands of sea-gulls. A sudden breath of wind let loose, seized us and whirled us along to the rich brown stricken rocks, that grazed our frail bark and threw us starboard and larboard without the least regard to any prejudices in favour of equilibrium, and we were sprayed from head to foot before we landed.

While the girls filled their bags with shell-fish and eggs, I resumed my researches away from the sun in the dark crannies of the branching caverns, all crusted with sponges and corallines, tufts of sea-moss and starfish. I scattered a rural population of crabs and sea-urchins which rapidly made their way into pools where the tide swept the snake locks of sea-weeds, and stray fish of brilliant hues chased each other in and out of hidden cells, and bright blue shrimps shot to and fro and wouldn't be caught: from unseen caves came the chime of dropping water, and over the black, jagged cliffs jet sprays rose spouting out columns of foam, then pausing to bubble and break again in and out of deep chasms, leaving behind them a white, seething sheet of foam.

With graceful ease and strength my two sea nymphs rowed me back to the shore again, to a palm-fringed hut buried in a thicket of bananas, and here I joined Mrs. Jardine. We squatted on the floor in accordance with local manners, each choosing his neighbour according to his sympathy, and made our tea off shell-fish and yams. Heaven, as a counterpoise to my felicity, had mixed with its honey a strong dose of bitters. A liquid decoction of cocoa-nut flowers (which for politeness' sake I had been over-persuaded to drink) had such a bad effect on me, that I feared for a time I was going to be detained for ever in this land which I intended to quit next day. Their usual practice here of cutting the skin and drawing blood from the affected parts was too heroic a remedy for me, and I had to forget for a day the necessity of eating.

We bargained with tobacco for curios. The natives sang and danced until two in the morning, making the night hideous with yells and shouts of revelry; and at six next morning, when we were ready for a start, there wasn't a native stirring in camp.

At eleven next day we anchored off Stephen's Island, a small fertile one about a mile both in width and length. We walked across it, followed by a trail of natives in every variety of dress and undress, through patches of jungle, groves of plantations and cocoa-nuts, and gardens of taros, to a small village of ragged huts, where we bought mats; and then followed the shore back, where we sat under the shade of two magnificent wongi trees, whose thick branches, laden with date-like plums in every stage of ripeness, formed an impenetrable shade.

In the village close by we bargained for fowls, 'man hen four shillings, woman hen two,' which showed that they knew the value of money. There were more horrible sights here than you ever see in the crowded bazaars of an Eastern city. One boy had a head which we measured, it was thirty-one inches round; we saw a woman too, whose nose and eyes had so completely gone, that the skin had grown smooth and tight over them; her mouth was always open, the lips gone, and the teeth sticking straight out from the gums. They say that many of these deformities are caused by eating certain kinds of native fruits, and human flesh in a decomposed state. Two women here were rasping cocoa-nut with shells to use in cooking their yams, and in pots close by we saw the fibre from the leaves steeping in water, before it was made into ropes and lines for their fishing-nets.

From Stephen's Island we went on to York Island, very low

lying, and about three or four miles round. We walked all round it, ploughing our way along stretches of heavy sand, then over sharp rocks where the sea came in with a loud roar from the wide, open ocean, and, rushing upon the rocks, leapt high above them. A long trail of natives followed in our rear with only the scantiest of clothing.

We certainly are far from the fetters of civilisation here; the two native villages we passed were most unsavoury, with a strong suspicion of dead shark and other such delicacies about them. Here we bought curios from the natives, who seemed a surly race. I bought a curiously-shaped spear, very heavy, with an oblong-formed end; the natives told me that it was more than a hundred years old, and was used in battles long ago by the chief of the tribe, who carried it. It is curiously marked all the way down with lettering, noting the battles it had been used in. They would not part with it for a long time, but at the last moment, as we were leaving, they brought it to me, and I bought it for five pounds. As it is about twelve feet long, it is rather an awkward treasure to carry.[1]

A strong hot moist wind was blowing, and we were glad enough to get back, and to sit under the shade of the cocoa-nut palms; a thunderstorm was coming on, and the air swarmed with insect life. Birds, who are always good barometers, were flying in from the sea for shelter. The whole air resounded with the shrill cry of gulls and gannets; a shoal of small fish, like herrings, came close in to shore, and the birds above kept dropping like stones on them, sending up fountains and sprays of water all round; as the shoal turned from the coast and went out to sea again, they left a long rippling trail of water behind them, and far into the dim distance our eyes could follow their course by the cloud of sea-gulls which hovered above them.

We bought some biscuits from "Yankee Ned", the only white man here, who keeps a primitive kind of store, and trades with these islanders.

It was almost dark before we got on board; the storm that was brewing over our heads in one tremendous crash of thunder, and the rain came down as if it was quite in earnest; in half

---

[1] It was subsequently lost, and after some months of travelling along the coast in different steamers, it finally found its way back to me.

an hour it was all over, and by the time the anchor was up and we were away, nothing was left of it but the long swell of the sea. Moisture, stickiness, and general discomfort were everywhere, and bed being the least objectionable place, I got there as quickly as I could.

At six next morning we were on our way again, pounding and driving through a heavy sea and tide to Somerset. The water went swishing backwards and forwards over the decks, and how thankful I was to leave the *Albatross* for a good night's rest on shore!

We were on board again at six next morning, and at ten anchored off Thursday Island. I sent my luggage up to the Grand Hotel, and have spent a fortnight here waiting for a steamer to Port Darwin. What with two dances, races, and a theatre going on, we have had quite a gay time; but it has been getting warm, the steamer has been detained, and I have a vague sort of uneasy feeling that I cannot go on, but must give up my trip to Port Darwin, and come back to you. You will laugh at my foolish fears, but never mind; to-morrow I turn my face southward from sunny Queensland to home and you.

Letters from New Zealand

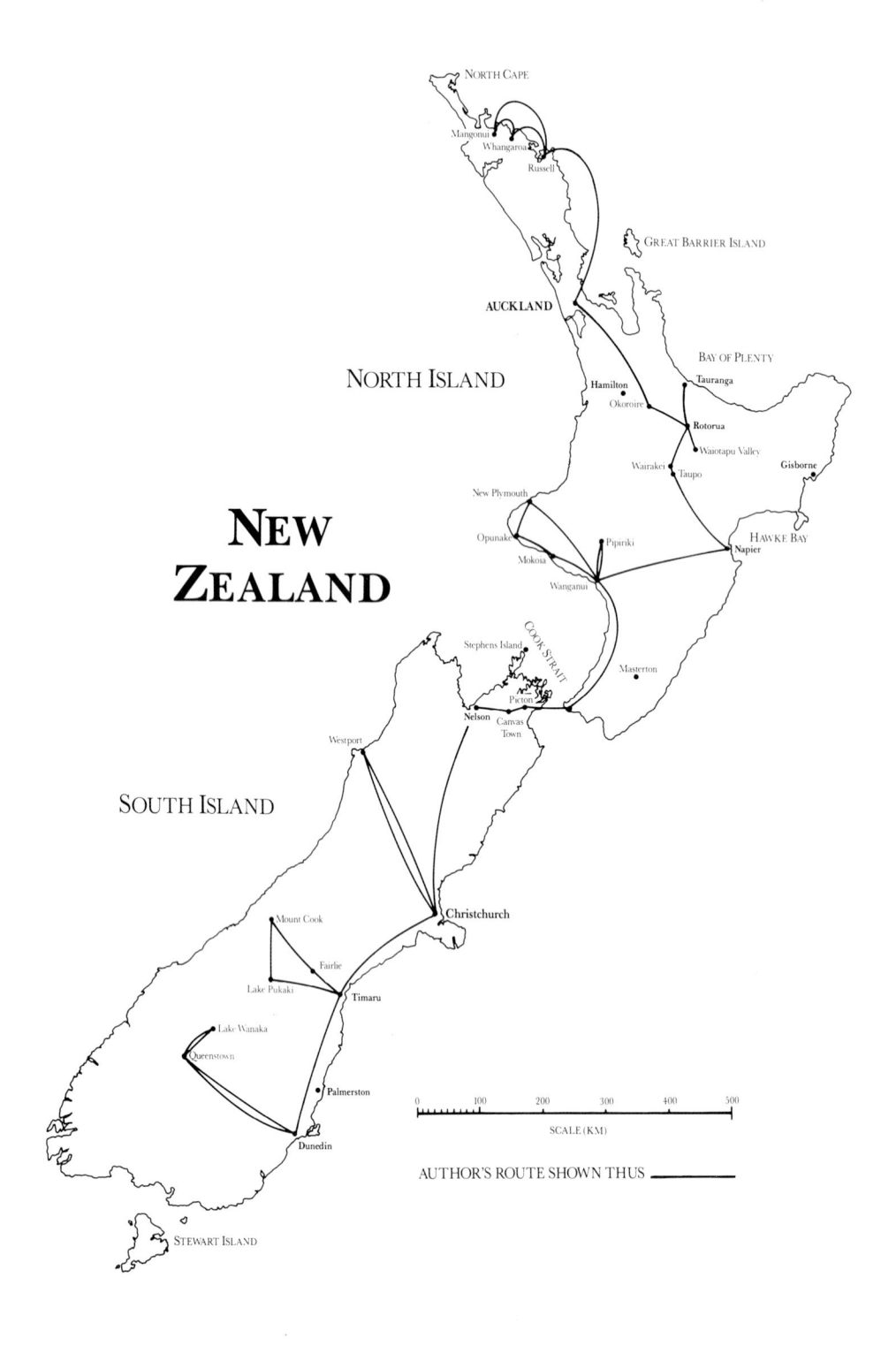

NEW ZEALAND

NORTH ISLAND

SOUTH ISLAND

SCALE (KM)

AUTHOR'S ROUTE SHOWN THUS ———

The Cradle of New Zealand

Auckland

What a day for a start! Even the substantial pier shook with the force of the heavy waves as they rolled and dashed like mad things, first under, then over; the sea-gulls cried above us, and the wind moaned and shrieked through the rigging like evil spirits trying to get loose. A few hurried shakes of the hand, a farewell wave of a handkerchief, the shrill ring-out of the ear-piercing whistle, then the vibration, thumping, and clanging of the engines as they battled with the surf, and we shouldered off the heavy folds of water, showering spray in every direction, one misty glimpse of a drenched town, and Sydney was lost in rolling, spreading clouds, whose thick curtains now and then for a moment slipped aside and gave us but a fleeting glimpse of the beauties of this world-renowned harbour. A wan, pale look settled on our faces when through the Heads we got the full force of the storm; things animate and inanimate began to take wing, and one by one the disappointed passengers went below. Thud went the rolling breakers over the stern, and whirr went the propeller, vibrating and shivering the vessel as she rose on the waves. Now she tossed and groaned, the swish of water was to be heard everywhere, and all the elements, combining to play havoc on deck, were holding high carnival.

For three days we bore the misery of the storm as best we could, but all things have an end, even sea-sickness, and most of our passengers had by that time gained their sea-legs.

Passing the North Cape of New Zealand (the first land we saw) we went through a school of whales, and close beside us watched a most exciting fight between one and a "thrasher". The latter, apparently, was victorious. The whale lay its full length on the top of the water almost motionless, and, judging from the constant flapping of its big tail backwards and forwards, it was evident that its energies were nearly spent. Through the glass we saw thousands of sea-birds on the rocks, and on the point of one a whole colony of gulls sitting on their nests. As the sun went down we passed through a narrow passage between curious-shaped rocks, one forming a huge archway, and at daylight next morning woke to find ourselves at anchor alongside the wharf in Auckland, in such a downpour of rain that we were greeted only by a sea of umbrellas and dripping cabmen.

On Sunday morning we went across in the ferry-boat to the North Shore for service on board H.M.S. *Curaçoa*, now lying in dock, and afterwards up Mount Eden, which is to Auckland what the harbour is to Sydney. The mountain has still the remains of its terraced fortifications, and the vast basin of the extinct crater at the top is about 200 feet deep. Judging from the many such you can count in all directions, this must have been a warm and exciting corner of New Zealand. For sixty miles round you can look down upon a panoramic world of beauty—city, meadow, mountain, inlet, sea, and lake stretching far away into the dim distance; but I leave it to far abler hands than mine to describe. The fresh sweetness of grass and scent of pines were everywhere, and the larks, soaring high above us, filled the air with melody. Everywhere seemed sunshine and gladness. Coming back under the shadow of the mountain, the gardens were a confused and tangled mass of loveliness; their moss-grown stone walls all covered with roses and honeysuckles, and masses of arum lilies growing in wild profusion. Our walk under the fine willows that lined the streets was a warm one; the sun blazed overhead, and they gave an insufficient shade, so presently we turned through a little gate into the cemetery. Here were coolness and shade, under the heavier oaks and limes. Ferns and grasses grew at their own sweet will among the resting-places of the dead; there was no formal arrangement of shrubs or plants, nature here had been allowed her own way. Down the steep incline, all in winding terraces, we came upon Judge Manning's tomb, one of the old pioneers of New Zealand, and well remembered by that characteristic book *Old New Zealand*; he died in England, but his last words (printed here) were that he might be buried in the far-off land he loved so well.

We were up at daylight on the morning of Tuesday, and, as

we went on deck, a breath of summer wind laden with a resinous scent of near woods greeted us, and what a sunrise! Golden gleams shot across the land-locked harbour from cliff to cliff, tipping each crested wave and bathing the hill-sides in wonderful shades of purple and gold; here and there, red-brown sails of fishermen's boats went by, while close to shore other boats were trawling their nets as we rounded a point where chattering gulls were searching for food on the ebbing tide. The sunlight danced on the roofs of the houses when we anchored beside the old barnacle-hung piles of the Russell pier. This little town of Russell is the oldest in New Zealand and perhaps the most historical. It was here, across the bay at Waitangi, that the first treaty with the Maoris was signed by Governor Hobson. After we had walked round the "everything-gone-to-sleep-looking little town", and into the first English church ever built in New Zealand, we sailed across the three-mile bay with Miss. W. (who took us in her own little boat as captain and oarsman) to the old Residency. Here we found the house tenanted by shearers, and shearing going on in what was once the old kitchen. From here on to Long Island, where we hunted for and found two of those rare shells *Muresc angasi*, said to be found nowhere else; then on to the old mission station, where, in the overgrown churchyard is a handsome monument erected by the Maoris to the memory of Archdeacon Williams. In the garden close by we boiled our kettle and made tea; here we were charged by two cows, who thought better of their first intentions, whisked their tails in the air and went off; two Maori girls, riding bareback, stopped for a few minutes and chatted to us in broken English. In the cool of the evening as we rowed back, a large shark went by, and its fins on the top of the water showed us that it was as big as our own boat; and as we approached the shore the sun went down behind the indigo-tinted mountains, touching up each promontory and rock with a burnish of gold. We walked up and down the one primitive street by moonlight without our hats, until one by one each light went out.

We sailed again at three in the morning, and at daylight we were on the bridge. And such a morning! Not a ripple on the water, and the rapidly-changing panorama of cliff and island was beautiful beyond description. We anchored at the little town of Whangaroa for an hour. On our right lay a small town where a ship was being built. Inland was the curious-shaped mountain called Taratara, where on the top the Maoris bury their dead in caves. The bay below is memorable for its gruesome association. The *Boyd*, a six-gun brig, was taken by the natives, who murdered and ate all the crew and passengers except one woman and her two children, of whom the chief took possession, but three years later they were rescued by whalers. As for the *Boyd*, it had a tragical ending itself. A number of natives went on board, and discovering some powder, put a lighted pipe amongst it, with the natural result that they and the brig were blown to pieces. As we passed a native village a boat-load of whalers came alongside us with the interesting intelligence that they had speared ten whales, having had a lively encounter with one, which they described as being "great fun". Two curious conical-shaped rocks on either side of the Pass presently arrested our attention; they call them St. Peter and St. Paul. A herd of Angora goats in the distance presented a picturesque appearance, running wild as they were. The missionaries brought them here originally. As we approached the remains of another old pah, they told us a pathetic story of Maoris being starved out by a more powerful one than themselves. They killed and ate their own children before they would submit, but eventually they were conquered, and their enemies, binding them hand and foot, put them on this small island and left them to perish. The bones of some eighty of them are still bleaching there and on the mainland. Each bay has some story attached to it.

At twelve we came to Mangonui, our journey's end. Our return journey was almost more enjoyable. We left as usual at five in the morning. As the sun rose and lifted the veil of mist off each mountain and headland the scenery was unsurpassed by anything we had yet seen, and as the day wore on under the semi-tropical sun, the rich colouring of the tinted rocks, the vivid greens of the mountain-sides, and the sapphire blue of the sea were beyond description. We took in cargo at several small towns, and at Russell, which we reached again at twelve, we lunched on shore with the bank manager and his wife, and afterwards went sailing and rowing by turns with Miss W. and Gertrude round several of the small bays; then, anchoring the boat, we climbed to the top of Mount "Tikitikiora", where we had a bird's-eye view of all the surrounding country, the broken outline of the coast, and the whole bay of islands below us in the valley. We looked down from the heights above upon a sea of fern trees, and the cattle seemed as tiny specks. The tide had risen so much higher while we were away that the boat which we had left high and dry moored to an old stump was now in water which would have been above our heads; but, nothing daunted, Miss W. climbed out along the rickety fence and brought her ashore. After our kettle had been boiled we had our tea under the shadow of the cliffs, and then Miss W. and Gertrude rowed us back, unmindful of the sun beating down on their bare heads and hands. One was irresistibly reminded of scenes in William Black's novels: for although in the Antipodes, and far from bonnie Scotland, the spirit of wildness and water was the same. Another bright moonlight night, and we sat on the captain's bridge while he told us more long-ago stories, heroic deeds of the missionaries, thrilling incidents of the early Maori wars, savage stories and struggles for mastery, cruel murders of the early French explorers, and brave and daring deeds of many of the natives. Can you wonder that they fought undauntedly for such a country? Almost every hill is the site of an old pah; every mountain, headland, rock, and island has some history of its own—some grim tale of savage barbarity, or pathetic story of love and courage.

At six next morning we were back in Auckland in the busy old-world life again, midst the sounds of wheels and the tramp of many feet, and the past was all left behind in a hazy dream amongst those beautiful seas and mountains, the cradle of New Zealand's early history.

Hot Springs and Mud Geysers

Whakarewarewa

A dusty train and a three-mile drive in the coach brought us from Auckland to Okoroire. It is all hill and meadow country, with numbers of sheep and cattle grazing everywhere, and as the sun went down behind the blue mountains, and a purple haze on the fern-covered hills, you might have fancied yourself looking over veritable Scotch moors. The sun is always very hot in the middle of the day; but a cool breeze springs up in the evening, and here the air was delightfully fresh and much more bracing than in Auckland, for the Waihou River runs at the foot of the hill, just below the hotel, and the springs for which Okoroire is celebrated are not three yards from the bank. There are three or four of them of different degrees of heat, and all strong mineral waters. We each tried them before going to bed, and also in the morning. They are only five feet deep, but the water is so buoyant that you can hardly keep on your feet, and the sensation of the bubbling water is not quite pleasant at first. We felt more confident next morning when in daylight we could see the clear crystal-looking water. The sulphur one (the Fairy's Pool) has been rightly named. It has a high bank all round it of beautiful ferns. The river just here is very swift, and is most picturesque when the water dashes in a mass of white foam over large rocks and under a natural bridge into a pool below. A few days can be very pleasantly passed here, for there is good shooting—pheasants, quail, and wild duck—and the trout-fishing is very good in this river. Next morning we drove out to the fish-ponds, and at five o'clock started for Rotorua. The line had just been opened to within eleven miles of the town. The carriages, which were most comfortable, were lined with finely-polished woods of New Zealand and cushioned with leather. They had an open platform on one side, and we stood at the railing in front the whole way looking out—first passing through high fern-covered hills, then down patches of high scrub, with immense trees and such a mass of ferns and beautiful climbing plants. At each small stopping-place there were groups of natives clothed in various articles of tattered European dress. One small child, with a shirt not covering half of his fat little body, had on a pair of old boots sizes too large, and tied to his ankles with twine. They always greeted us with the same "Ten a koe"—How are you? We had secured the box seats on the coach, and the driver chatted to us as we went along. Close to the town we passed the monument of poor Mr. Bainbridge who was killed in the eruption of Tarawera some years ago. We had a double interest in seeing this as we had travelled from England with him and knew him well. As we drew near to the lake the smell of sulphur became very strong, and in the moonlight we could see the steam rising from the several springs that we passed. Rotorua is the name of the lake; the township Ohinemutu, is really the capital of this great New Zealand wonderland. Our hotel, "The Geyser", about two miles from Ohinemutu and in the midst of the boiling springs, is at Whakarewarewa and the native village of that name is behind us. The Government sanatorium is close to the lake and about a mile to the east of the township. There there are other springs, but each has its peculiar and different mineral water, and they are world-renowned for their great medicinal qualities. Our first night at Whakarewarewa was a very disturbed one. We had been rather congratulating ourselves that in such a sulphurous atmosphere there could be no insect life, but oh! the mosquitoes! Next morning, scrambling down the cliff, we heard a rumbling noise, and came suddenly upon a recently-sunken hole of boiling mud. The earth kept falling in as we came near it, and we thought it better to retreat. Crossing the river and passing through the little Maori village, we made our way up among the boiling springs. What a sight it all was! Close beside a deep hole of unfathomable water of the purest blue is one of boiling, foul-looking black mud. Then between a wide cleft in the rock we peered down into a surging mass of white foam, tossing backwards and forwards in mad fury, with a spitting, hissing sound most uncomfortable to listen to. On the top of a small white terraced hill we looked for a moment into the depths of its crater, when there suddenly came a rumbling as of distant thunder, and, quick as quick could be, we darted back, for a jet of boiling water was thrown up about sixty feet into the air, and in a moment we were enveloped and half smothered by the hot steam. The water fell and rose again for a few minutes, and then was still. The surface of the hollow-sounding ground here seemed a mere shell, and the heat coming up through the cracks was almost unbearable, and our feet felt burning as we hopped by no means slowly over the hot stones. Now beside us we saw a huge cauldron of the purest white bubbling mud, and the rocks all round were pale sulphur colour, and in places painted with all the prismatic colours of the rainbow. It was all most weird and uncanny. The whole surface here has steam issuing from every crack and cranny and the ground underneath seems to be carrying on a regular fight with the elements, from the muffled sounds of bubbling, blowing, hissing, and snorting; and the surface looks as torn and fractured as if it soon must vanish altogether. The whole air reeks with the odour of molten and foul-smelling sulphur. Gertrude had led me on, and we had not known what risky ground we had been treading until we got back, when our danger was most probably exaggerated. As we came back through the native village the women were cooking their potatoes in rush baskets in the boiling spring. All their food, even bread, is cooked by this and steam. In the cooler baths these brown Venuses presented themselves in a variety of attitudes; it was sort of bathing thoroughfare, and the little half-aquatic broods are never happy unless disporting themselves in the tepid water.

Our next excursion was to Waiotapu Valley, a drive of forty-four miles there and back. On the road from Mt. Pareheru we had a splendid view of all the surrounding country under Mt. Tarawera, and of the black yawning crater at its side. The whole country round it is covered with a thick deposit of gray-looking sand now crisp and hard, and desolation reigns everywhere. In several places on the road there were deep rents in the ground, and in one place (Earthquake Flat) the whole valley had sunk several feet. The country is one range of fern-covered hills and mountains, desolate and dreary-looking in the extreme. Its only beauty rests in the rich colouring on the bracken, the brown and gray rocks, the river below with its grass-lined banks of waving yellow toe-toe grass and red-brown flowers of flax,

Hot Springs and Mud Geysers

Alectryon excelsum Forster, *New Zealand, watercolour, 54.5 x 38 cm*
Reproduced by permission of the National Library of Australia

and the never-ending shades of blue in the distant mountains. We had our lunch under the shadeless ti trees, and the Maori guide who met us at Waiotapu took us over a small bridge across the river to the springs beyond. The great mud geyser is only in action at eight in the evening, and we merely looked down into its black yawning chasm with steam hissing up and a sound as of giant bellows being blown. Farther on we came to the Champagne Lake, which, when earth was thrown into it, all bubbled and fizzled like a seidlitz powder. From the bank we looked down upon it with its yellow water all steaming. Another pool is of black boiling mud. Beside it is one of the most brilliant yellow-green water, and another of opal blue. They were all, with the exception of the last, boiling. Mud was seething in every direction. The White Terrace is a rippled slope of white silicious deposit. Then there is a sulphur fall, the brightest yellow; alum cliffs, acid and alkaline lakes, and pools of every colour. Last, but not least, is the Opal Lake, the largest of all, with the most beautiful transparent turquoise-blue water. The red cliffs, the dark-green clumps of manuka scrub, and the rich blues of the near and distant mountains made a wonderful picture of colour. Some ducks flew over our heads and it occurred to us what a shock it would give them if they unsuspectingly alighted on one of these burning lakes. Gertrude suggested to the guide that it would be a quick and easy way to get boiled game, but he did not smile. I asked what the natives lived on in olden times in these bare regions. He said "Old man long ago old times lived on this (pulling up a fern root, which he said they roasted) and birds." We wrote our names in his visitors' book, filled with other autographs from every part of the world; but we didn't envy him in his hut and his loneliness, and, even with all its wonders, were not sorry to turn our backs on Waiotapu, so, wishing him good-bye, we started homewards.

Maori Mythology

Ohinemutu

We made up a party next morning and drove to Rotorua and from thence took the steamer across the lake to Han-marana. From here we went in a boat up a small picturesque river to its source, where the clear icy cold water wells up from a very deep chasm in the hill-side. Pennies and other things we threw in quickly came back to us, from the great force of the water coming up. Gertrude tried hard to push her oar down, but had to confess herself beaten. In January and February the natives fasten a net across the stream and catch blind fish. After lunch we steamed over to Mokoia, an island in the lake which they say the Maoris have cultivated for 400 years. Here we saw on the edge of the shore Hinemoa's steaming bath, and heard as pretty a love-legend as many in classic lore. In fact the story of Hinemoa and Tutane Kai occupies as important a place in Maori folk-lore as does that of Hero and Leander in Grecian mythology. The story goes that Hinemoa was forbidden by her tribe to meet her lover, who lived on this island of the steaming water. To prevent her from escaping to him all the canoes the tribe possessed were collected, fastened together and hidden. But love, who laughs at locksmiths, must have tittered at the idea that any such clumsy device as this could keep true lovers asunder. Hinemoa wandered down to the shore, and listening to the soft notes of Tutane Kai's lute, the signal that he was waiting for her, determined that, canoe or no canoe, she must keep tryst. So she took a number of empty gourds, and using them as floats swam successfully from the mainland to her lover's island, resting *en route*, so legend says, first on a sunken rock and then on a floating tree (which one may suppose the kindly Maori divinities sent that way). Arrived at the island, Hinemoa hid herself in the steaming bath, and waited a fitting moment to declare herself to her astonished lover, which moment was found when a slave came to draw water, when Hinemoa, seizing the calabash from her hand, dived like a sea-maiden under the wave. The slave, terrified and confounded, rushed to tell her master of the apparition, and he came at once to the water. The rest of the tale may be left to the imagination, but the lute, which played the part of Hero's lamp in the older tale, is now in Sir George Grey's collection in the Museum in Auckland.

In ancient times the great Taniwhas, or sea monsters, lived in these lakes, says legend. Of course their favourite food was human flesh, and of course every evil that befell the natives was caused by their witchery. Once upon a time, too, there was a giantess called Kurangituku, who did much mischief, and was greatly feared. After inveigling and doing to death many brave men, she at last lured a chief called Hatupatu from Tarawera, where he was spearing pigeons. She fastened him in her house quite securely, as she imagined, and then she went out hunting. While thus enjoying herself she heard the chirp of her little pet bird in her ear, "Riro, riro," it said, which meant "Gone, gone." Kurangituku dropped her spear and rushed back at a great rate to her house. Yes, Hatupatu was gone indeed, and looking up at a steep cliff the giantess beheld him scrambling over its top. After him she went, and the native guides will point you out the marks of her finger-nails on the rocks as she clawed and climbed up their surface in hot pursuit of Hatupatu. He, meantime, had run for dear life to a hiding place he knew, whence peeping out unwarily he was seen by the enraged giantess as she panted at the top of the cliff. She must have been sadly blown, for Hatupatu managed to keep ahead and gave her a fine chase across country to Ohinemutu, where he disappeared into a spring. Now this spring was surrounded by a thin crust of earth under which was a boiling pool, called Whakarewarewa. Hatupatu being light skipped safely across, but the giantess broke through and was boiled to death, to the gratification of her neighbours in general and of Hatupatu in particular.

There were several dug-out canoes round the island with natives in them trawling for small fresh-water crayfish. We bought a kitful, and cooked some of them there and then over the steam of our boiler on board; but our palates were not sufficiently educated to appreciate these delicacies, for we thought them very fishy. In a little wooden house, now carefully protected, is a large stone idol, their god "Matuatonga". This was formerly used as a religious emblem, representing the more sacred relic which the pilgrim fathers brought with them from the legendary Hawaiki, and which is now in Sir G. Grey's collection in Auckland. He also, many years ago, when Governor of this Colony, found as an ornament in one of their whares the leg and arm bones of a man, who must have been over nine feet high. The man's name was Tohourangi; the bones are now I believe in the British Museum.

We landed on the opposite shore, where a buggy was in readiness for us, and we drove on to Tikitere, the site of more boiling springs and fresh horrors of volcanic forces and fiery furies of the earth. We were, I think, more fascinated with the weirdness of these satanic-looking fumaroles than any we had yet seen. Dante never imagined a more gruesome picture than the (so-called) Gates of Hades—a small ridge of rock between two boiling lakes of mud. These had been, they said, unusually active the last few days, and we felt almost suffocated in the hot, evil-smelling steam as we passed over. The earth throbbed and thumped all round us, steam issuing up from every seam in the rock, while small holes of bubbling mud in every direction told only too plainly what a thin crust lay between us and death of the most ghastly description. It was not a pleasant sensation that we felt. Farther north is the Inferno, a black, yawning pit, where the scattering waves and mud dash in mad fury against the rocky sides; it gives the stoutest heart a thrill of horror looking down into its inky blackness, and one almost expects to see a forked-tailed monster issuing forth. Beyond this again is the large crater basin of Ruahine, with the black lake, a mass of boiling mud and water with here and there geysers throwing up jets of their thick black slime from one to three or four feet high. It was with a feeling of thankfulness that we climbed the hill above, where from a distance we could look down upon its wonders, and from where we had a magnificent panoramic view of the whole of the surrounding lake district.

The last place to be visited before leaving Rotorua was the scene of the eruption, seven years ago, at Tarawera. We rode ten miles, as far as Wairoa, where you see the ruins of the hotel and other buildings, cruel evidences of the horrors of that dreadful night; from here we were rowed across Lake Tarawera by Maoris, and then commenced our ascent up to the great rift. We passed the site of several deep craters, and higher up the mountain nothing could describe and weirdness of the scene; not a tree, not a shrub, not a green thing of any description, nothing but a vast panorama of desolation as far as the eye could reach, a gray crust of earth scarred and seamed in every direction, and above the great, frowning, deeply-furrowed cliffs overlooking this once beautiful lake the silence was death-like in its intensity, unbroken even by the flutter of a wing. The sense of loneliness chilled you, and with an infinite feeling of relief I turned my back on it all. A few days after I went to stay with Judge and Mrs. Gill and we spent a delightful week with them at the old-fashioned town of Tauranga, with its long avenues of poplars and willows. During the last war in New Zealand it was the scene of many battles, among them that of the well-known Gate Pah disaster, when the Maoris so bravely defended it with only 300 men against 1500 of our troops. The natives had made a redoubt in a narrow neck of land between two swamps, and palisaded and defended it by lines of rifle-pits. These were thatched with fern, and the eaves of the roof so raised that they could fire on their besiegers. Early in the morning our troops opened fire on them, the natives in their burrows listening hour after hour to the sound of shot and shell, thinking certain death awaited them. Late in the day the seamen, marines, and soldiers forced an entrance, and the pah was almost taken, when a panic seized our men, and they rushed pell-mell out by the breach, crying out that there were thousands of them there. The officers did their very best to rally them, but it was useless, and the natives, taking advantage, fired on them, and twenty-seven of them were killed and sixty-six wounded. A handsome monument has been erected in the old cemetery here to the memory of those who fell. Three miles away, at Te Ranga, another engagement took place, when our troops, under Lieut.-Col. Greer, were successful.

A year after this Hauhuaism first broke out—a religion started by a native called Te Ua, who said he had been visited by angels who told him all Europeans were to be exterminated, and that those who believed in the new faith would be invulnerable. His followers, eager to test the truth of these assertions, promptly killed seven men; then, under a chief called Titokowaru, attacked a British entrenchment near New Plymouth, and were defeated with a heavy loss. But this check did not deter them from banding together to attack Wanganui. Some of the hostile tribes, however, resisted their passage through their country, and in a great fight on an island called Moutuoa, the Hauhaus were again defeated and many taken prisoners. Hauhauism was practically put an end to on the east coast the following year, when several of their pahs were captured by our troops and 1000 hostile natives taken prisoners. Among the captives was the chief called Te Kooti, who, with a number of others, was sent to the Chatham Islands; but he escaped, and, though hunted down for many years, always evaded capture. Two years ago he died an old man at Rotorua.

Many places in the neighbourhood of Tauranga are "tapu" (rendered sacred), and across the bay is the site of an old burying-ground. A landslip on the cliff had quite recently swept away the graves and some old carved monuments. A year ago Judge Gill tried a curious native case in the law court here. A woman brought an action against an old man for casting his evil eye on her husband, who died in consequence (so she said). His own grandchildren gave evidence against him for having bewitched a child, who had pined and died a few weeks after it was born. They are most superstitious about such things. Some years ago a native servant that we had, having taken more wine than was good for him, stuck a lighted match into a chief's beard, when in an impressive manner the chief told him in three days he would die—and he did, though my husband and I did our utmost to persuade him to take food, and that there was nothing wrong with him. Reinga, on the North Cape of the North Island, according to their notions is the earthly portal to the entrance of their final home—the flitting souls glide noiselessly along through a deep cave in the cliff, then they ascend a high hill, and journey along a valley, where on the margin of a lake a canoe awaits them for the island of Hawaiki, and place where their fathers came from and to which their spirits return. After all battles (so their legend goes) those on earth near this cape can hear the flutter of their wings as they go through the air. The chiefs ascend to heaven first, leaving behind them their left eye, which becomes a star.

The entrance to Reinga is by a Pohutukawa or Christmas tree. If the branches were cut by a white man the road to eternity would be destroyed for ever and the island annihilated. In the tussocks of grass on the sand-hills here the poisonous spider, Katipo, is principally found, though it is in other parts of the island as well. This is the only poisonous insect in New Zealand. At different periods of its age it varies in appearance. When young the stripe on its back is bright red. When fully grown, a deep orange. The hills all round here are covered with toot—a low, broad-leafed bush, with long bunches of claret-coloured berries, which the natives make into wine, though the seeds and stalks are very poisonous and often kill sheep and cattle when eaten too greedily. Great quantities of flax grow in all the valleys and along the banks of the Snowy River line. It is all in blossom now, and the native children are very fond of getting honey from it. They will sometimes get half-a-pint from the flowers on one plant. At the root there is a kind of semi-liquid gum, which the Maoris eat and use as glue and sealing-wax. The leaves, with a sharp-edged shell, answer the purpose of writing paper; they make fibre out of it for cords, nets, lines, etc. It is used in building their huts and canoes. The women make baskets with strips of the leaves, which serve as plates and dishes, and their beautiful mats and garments are all made from the finest variety, which

is very silky and almost a pure white. It is far superior to the European hemp fibre, and is becoming every day a more important export. For dyeing black the natives use the bark of the Hinau tree, and for red the Tawaiwai or Tanekaha tree.

Making an early start by the coach for Napier, I found, alas! that the box seat had already been engaged by a little German doctor, as broad as he was long. "Take great care of him for he looks very precious," were Miss Gill's parting words to me.

It was a glorious day, the sky that intense blue which has no equal, and under the bright sun and the wonderfully clear air the colouring of mountain, sea, and forest was almost too vivid in its intensity. We halted half-way to change horses and have lunch at a little wayside inn, and the sun was just setting when the first whiff of the sulphurous air reminded us that our journey was at an end for that day. The little village of Ohinemutu was unusually active as we passed through, for native elections were going on, and the Maori women were resplendent in all the colours of the rainbow, with the inevitable pipe in their mouths. At the hotel all the old faces had gone, and at the table I saw a long row of strange people. There was a little, long-haired, carelessly-dressed, spectacled professor, with his kindly, homely little wife, a contrast to "her ladyship" opposite, who eyed us through her glasses as if we were minute specimens, and quarrelled with her food until we were driven to wonder why she ever left the comforts of her own home, if she could not bear the ordinary trials of travelling. Her husband, a tall, military-looking Scotsman, bore all her complaints with the resignation of long habit. Next them sat an Irishman with a tread-on-the-tail-of-me-coat-if-you-dare expression that warned off intrusion and friendliness too; then a dear old Scots couple, who were full of tales about the early days of their settlement and the gradual growth of the colony. The tall Engish gentleman next I knew was a splendid specimen of the old-time squatter, one of those who have helped to make Australia what it is, and my heart warmed at the sight of him and his wife. Opposite these were two pretty American girls and their maiden aunt. The girls were full of life, and amused us all with their naïve and original sayings. The aunt was a very starchy spinster, of the "prunes and prism" variety, with a mouth always in the first position. A British matron sat in silent dignity next her good-natured, wealthy, ship-owning husband, of whom she seemed proud, though she failed to imitate his urbanity. A rheumatic farmer carried a liberal sample of his own soil about his person; a man sat beside him who was afterwards so continually popping up again on our travels that he merits a more lengthy description.

He was my travelling companion of the day before, a little German Jew, a doctor by profession, and he was here partly for his health, I imagined, and with the most laudable desire for information was taking snap-shots and notes after the manner of the immortal Mr. Pickwick, whom he resembled in another way—he was very fat. His credulity was unbounded—he believed everything that was told him, and put it all down in his note-book with the utmost gravity. He carried an immense brown bag, and whenever he wanted anything out of it that thing was certain to be at the bottom; and to find it, the little man invariably turned out the entire contents upon the floor of any room or place where he might be; we thus became intimately acquainted with his belongings, and I could describe to a nicety his entire wardrobe, so often was it distributed into its component parts before my reluctant eyes. He was writing a book, he said, and I have often longed to see it, and its marvellous stock of traveller's tales.

The two English tourists wish they were elsewhere, and the newly-married couple coo and cast sidelong glances at each other, much to the amusement of two black-eyed amusing little children, daughters of a book-maker, who made his "pile" on the last Melbourne Cup. The remainder of our neighbours wear no particular identity, and a long summer's day spent with them would not be a joy to look back upon.

One more day among the geysers around Rotorua, when the largest one in the district, Pohutu, played for the first time for four months, and we set off, three of us, by special coach overland for Napier, making an early start at five in the morning for Wairakei, to see the geysers there while it was daylight. The first part of the road was all mountainous country, a succession of fern-covered hills and deep ravines; the mountains gradually became higher, bold, and rocky, then patches of forest lands, and here and there native settlements, generally under the shadow of the mountains. We crossed the Waikato River at the half-way house at Ateamuri, a wilderness of detached rocks. The highest cone, rising 800 feet above the banks of the river, was the scene, years ago, of a great native battle. Six weeks ago the most wonderful geyser broke out at Orakei-Korako, twelve miles from here. It is considered now the safety valve for the whole district. It can only be reached by riding, and those who have seen it say there is nothing to equal it. We were not able to give up the time for going there, as it plays only every nine hours. The Taupo correspondent of the *Auckland Weekly News* gave the following account of it: "No language can describe the utter ferocity of the outburst, which appears as if it would tear up by its roots the foundations of the earth. Pohutu, at Whakarewarewa, is a stately pillar of water hitherto unparalleled, and Whikiti, at the same place, is a picturesque fountain of spouting jets and feathery spray. The Crow's Nest (at Taupo) spits out a jet of water for a moment's duration every half-hour; and Kerapiti, the great steam-hole near Wairakei, blows a spiral column of steam with remarkable energy high into the air; but this terrific geyser out-herods Herod. For two hours it rips and tears out of the earth in a fierce terrible manner, quite unique even in this district of thermal energy. It rests every eight or nine hours between its outbursts."

Not long after leaving Ateamuri, the rain came down in torrents, but on reaching Wairakei at three o'clock, we tucked up our dresses, put on our waterproofs and best walking gear, and started off in the downpour to see the geysers, which were the finest we have yet seen, and their beauty was enhanced by the numerous fern-covered winding paths overhung with ti-tree and climbing plants. We visited by turn the Champagne Cauldron, which played up every seven minutes; the Fairies' Pool; Donkey Engine, which hissed and blew out with the sound of a dozen snorting giants; the Red Geyser, so called from the colour of its clay; the Prince of Wales's Feathers, which from an insignificant opening with pent-up force every few minutes throws up this beautiful-shaped fountain; the Dragon's Mouth; the Devil's Toll-gate, which at this particular time was most unpleasantly slippery to approach; the Steam Hammer, which gave out the sound of a dozen anvils; an unwholesome-looking mud cauldron, where two years ago a pack horse fell down and disappeared, rendering it for three months more active: and many others were visited too numerous to mention. We came back looking like wet fowls with rain dripping from every feather. Next morning horses were brought round for a ride to the Rapids. Here the Waikato has narrowed to fifty feet, and the foaming torrent falls many hundreds of feet in half a mile. It pales in comparison with the Huka Falls, three miles higher up the river along our road to Taupo, where the overland journey would be well repaid by a sight of the river alone. We crossed a small suspension bridge over the Rapids and stood on the edge of the cliff, looking down on the great fall of the foaming torrent as it went noisily tossing and tumbling over the rocks, and in one great mass of water formed a huge blue wave as it took its final plunge a few yards below. The mighty stream here rushes on with indescribable force between high walls of rocks. I tried to think what words could express its grandeur as we stood looking down into its foaming depths, but none would come. The colouring of the water is so beautiful. Sometimes it is a showery mass of white foam, through which, as it parts, it shows the most vivid blue, and then, eddying under the banks, dies away in every shade of transparent green. The last sight at Wairakei which we walked to see was Kerapiti, or the Devil's Trumpet, which is a blow-hole emitting, they say, 180 lbs. of steam to the square inch. Good-sized sticks thrown over it are tossed like feathers in the air, and the sound is equal to that of a dozen engines letting off volumes of steam.

We had a delightful drive of six miles to Taupo, the largest lake in this island, being twenty-six miles long and nineteen wide. In the distance, across the water, are the two giant volcanic cones of Tongariro and Ruapehu, 6000 feet and 9000 feet high, the latter extinct, and covered with perpetual snow. Tradition says a third giant stood between them, but having quarrelled he fled to the West Coast, and his snow-capped head is now the exile in Taranaki—Mount Egmont. The whole of this thermal district lies between the active volcanoes Tongariro and White Island, and at intervals along this volcanic line the smouldering fires in the depths below occasion the countless grand and healing springs.

A Lush Beauty

Napier

For many miles of our journey from Taupo we drove along a most dreary waste of flat, hungry-looking country, with no sign of any living thing. Then followed the mountain ranges, through which, for the last day of the drive, the horses literally climbed a narrow zigzag roadway. The deep gorges were hundreds of feet below, and the river, that always seemed to follow us, was still madly rushing over its rocks and falling into cascades in every direction. By the old roads the coach used to cross the river forty-three times in the one day's journey. At the highest point on the range, 2600 feet, we passed through a flock of 5000 sheep. I don't think that our horses quite liked it, and I am sure that the sheep did not, for many of them rolled in the most uncomfortable manner down the steep mountain-side.

As we came near Napier the fern-covered hills became lower and the country more fertile; then down in a long valley we came upon an English-looking landscape, with cultivated fields on both sides of the road, and homely-looking cottages. The Harbour presently lay before us and in the distance the town of Napier, part of which is built on high cliffs, with the principal streets at its foot, facing the open sea. It is approached by a long, low stretch of shingly beach which marks the deep bay for many miles along the coast. This town is the centre of the great agricultural and pastoral district of Hawke's Bay.

A few days later I started at ten in the morning by train for Taranaki, passing through rich pasture lands, trim hedges, comfortable homesteads, thriving little villages, rich grass lands, with flocks of sheep and sleek, well-fed cattle grazing contentedly in happy ignorance of freezing-works. Then through patches of dense scrub to Danneberg, with everywhere its sawmills and stacks of red timber; then on to Woodville, the largest and most thriving town in this part of the island, and through the Manawatu Gorge with the bubbling river many feet below you, and the high hills above, to Palmerston. The rain was coming down now so heavily that we only had glimpses through the thick mists of outlines of hills and trees, and now it became mistier still, until all was wrapped in darkness, and we rolled our rugs around us, and, tired of each other's chattering, soon fell asleep until half-past nine. When the day's journey was over at Wanganui, a short drive brought me to the Victoria Hotel, supper, and to bed.

At six I was up next morning, and at seven steaming up the river in the *Wairere* to Pipiriki, the outskirts of civilisation in this district. A monument stands close to the starting-point, and I had just time to read the names on it of the friendly Maoris who had fought and lost their lives here in our service.

The country recalls endless memories of Maori history: every height and bend of the river is the scene of some battle famous in legend and song. Above us are remains of many old redoubts, monuments of men who fought for hearth and home. Montoa Island, twelve miles down the river, was the spot where the famous battle of 1864 was fought between the friendly natives and the fanatical Hauhaus, the former fighting so gallantly to save the town. The precipitous cliffs, hundreds of feet in height, are clothed in every variety of vegetation, and little native villages are perched here and there on every spur where a footing can be found. In the last seven miles the scenery became wilder and grander, and the cliff tops showed out high above us through the thick mists and driving clouds, adding more grandeur and mystery. The river below was brawling along with a headlong flight swelled by last night's heavy rains, and though we had started in bright sunshine, the rain now came down in torrents. Truly the freaks of the climate here are of wonderful interest. At Pipiriki, our landing-place, seventy miles from the town, a crowd of lazy, dirty natives were on the bank to greet us, and the cliff was so steep and slippery that for every two steps we slipped one back. I stuck several times in the deep mud, and a very tipsy man who had made himself most objectionable on board, and had already fallen twice, offered to take me on his back. I asked a native to carry my bag a hundred yards; he wanted five shillings for doing it. One of the men on board kindly took it from me. Then I stuck again and had to be pulled out, and I wished I had not come. I was angry with everything, and came to the edge of my temper at the accommodation house, where they said they had not any room for any of us, as thirty or forty men were already there, driven in from their road-making by the rain; but they were very good after all, and, though I did have another wade across to my bedroom, it was clean and comfortable when I got there, and had brushes and combs provided for me. I was afterwards left in undisputed possession of the one small sitting-room, and I sat there in my wet clothes until the cold drove me to seek solace under the bedclothes. From my window I looked right down upon the river, a mad torrent of rushing, rising water, and across on the opposite side a native village, with wooded cliffs towering high behind it. It was all very beautiful, notwithstanding the elements, which seemed through the night to threaten to uproot us altogether.

Next morning I watched a native paddling a canoe up the stream. The sight decided me that it could be done, so after breakfast I made arrangements to hire a canoe, and three men to paddle me up the river. They didn't like going, and were very sulky at starting, and if it had not been for the beauty of each fresh bend, which became grander the higher we went, I don't think I could have had courage enough to brave the current, which at times was so strong that it was a hard battle to fight against it. We kept close to the bank, but now and then an eddy, strong from some hidden rock, sent the water whirling in such circles that we had to dodge out into the middle of the stream. My oarsmen could not speak English nor I Maori, so we were not a merry party, and might from our looks have been officiating at our own funerals. We made a halt at some caves three or four miles up, the first with masses of ferns hanging from the roof and sides, the other very dark, and we had to use candles; but it was so muddy that I did not care to penetrate far into the blackness and slime. Here the men wanted to turn back, and, having made up my mind to go on, I had to insist. We passed several villages inhabited exclusively by natives, and at one larger than the rest we were told there was an accommodation house. I landed and went up. There was one solitary white man there. I didn't like the look of the very unprepossessing surroundings, so I gave it up, and we turned back. The paddle down stream was very easy work, though at times the current swept us uncomfortably swiftly.

After another wet day, at ten on the following morning I slid back to the steamer; they were still unloading, and it was an hour before they started. I sat watching the stores being taken up the hill on sledges and trollies with strong wooden wheels, while the crowd of chattering natives seemed all mixed up in a jumble of mud, kicking horses, and discomfort altogether. The only good the pelting rain did was to clean my umbrella from the white clay stains—a momento of the overland journey, which nothing else removed. The sun at last began to shine again, and the thick mists unveiled one after another the wooded cliffs. Small waterfalls fell in all directions from the heights above in showers of spray, and here and there the gray rocks showed themselves through a mass of beautiful fern fronds and lichen-covered forest trees; now and then a giant tree stood out above the others from the mass of tangled undergrowth, a wild wealth of beauty. We made a great many stopping-places on the way back. A fat Maori boy was first landed at his native village, and he greeted his friends with such an unsteady pair of legs that he lost his balance in the slimy mud, fell over, and rolled into the river, to the intense amusement of all his dusky friends, who never moved a muscle to help him. Farther down, at one of these towns, a man, and his wife resplendent in a tartan skirt, with bright green trimmings, scarlet shawl, and blue handkerchief round her head, landed, and after silently rubbing noses all round we watched the bit of bright colour disappearing for a long way up the hill in the distance. As they went, no one turned even a head to say good-bye, but sat, stolid-looking bundles, with apparently not an interest in life beyond the steamer below. Jerusalem, Corinth, Athens, London, and so on, are the names of these villages.

The steamer has a primitive way of landing her passengers. Backing anywhere into the bank, a plank is laid across for women; men are supposed to make the jump. Now and then a child ran along the bank with a letter to throw on board. When the steamer stops, these merry imps clamber on deck, and as she backs out into the stream they quickly go splashing helter-skelter on to land again or water, to them it doesn't make much difference which. Four men ran along the shore calling for "tucker"; they were surveyors who had run out of everything, and another stoppage was made. Lower down still an old woman waved her bundle; the plank was laid on shore and she came on board.

She had been spending a week with her sister who had just died. Her husband was away, and she was going back to her little farm very sorrowful. "If I had but a bit leddie to bide wi'me," she said wistfully, "maybe I'd greet less the nicht." A lady had once gone to stay with her, it seems, and she wanted me to follow her example. Besides, I was in mourning, and she felt that I could feel for her in her trouble. There was really no reason why I should not yield to the impulse which prompted me to say "yes" to her modest, but evidently heart-felt request; so I went with her at the next stopping place. By turns she carried my bag and I her bundle, until we reached her homestead, about a mile off. It was a clean little place, with a few sheep and cattle about; they sold the butter they made, with eggs and poultry, to the neighbours round them. Two strong active lads were clearing the land where grass would be sown, and they would rear more cattle, but it was "muckle work" commencing. The boys were in a great state of wonderment at my appearance, at first thinking me a new "help", and my proven ability to make scones elevated me to a pinnacle of esteem and favour that I trust I had not forfeited when I left. I took my first lesson in knitting that evening when my hostess had leisure to give it, and then at half-past nine she read a chapter in the Bible, in her quaint way, and we went to bed. Her husband came home unexpectedly next evening, and I shall not soon forget his hearty manly greeting of us both. "Weel, lass, what's the maitter noo?" he asked, as she burst into tears at the sight of him. I was "a bonnie bit leddie", a "dainty leddie". Nothing could exceed his chivalrous courtesy, or the kindness of both to me. I left next day, and his last words were "Dinna forget us": nor shall I.

Next morning I rode to meet the coach, and arrived at the "Victoria" at Wanganui in time for a bath and dinner, having had a glimpse into another phase of human nature. My hostess had offered me the best of all she had, not even knowing my name.

Not every inch of New Zealand is fertile land. Fortune does not always await the farmer, and for the intending emigrant there are many rocks ahead. It is as uphill work here at first as elsewhere, and no one should come without a friend or relative on the spot to advise them, certainly not to be led by promises of the colonising agents, who are naturally interested in disposing of the land, large areas of which are at present an incubus on the bank and loans companies, and must be got rid of by hook or by crook. North of Auckland, about the Bay of Islands the land is in many instances very poor (though there are some rich parts), but the owners were naturally trying to dispose of it, and in one or two instances they used bone-dust with the grass seeds to show intending purchasers what the soil could produce, the unwary one not knowing that this fertiliser had had to be resorted to. Mr. W., who when up with us in the steamer to the Bay of Islands, was going, as an experiment, to sow gorse, then burn it off and feed the sheep on the young tender shoots as they came up. He had tried it in the South on a small scale with great success. The sheep had grown fat on it, and the wool was good. The result will be looked forward to with interest, as the land, which, as it is at present, is useless, can be bought cheaply. During Lord Onslow's term of office as Governor in New Zealand, he took the keenest interest in all pastoral pursuits, and, setting aside his viceregal dignity, he rode amongst the farmers, talked with them, lived with them, and made himself thoroughly acquainted with the whole workings of farm life.

Reminiscences

Napier

We left Wanganui at three in the afternoon by train for New Plymouth. The town was soon left behind, the homesteads became more scattered and the country broken up into fern-covered ridges, with deep gorges, running brooks, tall poplars, and waving willows. Then on, past wooded hills, scrubs, rolling downs, and on through swamp and sandhills close along the shore to the country towns of Patea and Hawera, with rich volcanic soil ten feet and twelve feet deep. As the sun went down, a fresh crisp air blew in upon us through the open windows, and the clear-cut snowy cap of Mount Egmont came into sight, with its perfect cone of 8200 feet, towering above us. No wonder that Taranaki is proud of its mountain and the many never-failing springs fed from its reservoir of eternal snow. I first made its acquaintance long ago, from the sea, when there was only an open roadstead at New Plymouth, and we were sent ashore in whale-boats. There was no breakwater there then and the iron horse was here unknown. As the train rushed into New Plymouth at ten o'clock at night, I strained my eyes through the sea of faces to catch some familiar ones I knew. Many were there, and only I seemed changed.

The little country town had grown into an imposing one, and rows of well-to-do-looking shops lined the streets. The fern-lands were cleared, and homesteads were dotted about, where before we had picnicked and gathered ferns in dense bush. Only the little river was the same, running over its pebbly stones and under the shadows of the great tree ferns, then through the town and the black iron sand to the sea, where the great peaked sugar-loaf rocks, Ngamotu (the islands) stand out against the sky, the old and strongest fortress of the Ngatiaroa tribes of long ago. We climbed up to Marsland Hill, the site of the old barracks, and looked down upon the old church and its holy acre, where so many of our brave men lie under the shadow of those great pines.

The Flower Hunter

Hoheria populnea, *New Zealand, watercolour, 54.8 x 38 cm*
Reproduced by permission of the National Library of Australia

My few days at New Plymouth literally flew by, but there were other memories to be renewed, and I left one bright morning with Mr. Halcomb, and drove out to his farm at Urenui—a splendid road the whole way and farms as far as the eye could reach. The dairy industry has made rapid strides here, for the warm, moist climate is so favourable to it. All the crops looked splendid. There is so little frost here that you can eat new potatoes all the year round. Waitara in this way had grown into a large town with freezing-works and a small shipping trade. From there, on we went through the same rich grass lands, cultivated fields, and browsing sheep and cattle. We turned into the gates of Ferngrove—this pretty homestead—just in time for lunch, and I ate my first New Zealand peach and fig, which were delicious. The afternoon was lazily spent in wandering round. What a glorious day it was; the bees buzzed in the thick clover blossoms, and the summer fly went by with a darting swish. High up from the edge of the hilly ridge where the house stands, you look down upon a deep gorge, with a clear-running stream, and beyond is a dense bank of tall trees and ferns, with here and there a scarlet mass of rata blossom. Hills and valleys stretch away into the distance, where the snowy guardian Taranaki rises in the background. The sea is in front of us, and the long coast-line of broken hills and high white cliffs, where we had made our home at Pukearuhe when first married.

These cliffs, which have been called the Key of New Zealand and have witnessed many scenes of violence and bloodshed, now look peaceful enough. One day I started off to revisit these old haunts. We crossed the mouth of the river on dry sand, where long ago we were once caught in the shifting quick-sands, that never-to-be-forgotten ride where for more than an hour we were struggling with death; then came another race for life round the point, with the tide so high against the cliffs that it meant a swim for our horses, or turning back by the river again. How terrified I was! yet too much ashamed to confess it before the two strange Englishmen who were coming to spend Christmas with us. What an experience for them, poor things! Once round the point we were safe, and then what a gallop we had on the long stretch of hard, yellow sands, and what canters afterwards in the early dawn of the frosty mornings: it was always a race between man, bird, and Maori, as to which would be first to pick up that most delicate of all, the frost fish, which only comes ashore in this particular weather and was never once known to have been caught with a line or a net. Those were halcyon days of sea-breezes and happiness.

To-day the sun is shining its brighest; for me the scent of gorse, of sea-cliffs, of wooded dells and hollows, made the memories grow stronger; and now we rode under the self-same tree of snow-white blossoms where long ago I had pulled my first wild flowers and crowned my hat with them. There was the very spot where we rested to have lunch; there in the distance the outline of the old home; the dear sad memories were all too strong for me, and on the threshold I had not the courage to go on.

Turning back, we went to see old Tom Bishop; he was an old 43rd hero, and what a welcome he gave me! He had a comfortable little home, and his pension and all. Despite my repeated assertions that I didn't want them, he insisted on picking me all his strawberries, ripe and unripe, and between his smiles and his tears (every few minutes brushing his sleeve across his eyes) he reminded me how I had begged him off from punishment, with many others, for "just this once". Just this once came very often, and I laughed as the remembrance came back to me of his oft-repeated pleadings for leave to go into town to see a sick grandmother, who must have died quite six times during the year. Then there was the bugler, who was always called "little Tommy", and I recalled his quavering notes as he used to sound the calls. Thompson, another old soldier, was now, he told me, "amicably prosperous"! Many of them were now rich farmers, hotel-keepers, and one the principal storekeeper at Urenui. Lloyd, an old one-eyed Maori, well known during the war, stopped to say his greetings, and several others nodded a recognition. We drove on to the farm of Mr. H.'s son-in-law: 600 acres of splendid grass land. The former owners had had recourse to a cruel way of clearing it. It was originally all covered with ferns, six and seven feet high; cattle were turned into it in the spring, when they lived on the young shoots as they came up. In time the constant nibbling destroyed the plants, and the poor animals were left to starve, eating at last even the roots. The grass soon grew after it was sown, but the cattle lay dead in every direction. It was less costly to improve the land in this way than by other means.

The last of the harvesting was finished as we got back; and I went to watch the long row of cows being milked. There are six young men here learning farming; they are all Englishmen and do the whole of the work, rising at five, when they have tea and something the eat, then breakfast at eight, lunch very often in the fields, and dinner at seven. They seem a very happy household. The farm is 1000 acres in extent, carrying 1000 sheep, 200 head of cattle, and 30 horses. The work is mixed—dairying, pastoral, and agricultural—100 acres being kept under the plough for turnips, oats, carrots, and other crops.

Even here in New Zealand they talk of "Queen's weather", and what a glow of sunshine came flooding into the room to herald the day, my last one in the little town that from old associations was so dear to me. We had planned a day in the country, and started early in the morning, first passing up the Devon line, where here and there a good-bye was said; then along an English-looking lane with tall hedges on both sides, past the old hospital—a picturesque Elizabethan-looking house, which is now turned into a home for old men; up the hill again to the cemetery, where a monument stands out against a dark background of pines, marking the spot where those who were cruelly murdered at Pukearuhe, the White Cliffs, lie. Now from a height we looked down upon the clear pebbly bed of the Maiwa-Kaiho River, with its water-race, and endless ladder of wooden steps leading to it, which we did not descend. With out faces turned homewards, here and there through the green hills we caught glimpses of the homely-looking little town, and round a sunny corner a Maori cart was standing. What a subject for an artist! The man with his brown face and great brawny arms, she with the sunlight all coming through her tangled tawny-coloured hair, and her eastern-patterned dress, a wondrous mass of greens, yellows, and blues. A little child, in a bright crimson frock, on his hands and knees, was drinking at the stream, whilst all through the twisted stems of the interwoven foliage, the lichens and ferns were turned to gold as the sun went down. One more good-bye at the corner of the church, and I passed through the gate into the rest and quiet of the pretty parsonage garden.

At eight next morning I was on my way again. We had had three of the hottest days that had been known for many years in New Plymouth. The thermometer stood at 93° in the shade, and it was unbearably warm in the train, and so dusty that we all looked as if we had been well peppered before we had gone a mile. Among the crowd of passengers who filled the one long carriage was the little German Professor, looking rather dilapidated from a week of camping out on Mount Egmont. As usual he turned the miscellaneous contents of his great brown bag out on to the floor, much to the amusement of the passengers, some of whom made "rude remarks", which in a muttering tone of voice he told me was "ferry bat taste".

At Haweia we wished each other good-bye. As I left the carriage, the guard, an old solider of the 43rd, addressed me by name, and reminded me that, close to the train line, we had passed through my husband's farm, which years ago he had sold for £10 an acre, some of which are now worth £500 each. Several other old soliders came to meet me on the road, some of them now well-to-do farmers. One, with his carriage and a good pair of horses, insisted on driving me to Mr. Livingstone's farm, the best and largest in the district, which in richness would vie with the finest English holding. Here I met Marian Bleazel, my dear and faithful friend who had lived with me for so many years in Victoria and New Zealand. She took me all over the pretty garden, and into the orchard, where the apple trees were laden with fruit, and two crab-apple trees were breaking down with the weight of their crimson berries. I had lunch off junket and thick Devonshire cream, and did not wonder when the two visitors there from Napier told me that they had gained a stone in weight in one month. Everything was home-grown and home-made.

I went on from there by coach to Opunake, which we reached about seven, after a very rough drive. It had been an oppressively hot day and the air was heavy with dense smoke from bush fires. The sun went down like a ball of flame, but the little coast town was all *coleur de rose* for me, for here I met my best friends in New Zealand, Major and Mrs. Tuke.

At one time during the war this was a very important town, and a great many troops were stationed here. The walls of a very strong redoubt remain, and some of the old military buildings are still left standing. People even now predict a great future for this town; but at present it is not by any means an exciting place to settle down in, the only beauty being its mountain, for here you see Mount Egmont from the west side, and each night we watched the moon in all her full-blown glory rise behind it.

Fifteen miles from Opunake is the largest native village in New Zealand, Parahaka, where the great prophet, Ti Whiti, lives. On the seventeenth of every month he holds a great meeting, when the natives feast for several days. We drove over to see the village, but the prophet would not come out to meet us. I was determined to see him, so we went down to a small enclosure where he was surrounded by about twenty-five of his followers, who never leave him. They were fine men; but, we were told, probably the most troublesome in all New Zealand, and ready to do anything their chief may put them up to. Some of them were playing draughts with shells and stones on the bottom of an old box. One, an immense man, was six feet four inches in height. I made him stand up to show me his height, but his arms were as soft as putty. These men lead a most idle life, doing nothing but sleep and eat. Ti Whiti, who is not a bad-looking man, with a thick gray beard and hair, was dressed like a European. He had a cunning but merry twinkle in his eye, shook hands with us all, but beyond that paid no attention to us, and we left him. This old fellow has probably worked more mischief in New Zealand than any other man in it. He knows the Bible off by heart, and is very clever in turning each prophecy to his own way of thinking. In 1882 he was taken prisoner for rebellion and shut up for two years, and again a year or two ago for debt, when he refused to attend when he was summoned. It seems strange that he should have retained his power over the natives for so long, for no prophecy of his has ever come true in one single instance, and he has a remarkable excuse always ready to account for this. He is always going to raise the dead to life again, and year after year his followers go up with their bundles of clothes ready for the departed ones to put on when they emerge from their graves and sweep, as they are told, all the white men off the face of New Zealand.

The other chief here, Tohu, was at one time his most staunch ally; but they quarrelled, and have now formed themselves into two parties—those belonging to Ti Whiti wear a white feather stuck in their hats or hair. At the present time a fierce quarrel is going on between them over a small piece of land a few feet square. Tohu built a house on it in his own part of the town.

Ti Whiti said it was his land, and ordered his men to pull it down. When he found he could not demand the land, as it belonged to the tribe, he commenced building another exactly in front of Tohu's European house, the largest in the village, but which he only uses on state occasions. He lives close by in a miserably draughty whare, where we went to see him, and found him suffering from toothache and looking very ill. He has taken the quarrel so much to heart that it will probably kill him.

He hardly took any notice of us, but gave us the key to go over his house, which is divided into long eating rooms upstairs and down, with only tables and chairs, and room for storing knives, forks, spoons, and dishes; for since living in prison they have adopted European ways, build their houses in European style, and sit in chairs on state occasions. The village would be a picturesque one if it were not for these hideous incongruities in the way of buildings. The native whares are all huddled very closely together, and some of them we went into were beautifully made, one in particular, with a neat little garden round it, made us quite envious. The walls were made of raupo stems inside, most evenly put together, and the floor all covered with well-made flax mats. Three really pretty girls were squatting inside, one making rush bags, and the other two combing and plaiting their thick black locks. Most of the other whares were uninviting, with just one entrance, and a sickening smell of closeness pervaded them. The women congratulated Mrs. T. on her well-grown *carpi* (good) daughters. Many of Ti Whiti's followers are deserting him, and this last meeting was the smallest that has been known for many years. He is always kept well supplied with money, but it is all spent in feasting.

We went over the ground where 1800 troops were stationed; but the only remains now left to mark the spot are some English weeds, growing rankly in what were once gardens, the foundations of an old stable, and the earthworks on top of the hill where the old redoubt overlooked the town. Before leaving we were invited to have some tea. A long table was spread with a cloth and plates of cakes and buns, the butter being put carefully in a lump on the top of each; tea without milk and a decanter of thick-looking wine, which we thought best not to try. We all did full justice to our repast, and, after thanking them for their kindness, we shook hands with a great many of them and made our adieux. I forgot to say that they showed us their billiard-room, with a full-sized table, and the walls hung round with Scriptural pictures of the most garish description. Among the whares is one larger and more ornamented than the rest, where, in olden times, the Tohunga (chief) lived, to whom it was held sacred. These chiefs obtained a great ascendency over their followers; they had the power of ventriloquism and practised the art of doctoring, making decoctions from astringent barks valuable for their healing properties. Like most other natives, they used clay for the healing of wounds.

Coming home, we passed the spot where poor Miss Dobie (sketching for the *Graphic*) was cruelly murdered by a native. The officers and men in the constabulary have put up a white cross in the little graveyard here to her memory.

Sheep-Shearing, Physicking and Dipping

Wellington

From Opunake I made my way by Patea to Wellington; my stay there was brief. On the second morning, after an early breakfast at eight, I started by train for Brancepeth, one of the largest stations in New Zealand. For some miles after leaving Wellington the line skirted the sea-shore under the shadow of the cliffs to the rich valley of the Hutt, then over silver streams where many a lusty trout lies hidden, through rich clearings and thickly-wooded hills to Mungaroa, where the line begins to mount higher and higher and the scenery becomes grander and more imposing; but, alas! the relentless fire has been here, and down the steep slopes of the mountains are the blackened stumps, all that remains of the once magnificent forest.

At Kaitoke two powerful Fell engines were put on, one in front of and one behind the train, for they want all the force they can command to haul it up this steep gradient of one in fifteen. It is seven miles from here to the top of the Rimataka range. At a place called Siberia, in 1880, a furious gale, sweeping suddenly down the gully, hurled several of the carriages off the line, and the wonder is that only four passengers were killed. A strong break-wind has since been erected there. We parted with these engines some distance below on level ground. Here the Wairarpapa Plains extend to the head of the Pairau Plains, eighty miles distant, and the dreary, flat, and monotonous country, with its pebbly surface, looks like the bed of a wide river. At Masterton, the largest town in this district, our train journey was over. A waggonette and capital pair of horses met us, and after lunch we had a lovely drive over the hills to my friend's station, some twenty miles away.

Sheep-Shearing, Physicking and Dipping

The homestead lay nestling among a forest of pines. We crossed the bridge over the river, where the banks below looked refreshingly cool under the shade of great willow trees. Then a quick sweep of the road up the avenue of pines where the scent of our own blue gums and Australian wattles (growing better here than in their native home) was filling the air, and up through the garden gate to the many-gabled old-English-looking house, with its trellised roses climbing up the windows, and rich creepers clothing the walls everywhere. My friends were waiting for me at the door with words of welcome. How nice everything did look, and how pretty the drawing-room was, with its deep bay window at the end, and the conservatory beyond with ferns and trellis covered with ripening grapes. The low French windows opened out on to the smooth well-kept lawn and tennis-ground, and beyond it was the garden gay with groups of tall sunflowers, lilies, and such a wilderness of scarlet poppies. How big my room looked too, and how comfortable, after my three months' experience of hotels, and what a fresh sweet home-look there was about everything and everybody!

In the cool of the evening, after tea, we had a walk round the garden, and made our way to the peach trees, which looked most tempting. The raspberries were almost over, but the apple tree was laden, so were the plum trees, and a hedge of blackberries was quite a sight to see with its masses of ripe fruit.

Next morning the horses were brought round for those who wanted to ride or drive, and off we all started. Shearing was just over, and they had shorn 100,000 sheep; but station life is always a busy one, and each day there is something new. This day the lambs were getting their dose of oil and turpentine. Their mouths were held open and it was squirted down their throats with a small syringe—a most ingenious way of giving physic. They didn't seem to mind the operation, it was so quickly over; and they went off without even a shake of the head; 7800 were dosed that day. Then we drove on to the big substantial wool-shed where a few stragglers were being shorn—here, as on most of the large stations, the Wolseley shears are used; one shearer's record with them, which was written up here, had been 250 sheep in a day. Passing along the road, we watched the reaping and binding machines at work. Clover had been sown with the oats, and instead of the bare stubble the paddock was thick and green with it. Later on, down by the river, we boiled water, and had afternoon tea under the shadow of the overhanging cliffs and tall bush trees, which here in patches have been saved for shelter for the stock. Those who were energetically inclined afterwards played tennis, while my friends took me round to see the stables, the large poultry yards, and the well-stocked station library, where all the new books and papers were to be seen. The station, with its many outhouses, looked like a small village, and I wondered, but did not like to ask, how many hands were employed to work it.

Next day we went to see the sheep being dipped. They swam and ducked them into a deep trough of arsenic and water, 10,000 going through in one day. Drafting, too, was going on, and all hands were very busy. The frozen meat trade, too, is taking such strides that the squatters' hearts ought to be jubilant with such a promising future. Coming home, we met the rabbiter with his pack of dogs; for this troublesome pest is not yet a thing of the past. How quickly the time seemed to fly! but I had to hurry on. My visit ended all too soon, and once more came the good-byes. The rain fell just enough to lay the dust. Then into the train, where a crowd of natives in the next carriage were going to attend a big lawsuit over some land dispute, and the small owner, a boy of four, together with his relations, ate and slept by turns until Wellington was reached at eight P.M.

Next morning I went over the Wellington Museum, which is well worth seeing. Sir James Hector has had charge of it since its foundation in 1865. The Maori carved house here, which was originally built at Tauranga by the Ngatikaipoho tribe, is the best I have yet seen. It is hard to realise that such elaborate carvings could have been produced by those rough old stone weapons that are shown in the case in the same room. A big glass jar reminds one of Victor Hugo's *Toilers of the Sea*, for it contains a single feeler, 14 feet long, of an octopus which was caught in this harbour, and nearly cost the boatmen their lives by upsetting them into the water. The creature itself was 52 feet long. The collection of New Zealand birds has not such a stuffed look as most that you see. They are all here, from the Kea (the long-beaked evil-looking parrot that picks the livers out of the sheep) to the great handsome green Kakapo, or owl parrot; the beautiful large pigeon and funny little black Tickes, with dull-red saddle-shaped markings on their backs; long-tailed cuckoos; the Pukeko, or swamp hen, with its long legs, blue breast, and bright-red beak. There are kingfishers, parson-birds, wattled crows, bell-birds, many kinds of ducks and sea-birds.

In the afternoon I drove out to The Hutt, where at M'Nab's Gardens (the principal public ones of the kind) I saw a splendid collection of asters. The seed had come from Amsterdam. We had tea under the shade of the trees, and drove back as the sun was going down, and the landlocked harbour and mountains were all bathed in tender purples and gold. No wonder that Wellington is proud of her beautiful harbour. Soames Island, the quarantine station, lies near the entrance; Point Halswell beyond, with its battery of heavy guns, and above it still, at Kaiwarra, another heavy battery. The city, which lies under the shadowy surrounding hills, is well guarded, and it would be no easy task to approach it in time of war. When the seat of Government was moved here from Auckland in 1865, this "fishing village", as it was then called, was made the fourth most important city in the colonies. The "gay" session time is in the winter.

In this land of earthquakes almost every building is of wood, and a stranger may not on first sight be impressed with the town's appearance. But if he desires to form a just estimate of its remarkable position and picturesque surroundings, let him take a walk to the top of Mount Victoria, with its signal station, where he can get a magnificent panoramic view of the whole of the surrounding country, the open sea with its high headlands, the entrance to the harbour between the heads, the whole course of the bay, and the drive "round the rocks", a picturesque road that hugs the harbour and the town below, with its rugged background of mountains. Then let him make his way up endless wooden steps behind the town to the Catholic cemetery, where from above he looks down on Te Aro, the industrial portion, with the hospital, college barracks, and basin reserve, and on the other side on Thorndon, the fashionable quarter, with its pretty villas and gardens, and below Government House, Lampton Quay, the shipping, and principal thoroughfare of the town.

Ruthless Deforesting

Christchurch

It was with difficulty I could tear myself away from kind friends in Wellington, who hoped to the last that I would miss the steamer. On the contrary, it had been put off for an hour, so we were in good time. We had a five hours' run across to Picton. The storm which had been blowing had quieted down, and left the sea with a long heavy swell; but after passing the tide rip at the entrance of Tory Channel, with its breakers ahead, we came into smooth water in Queen Charlotte's Sound. On several of the hill-sides are the remains of gold workings, and here and there are old whaling stations, but nowadays whales are seldom see here, and only porpoises chased each other and our steamer too, in sport, as she glided smoothly in between the endless succession of high hills and deep indented bays. The little town of Picton lay nestling at the far end, locked in by an amphitheatre of hills. They told us that most splendid fishing is to be had here, and it boasts of having one of the largest fish-curing establishments in New Zealand. It was just dusk as we came alongside the pier, and the Bishop of Nelson (who was on board) kindly went on shore and engaged me a seat in the coach, for, alas! to my dismay I found that I had a drive of twenty miles into Blenheim (in the centre of the Wairau Plains) that night to catch my coach next day to Nelson. This was not a pleasant surprise to me: there were no cabs, so my luggage was sent along in a wheelbarrow. It was pitch dark inside the coach, where we were packed like herrings in a tin. I knew that a boy was beside me, for in a few moments he had fallen asleep on my shoulder. Two women in the far corner made an incredible noise with their perpetual chatter, and a man who evidently "enjoyed" bad health was very plaintive over his many ailments; the friend beside him was unsympathetic. At ten o'clock there were gleams of lamp-light and we drew up with a flourish of trumpets in front of a substantial-looking hotel, feeling ready for supper and bed. It was the cheapest drive I had ever had, and even with my luggage, which was by no means light, cost only five shillings. After a sleepless night I was up at six next morning, and at seven we started on our way by coach again. Blenheim was still sleeping and nothing was astir along the road but the milk-carts *en route* to a big butter factory, which we passed by the way.

The river had risen so high from the last rains that we had to go an extra eight miles round. It was a pretty, homely-looking country, and we drove between hedges of hawthorn, barberry, and sweetbrier, with fields on either side, small homesteads dotted about, and gardens with apple trees laden with fruit. We passed numerous rustic wooden bridges. Under the shade of tall poplars and willows ran the Wairau River. The road for many miles skirted the plain, famous in New Zealand history. It was here that in 1843 the first serious fighting took place, and Captain Wakefield and many of the pioneer Nelson settlers were murdered by Te Kauparaha, who disputed possession of the land which the Europeans were surveying, and drove them off. Some say the motive was revenge for the death of a Maori woman who had been accidentally shot by a white man on a small hill above the road. A monument is erected to the memory of those who were killed. The plains themselves extend for sixty miles, and are wonderfully fertile, growing sometimes twenty tons of potatoes and sixty bushels of wheat to the acre. Leaving them behind, we came to the long fertile valley of Kitue. Here on all the mountain-sides, some so steep and the land so poor that no sheep could find a living on them, the ruthless deforesting of the country is going on. Can no one put a stop to it? The beauty of New Zealand is quickly being destroyed in every direction. On an arm of Pelorus Sound we passed the picturesque village of Havelock. Some years ago this town grew to the size that it is, in consequence of rich gold discoveries at Mahakipawa, but very little is coming from there now, and the place has a destitute look. A few yards farther on large sawmills came in sight. What a picture it made. The stacks of red cedar in the river; the background of deep indigo-coloured mountains high above, with the blue peaks growing fainter and fainter away into distance, with every gradation of shade upon them. Along the roads were willows and English trees just in the first yellow wane of autumn, and the briers and hawthorns were scarlet with berries, while tangled masses of blackberries with every shade on their leaves covered the ground.

From there onwards for many miles we followed the swift, deep, winding Pelorus River, the waters of which were of the most peculiarly vivid green colour. High forest-clad mountains towered above on the farther side, and the banks were lined with wild masses of beautiful scrub: at Canvas Town (which has no canvas), the half-way house, we stopped for lunch. There were two tourists who had come for trout-fishing and deer-stalking; the license fee for the latter is twenty shillings and entitles the holder to kill (in this Nelson district) six bucks—in Wellington and Otago it is three pounds for four stags; shooting begins the middle of February and closes the end of May. The rules, they say, will be more stringent as the time goes on; no customs duties are charged on guns or sporting materials which are *bona fide* property of any one landing and in use by him. The deer have increased very much here, so have those wretched little pests the weasels and stoats, which were imported to kill rabbits, but not caring for the more open country where rabbits are found, they have left them alone for the thicker shelter of the hills, where they live on quail, pheasants, and other birds, and sometimes young lambs. We passed flocks of English starlings, and saw an exciting fight between a black cat and a rabbit. We watched puss stalk her game, and saw it eventually killed. The settlers give from sixpence to a shilling for every cat they can get, for, after all, they are the greatest enemies the rabbits have. There is an amusing story told of a man who took over a shipload of them, which were turned out. They were all domesticated ones, and the morning after he was awakened by the dismal mewings of hundreds of them round his house clamouring for food. History does not relate how he dispersed them again, which in a cat's case is no easy matter. In Victoria there was a case of a cat and rabbit having lived together, and at the Zoological Gardens there you may see some photographs of rabbit-cats. We seemed to have come into a land of rabbits just here, soft little gray heads and ears pricked up in every direction, and scurrying forms darted here and there across the road into the tangled thicket and the many holes. Beyond Canvas Town the scenery became wilder and grander, and the road a mere narrow track through wild unbroken bush. We crossed several small rivers hurrying on with such speed that the day seemed too short for them. The waters often were over the tops of the wheels. The streams go down, the driver told me, as quickly as they rise, and all flow into the Wai River, which now ran beside us. Crossing a bush track to our left, the driver pointed to a high mountain peak above, where the bushranger Sullivan and his three mates committed so many murders. There, away up in the wilds, they used to lie in wait and kill the diggers who went by with their heavy bags of gold; then went into Nelson, and in a lavish way spent the money. Suspicions were at last aroused, and Sullivan turned informer. The feeling against him was so strong that it was with the greatest difficulty the crowds were kept from lynching him as he was taken backwards and forwards from and to the gaol. He was afterwards imprisoned for the suspected murder of a young surveyor, and sentenced for life; but finally let off. Burgess, the other principal witness, before his execution wrote a history of his life, relating the whole affair, and the various other murders they had committed in Australia. Sullivan, he said, was always the leader. His evidence could not, however, be relied on, as his one idea was to hang the man who had so treacherously betrayed them.

The telegraph station on this road is the most important in New Zealand, and here are distributed all messages from the North Island to places in the South; in addition to this the Eastern Extension Company's cable ascends from the bed of the ocean at Cable Bay, the other end coming to the surface close to Sydney. The roads now became steeper at every mile, and under the deep shadow of the cliffs above and of overhanging trees we came into almost gloom, then out again into the bright sunshine, where every leaf sparkled and the beautiful woods above and below us looked as if perpetual youth were in the green ferns and the creepers that weirdly coiled and twined round every stem. Far away below us we heard the rush of the river hurrying along, tripping over pebbles and leaping down rocks; now and then we heard the pigeons coo, and in the distance the ringing note of the tui. Higher and higher we went, until from a spur 1600 feet, the highest peak on the Wangamoa Range, we looked over a vast panorama of blue mountain-tops and down the steep slopes of densely-wooded ranges. Then we gradually descended until the plain was reached, and to the right of our road the sun sank across eight miles of prosaic mud flat before we reached Nelson. It was half-past six, we had driven over eighty miles, and changed horses five times on the road, and I was fresher than when I started.

I found that the longer I stayed in Nelson the less I felt inclined to leave it. The ever summer-like climate never seemed too hot nor too cold. They say that the thermometer seldom rises above 75° and in the winter seldom falls below 50°. Everything seems to thrive here; unlike the rest of New Zealand, grapes grow out of doors. The town has a clean, neat look about it, and every cottage has its well-kept garden of vegetables and flowers.

A lady and gentleman who had come the long coach journey through from Christchurch advised me most strongly not to go that way—they had, they said, come at the risk of their lives. The road was terrible, the horses and harness worse, the rivers were almost impassable, but—the scenery was beautiful. This decided me, and next morning at ten I was on my way. Away again through the hills and into the rich Waimea Plains, skirting for many miles an inland bay, past some hop gardens where the pickers were busy at work, and on to Belgrove, 24 miles away, under the brighest of blue skies; the coach was there waiting for us, but it took some time to stow away its many mails and miscellaneous freight of boxes, bags, etc.

Our road went winding round and round the mountains until we reached the summit at Hope's Saddle. Here all the beautiful bush had been destroyed by fire. Smoke made the distant mountains an intense blue, and the tall, gaunt stems of the bare trees were sometimes gray, sometimes black, and at others showed a snowy white; against such a background their very weirdness was beautiful. Once over the spur, we went like the wind down into the valley, the narrow roadway winding in the most unpleasantly sharp turns down the steep inclines.

We crossed the Hope River, and the finest scenery began where the waters from Rotoroa, a small lake among the hills, flow into the Buller and Hope Rivers. From this point there was dense vegetation, and high bush on either side of the road, but it soon grew too dark to see more. A cold damp mist had come up from the river, and crept over everything, and the sound of dogs barking in the distance was very welcome, and meant that Longford, our stopping-place for the night, was reached. The coach from Westport had arrived before us, and everyone was sitting round a huge log-fire; we were in a land of horse-hair sofas and primitive china dog ornaments; an oleograph of "Sweet Anne Page" looked down from above on us with a smoke-dried face, and the wall beside this was decorated with four horseshoes, covered with black velveteen and pink ribbons! We were all very hungry, and made a substantial meal off roast mutton, eggs, scones, bread and jam; then up the tiny staircase with small passages and innumerable rooms everywhere, and to bed. Everything was clean and everyone most obliging.

How cold it was next morning as I dressed by candlelight, and how inhuman of the coach arrangements to start us at six! We drove along through a thick mist silently for two hours, and then, through a near break in the trees, saw the Buller River running hundreds of feet below; and the notices on the rickety wooden bridges, "This bridge is unsafe for traffic", just reminded us of previous warnings, but before one's wits had had time to gather themselves together to be frightened, with a dash we were over. An unpleasantly sharp turn of the road showed us where last year the outside edge gave way, and the coach fell 200 feet down the cliff. The proprietor's wife was killed and two passengers

THE FLOWER HUNTER

Coral tree (Erythina Lysistemon), *watercolour, 54.7 x 38 cm*
Reproduced by permission of the National Library of Australia

injured for life. The river was not very high or they might have been swept down, but they fell on a small sandbank, which saved them.

What a land of loveliness it was! Such magnificent birch trees, and such ferns! Hundreds of feet below, the Buller, with its bluish-green water, deep, wide, and swift, rushed, sometimes between sandy banks, then forced an entrance through giant rocks. The road wound round and round each headland, and we went spinning along the narrow track with the high wooded cliffs above and the ever-changing scene in front. We passed a dredge at work—one that in the last floods was turned over and its two occupants swept away down the roaring stream; and now John Chinaman has his sluicing-boxes close beside us, and the cliffs in many places are honeycombed in the quest for gold. Here and there a chair swung on wires is the only means of access to the other side, and later on, for a new sensation, I went across in one; a tipsy man had not long before fallen out, 70 feet, into the river below. The ducking probably sobered him, and he swam ashore, much to everyone's astonishment. At lunch time we came to the picturesque town of Lyell, a small mining township cut out of the hill-side, the backs of the houses all built up on high piles. Then we came to Inangahua junction, a most uninviting-looking spot, where the coach roads for Reefton and Westport diverge. I was undecided which route to take. The most beautiful part of the Buller Gorge was still in front of me, but if I had descended it to Westport it would have necessitated my remaining there for four days for a return coach. We therefore changed horses and I went reluctantly on to Reefton, which we reached at six in the evening. It is a corrugated-iron-roofed, straggling mining town on a flat, with wooded mountains all round.

The mines, which are of quartz, are on the other side of the mountain two or three miles away, but it was too late to see them. The coach took twenty-eight of us and our luggage to the station. The railway from here to Greymouth is a private line, and not particularly interesting, first through forest clearings and bush lands. At Nghara there are large sawmills and an aerial tramway, four or five miles long, from the mountains, which brings coal to the station. A lady I met in the train hearing me say I was going to the hotel, invited me to lunch with her at

Greymouth, which is a seaport town, and of no particular interest, but I spent a few pleasant hours there, and at three o'clock started in the Government train for Kumara, as yet only a small stopping-place on the line. From this station to the town we drove seven miles through a pretty bush track which, probably, by next year will be a land of tree skeletons, as the waste lands are being thrown open in every direction for selection, even along the beautiful Buller Gorge where goats could not find a footing on the steep mountain-sides.

Extensive mining operations were going on all round this town, and they told me the hydraulic system was the largest in the world.

I went for a long walk to the Teremakau River, and watched the mighty force of water coming through the nozzle of the pipes and washing the cliffs away. Where the stones have lain exposed to the air for some time a bright red moss grows over them, from which a strong scent is made.

Large dams have been made in the mountains here, from which the water is brought down in great flumes and pipes. The sight from Dillman Town, half a mile from the town where all the miners live, is very curious, the whole flat below the Teremakau River being a network of channels and boxes, and the water itself first yellow and then blue with sluicings from the sludge channels. I was up at six next morning, and before nine o'clock breakfast had had another long walk. At ten the coach started, and for miles we went through an avenue of magnificent birch trees. It was the last trip of the coach along this portion of the road, for the next day the railway was opened to this point. We changed horses at a small roadside hotel here, and took in some fresh passengers, among them two men of sorts; one of them tried hard to turn me off the box-seat by offering to pay more; I had already booked it days before, however; not to be done, he squeezed himself in between me and the driver, giving me the outside edge and barely anything to sit on; then he objected to the way we were being driven, and once or twice seized the reins; I thought for a moment or two the driver and he would come to blows; finally the other passengers interfered, and amidst a shower of abuse they compelled him to take a back seat. Eventually they left us altogether to get on to the opposition coach, where, later on, they got their deserts by being upset.

Ruthless Deforesting

From the Otira Hotel where we lunched our ascent commenced. The zigzag road is cut out of the solid rock. The Otira River runs below, and our voices were drowned in the deep hoarse roar of its waters as they fell over and dashed round great masses of broken rock. The perpendicular cliffs towered above us, some thickly clothed with vegetation, and beyond them again others hid their bare peaks in the clouds. The Rolleston Glacier lay to our right, with the sun glistering on the ice. As we mounted higher, the scene became grander as other peaks came into view, and the valley lay behind us 7000 feet below them. I have seen much beautiful scenery, but familiarity deepens my awe of Nature at her grandest. I sat silent beside my one companion (all the passengers but this one girl and myself were walking), and she seemed as impressed as I was. At last she heaved a profound sigh and stealing a glance at me remarked, "Ain't it pretty?" It brought me rudely back to earth again.

After Arthur's Pass was gained, the others all took their seats in the coach again and away we bowled down the other side. The character of the country now changed, the forest disappeared and only here and there were patches of manuca scrub and the so-called birch. After passing the "Devil's Punchbowl" waterfall, the endless perspective of the wide river-bed of the Waimakariri opened for miles in front of us. It was a clear, cold sunset, and the mounains stood out black against the silver sky. The wind from those snowy peaks laid an icy hand upon us as we crossed the wide shingly bed of the river, now so swollen by the melting of the snows above that it came down a perfect whirl of waters, and it was a case of touch and go as we went over. Oh, how cold the wind blew along that valley! and weren't we glad when another half-hour's drive brought us to our halting-place for the night, its only recommendation being the great log fire which greeted us as we went inside! It was a small, crowded and badly-managed hotel. As for beds, there were none to be had, the hotel was full to overflowing. They could not be blamed for this, for two coach-loads of passengers from Christchurch were already in possession; but I did expect civility, which was entirely omitted from their bill. Those behind us, including the two men of sorts, did not take things so easily. It was a night ruffled by unrest; sleep was out of the question on a horse-hair sofa with one rug, and in the chilly dawn of the morning we had breakfast by the light of a strong-smelling kerosene lamp, and started on our way, bowling along with five fresh horses and a new driver.

We said good-bye here to the last of the trees, and the mountains ran down to the broad river-beds, with their steep slopes covered with rock and grass; gaunt-looking and desolate. I held on extra tight at some of the narrow passes down the inclines, for there was always a spice of danger in it, and one felt a sort of wondering excitement in picturing what the next sharp corner might bring. Now we went along the gorges, then up again on to the hills. We passed a small lake with reflections so clear and distinct that it was only the image turned upside down, and farther on again the road skirted round Lake Lyndon, with numbers of Paradise ducks and a pair of swans swimming about with the greatest unconcern; on the hill-sides giant rocks lay tossed about all round us. Once over Porter's Pass we gradually descended again; every rugged outline looked intensely clear against the vividly blue sky, and the wonderful shades of browns, yellows, sepias and grays made up a picture more like Arabia or Egypt than this southern island. On the level bits of grass lands sheep were lazily browsing, and we passed two station homesteads close to the road. Then down we went on to the great Canterbury Plains, looking just like a flat map with its marked-out fields. And how tame they looked after the wild scenery that we had passed through, with nothing but long belts of thick plantations of blue gums to break the monotony—and, I suppose, the wind, which must sweep with great force here, for every haystack was knocked out of shape.

The coach stopped at Springfield, where we caught the very slow train to Christchurch. It was seven before we reached the terminus and our journey was ended.

A few days later I took the journey back again to see the rest of the Buller Gorge from Inangahua on to Westport, and was well repaid. Grand and rugged as the Otira Gorge is, the Buller surpasses it in actual beauty. The wonderful bush, the arches of rock through which the road goes, and the deep winding river itself form for 45 miles such a drive as few countries in the world could equal.

Before leaving Westport I went to the Denniston coal-mines, where the coal is taken from the top of the mountain instead of from the bottom of a pit, and the small town, with its irregularly-built houses, is the most curious of the kind I have ever seen. From Westport, which is a great coal-mining district, I took a steamer back to Christchurch.

After my return to Christchurch, I went one day to Lincoln, twelve miles by rail, to the School of Agriculture, an institution for young fellows who intended making farming their profession. Mr. Gray, the acting-superintendent, took me all over the building, and spared no trouble to show me everything that was to be seen—from the well-kept stalls for the horses, and where the cows were milked, to the dairy, where the separator was at work and butter being made by hand, where layers of tempting-looking cheeses were being mellowed in their drying-room—thence to the large pig-sties where the last few months of the poor unsuspecting inmates were made as happy as possible in luxurious dieting of milk, and other pig luxuries pertaining to the making of good ham and bacon. Then we went to the fruit garden where the branches were bent to the ground with the weight of good rosy apples, and the blackbirds were making the most of their time too among them before they were stored away for the winter. Rows of beehives were here, with all the improved methods of arrangement, so that each pound could be taken when the cells were filled. In the flower garden there were masses of flowers, and a cosy summer-house where many a meditative pipe will be smoked by the young energetic Scotchman who has just come out to take charge of the whole institution. On the broad well-kept lawns are tennis, football, and cricket grounds, where, after the day's work is done, the pupils can amuse themselves. Inside the large handsome building itself, I had a peep into some of the neat little bedrooms. Each student has his own, and every two share a sitting-room. I then went to the large dining-room and laboratories, and into the different lecture and class rooms, where I studied bones and the anatomy of horses and cows, depicted in forcible pictures on the wall, and examined the cereal room, with its bundles of grasses, etc. I examined specimens of the bot-fly and its chrysalis, and learnt how it deposited its eggs on the horse, how they were afterwards licked off by the poor animal, and became attached in the chrysalis state to the lining of its stomach.

The students here get a thorough knowledge of the practice and science of agriculture; they are well instructed in chemistry, physics, and veterinary science, mathematics, land-surveying, and book-keeping. The fees, including board, washing, etc., are £40 a year. The students are allowed to earn wages at ploughing and at harvest times. The institution is supported by endowments, students' fees, and the net profits of the farm after working expenses are paid.

Cliffs of Ice

Christchurch

We left Christchurch by the eleven express for Timaru a few days after. The force of the strong current of the Rakaia River, with the late rains, had washed away several of the piles of the long railway bridge, and each of the motley crowd of passengers "humped" his own baggage as best he could across the very unsteady banks to the train awaiting us beyond. As we slowed into Timaru the long breakers on the shore were coming in with a booming sound in the distance, and we saw the spray of their white crests breaking over the rocky cliffs long before the sea came into sight. It was three o'clock when we steamed into the station, and half-past five before the other train started for Fairlie Creek, on another line, where I was to meet the coach for Mount Cook.

I had a cup of tea and some fruit at a clean little restaurant in the town, and then went to a bootmaker to get strong nails put into my soles. "You see," he said, "putting them sideways you gets a little more purchase," which I took for granted and paid my bill of sixpence. After a drive round the outskirts of the town, I caught my train again and reached Fairlie at eight o'clock.

At eight next morning we were off again by the coach. At Lake Tekapo, fifteen miles long, we changed horses, and appeased our keen appetites at a hotel on the shores of this turquoise-green sheet of water. Then "all aboard," and on again through the Mackenzie Country, so called from a shepherd of that name, who was the first to explore this district, and grew rich on the proceeds of his neighbours' sheep, which he trained a dog to drive on to his land. It was a desolate dreary country, great rolling turf-covered plains, and boulder-strewn hill-sides. Here and there was a small homestead marked by a plantation of pines, the only ones to be seen in this treeless country. We amused ourselves for some time watching exciting races between tumble-weeds, which, caught by vagrant breezes, went tumbling along the road, taking jumps and turning somersaults over each other as they went bustling along at lightning speed to join others in the chase. Over Simon's Pass we came to the homestead of that name, more tussocky grass, more huge rocks tumbling every way, with Mount Cook always before us. Then over a small spur, as the sun was setting, and Lake Pukaki lay below us with the most wonderful reflections on its smooth waters, of purple hills, and snow mountains all bathed in dying rays of a brilliant crimson and yellow sunset. I was the only occupant of the small hotel here, which was clean and comfortable. They gave me a good fire, I made my own hot buttered toast, and, after reading the published statistics of growing vitality in the pastoral industry of the colony in 1891 (the only book I could get hold of), and the various remarks in the visitors' book, I felt that my brain wouldn't stand any more, so went to bed, where I slept the sleep of the just, and tired.

Next morning at eight the coach went over the river in the ferry, and we travelled for miles along the side of the lake, then over the yellow downs of Rhoborough Station, and through the bed of an old river, where I sympathised with the man who got down to see if the wheels were square, for seldom in my life before had I been so thoroughly "churned up". It got beyond a joke when we rattled down a steep incline, over more boulders, and through a creek, and every bone seemed disjointed.

Our next stopping-place was at a small station, where the manager's wife gave me a cup of tea, and we rested the horses for an hour. They needed it, for we had yet to ford the worst river, where the last floods had played havoc with the crossing place. It had forced a new channel for itself and had rolled down huge stones. We dropped down the bank, and as the coach doubled over on to the horses, I put out my hands on their backs to balance myself. We got through I don't know how, but it wasn't a pleasant sensation.

We found a very merry party at the Hermitage at Mount Cook, who had just come back from a camping-out excursion, and, unfortunately for me, went away next day, when I was left in sole possession. The weather was perfect, not a cloud in the sky, and the air so crisp and light that I felt ready for anything when I started next morning with the guide; first skirting the base of

Mount Sefton and then along the Countess Glacier, eight miles long, which travels at a rate of twelve inches in twenty-four hours. It is some time before you can realise that you are on cliffs of ice, not until you first experience the slipping shingles, which in places leave the ice exposed.

We had our lunch under an immense block of ice. The day was intensely hot, and the snow water in our milk most refreshing. Afterwards our road was very much rougher. Climbing along the sharp high ridges of ice with deep blue crevasses below, a false step would have sent us rolling into space. Above us towered the snow caps of Mount Sefton, with cliffs 300 and 400 feet high of solid ice, with the Huddlestone Glacier rolling down its sides; while other peaks again were gaunt and bare, with little or no snow on them, and the rock-strewn gorges between them were all chiselled and fretted into jagged points from the constant waterfalls.

Leaving the glacier to our left, we climbed the back of the Seeley Range. This was more of an experience than I had anticipated. It was rather like climbing a greasy pole. You got up to slide down again, and the top seemed to recede the nearer you reached it. We rested several times to get breath and to pick snow-berries, edelweiss, and white gentian, then on again until we reached the top. Away 4000 feet below us lay the long Hooker and Tasman glaciers, with Mount Cook standing out glittering and majestic in the distance; on our right the rugged rocky peaks of Mount Chudleigh and Malte Brun, while peak after peak of others was lost in dim cloud and mist.

It is a mental awakening to see the new sights and hear the new sounds, in this wonderful place: peal after peal of avalanche thunders, and down and away the great ice-blocks rattle along the steep slides, gathering up others as they go, and falling broken and scattered into fragments on to the glaciers below. What a doll's house the Hermitage looks away below us; and out in the plains the Hooker runs, a rollicking boulder-strewn river, breaking up into endless streams as it flows away into Lake Tekapo—but what a slide down it looks to reach those plains. It was impossible to walk foot over foot on this steep, rotten and crumbling, shingly cliff, so, catching hold of the guide's hand, we put our feet together and slid down for the first 200 feet, then, chamois-like, we jumped from step to step over the slippery moss and great stones, through stunted bush and wiry grass. It went against the grain to ask for help, after coming against advice, so I struggled on alone till I could not now hold out without a helping hand, and even with that my experience was a painful one. I was a sorry-looking object when I limped into the Hermitage at half-past nine at night; no one gave me a word of sympathy, and I felt that it was a hard and unfeeling world.

I woke next morning with a flood of sunlight in my room, and went through various acrobatic feats trying to dress, but it was useless, My ten hours' hard tramping had so strained every muscle that I was a prisoner for two days. Then the rain came down in bucketsful, but time was too precious to lose another day, so braving wind and weather I started off with a guide, over the wire suspension bridge on to the great solid blocks of ice-cliffs, which here and there were being quickly undermined. While we stood watching, the flood carried one huge mass away, making the waters leap again in crested waves three and four feet high as they went rolling down.

Along the Hooker Glacier the mountains were all clad in mists. Here and there only a white peak was visible, and the world looked cold, gray, and dripping. Later on a fierce storm broke over Mount Cook, the nor'wester blew a hurricane, and for two days we were in dense masses of cloud and mist.

The next coach brought some fresh passengers in, among them the little German doctor, who when I showed him my sketches quietly put aside all the best: "They are necessary for my purpose," he said. I suggested that some day I too might make use of them for a book; however, as the rain prevented us from going out, he kept me at work from daylight till dark filling the lines which did duty as his sketches—a cross marked "tree" here, a line marked "a mountain" there. With him came two ladies, an imposing, massive, gray-whiskered man with a fat smile and a cheerful aggressive manner, and two of the genus globe-trotter, not wanting in appreciation of themselves, who talked as if they had just discovered New Zealand, and we belonged to the wilds of Timbuctoo; however, we organised a riding party next morning, to see in one day what generally takes two—this meant a start at four in the morning; the two ladies, perhaps wisely changed their minds at the last moment, especially as we had drawn lots for the only side-saddle and it had fallen to my share.

After making various unsuccessful attempts to get on his horse, the little doctor was at last lifted by two men (for he was no light weight) into the saddle; the gray-haired gentleman being the father of the party had the pick of the horses, and a wooden gray mare fell to my lot, while the others were on a miscellaneous collection. It was yet barely daylight and bitterly cold, but at any rate there was no rain.

When we reached the Hooker, swollen with the melted snow and last rains, it was rushing along with tremendous speed, and ice-blocks, most uncomfortably large, were now and then being carried down. One horse was sent across alone to test the depth. He tottered in mid-stream, then swam, then gained another footing, and finally reached the bank; but, coming to the conclusion that discretion was the better part of valour, we swam the rest across, and ourselves chose the cage hung on wire ropes, a primitive way of being hurled over one by one. The sun was just rising as we mounted our horses again. Away down the valley between the high range of hills rose a flood of crimson light, tipping all the mountain-tops and the shred-like fragments of clouds as they floated by.

Leaving the Hooker, we went along the shingle and boulder flats of the Tasman River, on to the moraine, and up a narrow gorge where the horses literally climbed the rocks. There was a delightful sensation of expectancy as to which steps would prove fatal, but horses reared in these rock-strewn mountains become almost like goats in their habits, and after a time you rather enjoy the sensation of wondering what they cannot accomplish. Then we made a breakneck and sensational descent which was too much for the doctor and the tourists, and they got off and walked, and as it was all they could do to keep on their own feet the guides had to lead their horses. We reached the hut at nine o'clock. This not over-luxurious abode is generally a rendezvous for the night. We boiled the kettle, made "Billy" tea, and had a second breakfast, Keas, large green parrots, watching us all the time with the greatest curiosity. They occasionally, as if in derision, screamed their hardest at us, and wheeled in the air so close that we could almost knock them over. These most destructive creatures are found in great numbers at the foot of the snow mountains and kill the sheep by fastening their strong claws to their wool while they tear the flesh and eat out their livers. The poor creatures are so terrified of Keas, that on one occasion when pursued by them, five hundred went over the cliffs into space below.

We were soon ready after our breakfast for our climb, and, armed with substantial alpenstocks and blue glasses, set off along the Tasman Glacier, which is eighteen miles long and claims the distinction of being the largest in the world. It moves, we heard, at the rate of eighteen inches in twenty-four hours. When once on the pure ice the great ice-cliffs became more broken at every step, and the deep blue crevasses deeper. We peered into the clearest, bluest holes, containing crystal-like water, and crept into an ice-cave with lovely transparent walls of the clearest topaz blue; but these beauties of detail were surpassed in fascination by the glorious view.

Away in front of us lay the long snow-white sweep of the glacier. On either side are stupendous cliffs of ice and the sky-piercing peaks of Mount Cook, a mountain of serrated and corniced ridges. Beyond that again, the Hochstetter dome of solid ice and snow, with the sunlight all dancing and sparkling on it—almost too dazzling to look at—and its wonderful glacier-fall of frozen cascades coming down 4000 feet in waves and pinnacles, towers and cubes, each crested point tipped with unconsolidated snow. Beyond, again, other snow peaks of spotless white rise one above another. There is a solemn silence, broken only by the rush of water somewhere below us. Then a sharp crack like a pistol-shot, clouds of snow and ice, and the avalanche falls. To us, away in those heights, it looks a shower to stand under, and it is hard to realise that it would sometimes cover 200 or 300 acres of ground. The pinnacles that look to us a step are 200 feet to 300 feet high, and those smooth, pure white flats above them three and four miles across.

What a memory for a lifetime it is. The wild wonderful beauty of these mountains makes one feel unutterable things. Far from the haunts of men, from the cares of a humdrum world, a new life and world seemed opened up—a foretaste of heaven. Ruskin in his *Modern Painters* says that "the slope of a great Alp is the best image the world can give of Paradise, and the sublimest revelation of the Giver of life". We Australians travel for thousands of miles to see the world and its wonders, and yet at our own doors are sights to be seen which even the Swiss guides themselves acknowledge surpass in beauty of detail their own Alps. These Southern Alps, running in an unbroken chain for a hundred miles, range from 7000 feet to 12,350 feet. The glaciers are far larger than the Swiss ones, on account of the snow-level, which is from 2000 feet to 3000 feet lower. The native name of Mount Cook (Aorangi) has many different translations—scud peak, sky-piercer, and light of day; the latter because it is the first to catch the sunlight, and the last to show the evening glow.

I don't know how many miles we walked, but it was no easy climb, and we were very glad when the hut was reached again. Here we had more tea, cold mutton, bread, and marmalade, which we ate with a relish. Then everything was washed and the tin plates and pannikins put away into the tin-lined locker, the door locked in the little cabin, and we turned our faces homewards. The gray mare which carried me resented the side-saddle, and pursued her way dejectedly, and at a funereal pace.

The river had gone down a few inches, and those who preferred took their horses over, while the others were hurled across in mid-air. I had not started with the idea of having a bath, but, as luck would have it, in the dark my mare got into deep water and had to swim; all I could do was hang on with a possibility of extinction. When we got on to some big rocks in the middle of the stream, then plunged into deep water again, my heart had another sink; it was intensely, bitterly cold, and once or twice the mare felt as if she would roll over. I tried to coax the poor, frightened creature as she clambered now on to another rock, shivering and stumbling, then another plunge down, a swim for a minute or two, a strong struggle, and she dragged herself panting on to the bank.

I was so numbed with the cold that I dared not ride farther, and the guide taking my horse, I walked the rest of the way home straight to bed.

A few days later we all left with strong misgivings as to how we would fare crossing the river, for the coach the trip before had been turned over by the force of the current, and Barry, our plucky driver, sent rolling down the stream, half drowned. They pulled him out none the worse, beyond a few bruises, for his ducking. The brightest sun was shining, and the view looking back on those grand peaks one not easily forgotten. The lower mountains were of the most intense blue—"sign of a coming nor'wester", they said—and one black cloud only rested on the solitary peak of Mount Cook. "Now, hold on, ladies, for the next five minutes are anxious ones," Barry said, and so they were, and we did hold on, for the tilts backwards, then forwards, and sideways, and upways, unseated us each time. The water once swished through the coach, and we gave a sigh of relief when the other side was reached.

The dense clouds now became blacker, and the thunder echoes multiplied a thousandfold among the mountains, then terminated in one ear-splitting crash, and down came the sleet and down the strong nor'wester on us. For a moment everything seemed in a glorious confusion, for the coach was an open one, and it was out of the question holding up umbrellas. Cloaks and rugs flapped and wouldn't be settled, and the wind, shrieking and wailing around us, seemed like a host of evil presences. It grew icy cold, and the sleet seemed almost to cut our faces. On the mountains the snow was coming down so fast that before we reached the hotel they were almost completely clothed in their white garments; and when we left again next day there were patches of snow on the plains, and we had another long, weary, bitterly cold drive.

It was six o'clock when we reached Fairlie. Another dripping journey in the train to Timaru, where everyone was blown into the carriages with red noses an blue pinched faces, then into the town itself, where we dripped about for two hours waiting for the Christchurch train, and watching the great rolling breakers crashing along the shore, a mass of foam and spray. Seven uninteresting hours, and then the substantial comforts of a warm fire in Coker's Hotel at Christchurch, and the still greater relief of bed, and the knowledge that that trip had been successfully accomplished.

Even here everyone was shivering, but I forgot the weather amongst Miss Stodart's beautiful flower-paintings in the Art Gallery. I had the pleasure of meeting her, and next morning went to see her whole collection. It was a new revelation to me to see such work hidden away, and I think she stands without rival the first and foremost of our flower-painters in Australia. Her grouping, colouring, form, and harmony were perfect.

Hearing that Akaroa was one of the most beautiful harbours in New Zealand, I started off next morning three hours by train to Little River, where we caught the coach and drove on to the little town, 20 miles away. The view from the crest of the hill was most beautiful. The bright blue waters of the bay with its small historical island, the many homesteads and the little town all nestling under the hills, lay below us. Down we rattled over a capital road and round the sharpest curves, with hundreds of feet above and below, and only the nerve and skill of one man to save us from instant death; but the horses are as steady and sure as the man's strong arm, and you never think of fear. At Moreton's hotel on the shore, after a cup of tea I induced the landlady's sister to take me for a regular tramp, first through the Government Reserve with its beautiful wild bush and winding paths, then up and down little higgledy-piggledy streets, with immense walnut trees lining the roadsides, the nuts too common here for even school-boys to pocket; and up on to the high rock-strewn mountain behind, where the whole outline of the many indented bays lay below us without a ripple on the water, and the fishing boats coming in left their long serpentine trails for miles behind them.

At half-past seven next morning I drove to Pigeon Bay, 16 miles off, and from there caught a small steamer to Lyttleton, the chief seaport town of Christchurch, with a tunnel 1¾ miles long, and a very fine graving dock and breakwater. The town is built on an extinct crater, and there are still one or two small thermal springs carrying on their volcanic forces. We had more than an hour to wait, so I found out the agents for that cargo of Akaroa cheese we brought from there with us, and bought two of them. They are supposed to be the best in Canterbury, and tasted exceedingly good.

Cliffs of Ice

Erythrina vespertilio Bentham, *Prince of Wales Island, watercolour, 54 x 38 cm*
Reproduced by permission of the National Library of Australia

A Land of Olives and Honey

Dunedin

Christchurch is truly English in character, and many are the associations awakened by Christchurch ways and talk, and the rich level meadows, trim gardens, and tall spires, on the dainty, willow-fringed banks of the Avon, where in the deep shady pools many speckled trout lie hidden. But I was not sorry to turn my back on it all. The weather was now intensely cold, and before I left most of the mountains were white with snow. Though the cold of Dunedin, my next point, is perhaps greater, it is a crisper, drier air. The express left at eleven in the morning, and in its variety the day's journey was a great contrast to one in Australia. At one time we ran for miles along the coast close to the breakers, and heard nothing but the sound of the swell, and the solemn boom of the waves on the shore. Then came Oamaru, the white city, with its break-water enclosing a basin of 60 acres. Then we pass through an agricultural district which boasts of the largest wheat and flour mills in the colony. Later, the line runs on to high cliffs, with the sea hundreds of feet below. But darkness creeps on, the lamps are lighted, daylight shut out, and nothing more is seen until the train slackens pace as at 9 P.M. it comes into the noise and bustle of the terminus of Dunedin.

From my window next morning, in the Grand Hotel, in the heart of the city, I looked down upon a busy thoroughfare. The substantial building of the Colonial Bank of New Zealand was opposite, built of white Oamaru stone. But neither this nor the view of Cargill's monument, with its drinking fountains, the post office and telegraph station, nor the terminus of the cable-tram line, reconciled me to the rain, which came down in such hopeless torrents all day that we had to make the best of our time indoors. Next morning I left by the eight o'clock express for Lake Wakatipu, passing through the Taieri Plains and Waihola and Tuakitoto Lake to Balclutha, over the swift-running Clutha River, which drains all the central lake.

Lumsden, 137 miles from Dunedin, is the junction with the Invercargill-Kingstown railway. Inland from here are the largest lakes in the South Island, Te Anan and Manapouri (sorrowing heart), which is, perhaps, the most beatiful of all. We did not reach Kingstown until eight o'clock. The train ran straight on to the jetty, and we transhipped ourselves and our luggage direct on to the steamer. It was blowing a gale. The night was as black as pitch and nothing to be seen, and the lights of Queenstown (our destination) at ten o'clock were very welcome.

Next morning I went on board with my luggage, intending to stay for two or three days at the head of the lake at "Paradise", relying on my guide-book that Kinloch was the nearest starting-point. When, however, the steamer stopped there for mails I found that my route meant either a twelve-mile ride across two flooded rivers, with no means of taking my luggage, or else a row across in an open boat, which, judging from the present height of the waves, would not be an enviable trip; so I determined to return to Queenstown. I ought to have taken the buggy waiting at Glenorchy where I had lunched. It all served me right for asking no questions. The whole way up the lake was one long panorama of magnificent mountain scenery, and Mount Earnslaw towered above them all in front of us with his hoary head of glistening snow. Several rivers empty their waters into the lake, and the long, shingly valley is enclosed by high mountain ranges with countless peaks of snow.

Turning our backs again on them, the little steamer ploughed her way through the great waves, for a gale was still blowing, and only now and then through the dense masses of rolling cloud could we distinguish each near headland and peak, which gave height and majesty to the surroundings. The mists all cleared as we neared Queenstown again, and the jagged and serrated cones of the Remarkable Range stood out in black relief against the steely sky. They well deserve their name; their inaccessible heights look like battered fortresses, and high up in their seamed and scarred ridges not even a blade of grass finds shelter. Nothing but the shivering shale and crumbling stones are here, no hue of life on buttress or ledge, and, as if in kindness to clothe the blackness of the cliffs, the snow nestles lovingly in corner and crevice along its steep sides.

Next morning there was a clear, crisp feeling in the air and the lake lay in front of us without a ripple on its surface. It was too bright a day to waste a moment, and, filling my pocket with biscuits, I slowly made my way up Ben Lomond. How lovely it all was; the tall mountains rising against the bright blue sky, the deep ravines clothed in sombre garb of native beech, and the little village below with sunlight on the roofs of its white houses.

Next morning every mountain was capped with snow as we left Queenstown for Lake Wanaka; and on reaching the long winding zigzag road up the Crown Range, I was glad of the excuse to walk, for it was bitterly cold, and the sleet was driving down on the mountain-tops. Now and again through the lifting clouds away down in the distance we saw the blue waters of the lake, the ragged pinnacles of the Remarkables, Ben Lomond, the winding Shotover and Kawarau Rivers, and small homesteads dotted about in the fertile valleys below. On the other side of the range we drove for miles between high barren hills, along the Cadrona Valley, crossing and recrossing the Clutha River, where the rocky bed has been turned over and over again in the unceasing search for gold.

But most of the old water-races are now broken, the mud hovels are in ruins, and only an occasional Chinaman is seen at the town itself. But the sides of the mountains are all being tunnelled, and the town owes its existence and prosperity to the rich finds of gold here some years ago. Before reaching Pembroke, Mount Aspiring suddenly came in view with its curiously broken line of peaks. Two or three more miles and Lake Wanaka lay before us, surpassing, I think, in beauty Lake Wakatipu, though the approach and the town itself are neither so picturesque nor so large.

There were no tourists in the primitive hotel, though, later on, two splendid specimens of young Englishmen turned up, fresh from a week's camping out at Lake Hawea. They had had capital sport, they said, but deer-stalking in Scotland was child's-play compared to what they had gone through here. Their poor valet succumbed, and had to be patched up on Liebig and brandy.

Next morning was glorious. Not a leaf was stirring, and the

colouring was beyond description. The tall poplars everywhere turning to gold were backed up by the intensely blue sky; and each mountain, near and distant, turned from russet to brown, purple, gray, and every shade of tender blue. The air was so clear every sound was heard across the lake, and so bracing you felt you could walk on for ever.

I was not alone on those hill-tops—rabbits everywhere, from the grim skeletons hung on the wire fences as a warning to others, to the nimble-footed ones which bobbed round rocks, in and out of burrows, and even on the pebbly shore. There was no other sign of life, for on the shores there is a death-like silence, and I started even at the swish of a big fly as it darted by in the sunlight. A little boat was moored to the rocks, and a long line of cork heads on the top of the water suggested trout for dinner, which is the standing dish here, the fish often weighing from 20 lbs. to 30 lbs. Away on the hill-tops a deer disappeared, and two eagle hawks went skimming by.

In strange contrast to this scene of solitude are the stories one hears of the times when hundreds of pounds of gold a day were scraped out of the crevices of the rocks on the Clutha River by the early settlers, and fabulous prices paid for tucker and whisky. Some of the "shanties" still remain, where many a poor unfortunate was drugged and robbed of his nuggets. What tales could be told, adventurous or pathetic, of those early gold-digging days!

Two more days at Wanaka, then back to Queenstown again, and next morning I made my second journey to Paradise, which this time I really did reach.

There were only two other passengers. Of the one I need say no more than that he exactly answered to Miss Austen's description of Robert Lewars—"he had a face and person of strong, sterling, natural insignificance". The other was a very grave, not to say saturnine personage, who conversed with an air of extreme sadness on many topics, as we journeyed on. I thought his pessimism was to have no relief; but at last, our conversation meandering round to funerals (by a very natural pathway, considering his prevailing gloom), I discovered that there was a ray of light. The comparative cheapness of these in our modern days seemed to fill his soul with ineffable joy, and he became quite lively over the subject. I was irresistibly reminded of the famous advertisement, "Why live, when you can be decently buried for £2:10s?" and have my suspicions that he was its originator. When we parted the mystery of his unwonted interest in this topic was revealed to me, for he presented me with his card, on which was engraved, "Thomas B——, Undertaker, etc.," and obligingly expressed his hope that we might meet again!

The first part of the twelve-mile drive was not pleasant. Following the course of a long valley, we had several rivers to cross, and a cold wind coming down from the snow peaks laid an icy hand upon us. I pitied the owners of the land, for we passed hundreds of rabbits before reaching Paradise through the Gates of Purgatory, and along the shores of Diamond Lake. It was growing dusk as we drove through a beautiful avenue of native beech trees with the ground underneath carpeted with ferns, and, under the shadow of some overhanging rocks, already the glow-worms were beginning to light their lamps.

Next morning I was away over the hills, which here are no longer bare and barren. The magnificent forest trees clothe the near mountains from base to summit, while those behind are veiled in white garments of perpetual snow. At the back of the hotel (a convenient centre for many of the best walking expeditions) and only half a mile away, is the valley of the Dart River with Mount Cosmos nearly opposite, and glacier after glacier in succession, until the ice-fields of Mount Aspiring are lost behind the bush-clad slopes of Mount Cunningham.

I drove one afternoon with the proprietor of the hotel to see two young miners at work in a gully on one of the mountainsides. We left the horses below and climbed over the great rocks and up the bed of the stream where they were sluicing. I asked for a tin dish to go fossicking, and washed up my first gold—two nuggets, which were afterwards weighed and proved worth nineteen shillings and sixpence. It was most exciting, and I bought one of them as a memento of my first venture in prospecting. We had our five o'clock billy tea with them in their tent; and the camp-oven bread that they had just baked was very good. They were two fine specimens of New Zealanders, and I thoroughly enjoyed my five-o'clock tea with them. Coming home, the sun had crowned Mount Earnslaw with a golden glory, and even the wind seemed hushed to sleep, as if afraid of ruffling the mirror-like surface of the beautiful lake.

Sitting over the fire, waiting for the lights to be lit, a native robin hopped into the room and pecked up crumbs at my feet, and then flew out through the window. I had heard of their tameness in the bush here, but did not realise it before. Next morning I fed them in the garden, and one rested for a minute on my shoulder. In the thick tussocky grass and the water pools the wekas (water-hens) are even more tame. Here they walk about with the most important-looking air, bobbing their tails up and down. Nothing in the way of food is safe from them, and if you are ever unwise enough to leave a lunch basket near them, you will find that everything has been sampled on your return.

The days went by much too quickly here. The lakes and rivers, they say, teem with trout, but there was no time to fish. I could not loiter on the way, and all too soon I was back. The Remarkables were all bathed in a soft, silver blue light, wrapping everything in a thin veil of mystery, and the moon suddenly rose up from behind them, flooding everything in her soft, mellow light, and dancing reflections in long rippling waves of light on the water. It was a most lovely scene.

Next morning I took my last drive along Skipper's Road, one that no one whose head will stand it should miss, for there is no road like it in New Zealand. Even on foot going over these mountain passes, one would require to have a great deal of the rock-wallaby element in his nature to carry him with any safety over them. Leaving the town, the road takes you along a narrow valley between high mountain ranges, then over the bridge of the Shotover River, which below rushes between high ridges of rock; and in the long sandy reaches the heavy gold dredges are at work, as also, further on, in a huge natural basin formed by ages of river workings. A primitive town of tent, and wattle and daub houses has grown up round its shores. Here the zigzag road mounts till the saddle is reached at 3000 feet.

The mountains towered above us in every direction, and away beyond were the blue waters of the lake, and the dotted houses of Queenstown. From the summit the road descends round precipitous cliffs, with great, fortress-looking rocks above, and away below the yellow stream of the Shotover River. Water-races run here and there in every direction round the cliffs, and perched up in most inaccessible-looking places were tiny homesteads of the miners. What a weird, wild life they lead up in these regions!

A wire cage crossed the river below us, and here the road wound round a sheer wall of perpendicular rock, just a ledge, only wide enough to allow the wheels to go over, but there is a foot-high wall of rock on the outer edge to save us from a dip in the river, hundreds of feet below.

From Queenstown I went by Invercargill to the Bluff, where I caught the steamer back to Dunedin. It was blowing such a gale that, even clinging to a good stout sailor, it was all I could do to stand against the wind, and it was with unspeakable pleasure I walked on land again at Port Chalmers. There is not sufficient depth for large steamers to come up the channel, so we went by rail, the line skirting close alongside the landlocked bay for nine miles up to Dunedin, which, when I got a longer range of vision than I did on my first day, proved the most picturesque town in the Southern Hemisphere.

The first person who greeted me at the hotel was my little German doctor. His carpet-bag was by this time crammed with the things he had been accumulating, all of which were important to his great work of collecting data about the country, and, of course, all were poured out at my feet, in order to get at the latest, which had somehow got down to the bottom. He was very curious about my sketches, and threw out various broad hints as to the mutual benefit we might experience, did we join in our work of edifying the world with descriptions of our travels. I was sorry to disappoint him, but feared my ambitions were so much less than his own that my co-operation might prove more a hindrance than a help.

Dunedin is purely a Scotch town, and all its streets are named after those in Edinburgh. The first early settlers were whalers. Then it was a land of scrub and flax so thick that every step of the way had to be hewn out. It went ahead very slowly until 1861, when gold was first discovered in the Taupeka district, and then at Gabriel's Gully. Population streamed in, and the town rapidly grew. It is built in an irregular way up the hills. To the left is a narrow neck of land connecting the city with the long peninsula which runs along the opposite side of the bay. The Maoris say that, in the early days, at high tide this was an island.

Two days after, I drove for twenty miles on the opposite side of the harbour, where I spent a delightful three days at Mr. Larnach's beautiful home. Here you get a magnificent panoramic view of Dunedin and the surrounding country, the entrance to the harbour with its broken coast-line, and the open ocean on the other side with its white line of breakers combing the reefs on the high rocky headlands and sweeping in and out of the sandy reaches. Every inch of the rich lands is cultivated, and pretty homesteads are dotted about the hills in every direction. Driving home again, the level road skirts close to the water's edge round bluff headlands and past sandbanks where the fisherman drags his net. In the evening the empty milk-carts go home, and two lovers walking hand-in-hand were all that we met as we drove back in the soft drowsiness of an autumn afternoon.

On the opposite shore again is a drive still more beautiful along the Blueskin road, so named from a Maori, Te Hickutu, whom they called Old Blue Skin, from his very tattooed face, which in this district was not a universal custom. The road runs along the top of the cliffs, with the whole stretch of the harbour and Port Chalmers below, thick wooded slopes on the other side, and in the distance one mountain peak behind another; while farther away still in misty blue are those with their perpetual garments of snow. High up in these hills, away from the busy crowd, the dust and glare of the city, you see it only as a picture, with the tall slender spires of its many churches of all denominations, foremost among them the steeple of the first "Auld Kirk", the Town Hall, University, and other fine buildings. At Ocean Beach, the southern end of the city, are two headlands, bounded on either side with a strong battery of guns. Here the great waves roll in from the open sea, and the long sandy stretch of beach is a favourite resort for those who ride.

Every sort of manufacturing industry is carried on, from timber, grain, brewing, tanning, fruit and meat preserving, boot and shoe making, coach-building, biscuit, soap, candle and brick making, besides others too numerous to mention. Several iron steamships have been built by Messrs. Kincaird, M'Queen, and Company, and all the dredges used on the harbour works. At the Roslyn and Mosgeil factories all kinds of woollen goods are made, and many hundreds of hands are employed. I spent a day going over the latter, where everything is seen from start to finish—the wool in process of being sorted in its greasy state, then cleaned, dyed, and finally the cloth in its finished state. A great many girls are employed here, and a small town, containing the many cottages of those working here, has grown up in this rich Taiera Valley, a land which not so very long ago was the site of an old lake, now a land of golden plenty. Lake Waiholo, at its entrance, is where the sportsman fills his bag with trout and wild duck. At Milton beyond are large potteries, flour and oat mills, coal-mines, and limekilns.

Many interesting stories are told by the old settlers of the early days—how the heavy bags of golden nuggets were doled out to the settlers in payment for their land, how this section and that was bought for a barrel of beer; and how, from a few pounds in the early digging days, the land rose to hundreds in a day. A good story is told of a Scotsman who owned a small bit of land in Princes Street, which he had originally bought for a few pounds, and did not realise its value until he was offered £16,000, which he stoutly refused. "Saxteen thoosand pounds for't!" he said; "ye canna ha' made your money honestly, mon!"

The early settlers of New Zealand had a rough time of it, and needed strong muscles and stout hearts to battle against the many difficulties. For years it was one long struggle for supremacy between the Europeans and Maoris. Now the dominant race and the subdued dwell peacefully together.

Every variety of scenery and natural beauty is found in this Southern Cross world, from bold rocky island-studded coast-lines to rolling hills and level plains; from towering heights of active volcano to a wonder-land of silica terraces and undying fires of a hot-lake region, unreal and weird in their plutonic grandeur; from inaccessible glacier peaks of eternal ice and snow, where avalanches wake the echoes of a hundred valleys, to the fathomless depths of landlocked fiords where virgin forests guard the shores with such garlands as only nature could weave; from wind-swept gorge and rocky precipice to the great cold lakes; along the shores of golden reaches to fierce broad rivers, to ideal summer haunts where, among wildernesses of ferns and mosses, sunshine steals in and goes to sleep; and in the words of the Scripture, A land of brooks of water, of fountains and depths that spring out of valleys and hills, a land of wheat and barley, and vines and fig trees, and pomegranates, a land of olives and honey.